# Self-Esteem

# SELF-ESTEEM:

## Paradoxes and Innovations in Clinical Theory and Practice

Richard L. Bednar

Department of Psychology, Brigham Young University

M. Gawain Wells

Department of Psychology, Brigham Young University

Scott R. Peterson

Research and Staff Development, LDS Social Services

AMERICAN PSYCHOLOGICAL ASSOCIATION
Washington, D.C.

Published by
American Psychological Association
1200 Seventeenth Street, NW
Washington, DC 20036

Copies may be ordered from
APA Order Department
P.O. Box 2710
Hyattsville, MD 20784

This book was typeset in Palatino by TAPSCO, Inc., Akron, PA.

Jacket and Cover Designer: Michael David Brown
Printer: Edwards Brothers, Inc., Ann Arbor, MI

First Printing: November 1989
Second Printing: September 1991


### Library of Congress Cataloging-in-Publication Data

Bednar, Richard L.
  Self-esteem: paradoxes and innovations in clinical theory and practice /
  Richard L. Bednar, M. Gawain Wells, Scott R. Peterson.
  Includes bibliographical references.
  1. Self-respect.  2. Adjustment  (Psychology)  3. Psychotherapy.
I. Wells, M. Gawain.  II. Peterson, Scott R.  III. Title.
  [DNLM: 1. Self Concept.  2. Psychotherapy--methods.  BF 697 B412s]
RC489.S43B43  1989  616.89'14--dc20  89-17673
  ISBN 1-55798-064-0 (cloth)
  ISBN 1-55798-150-7 (paper)

# Table of Contents

# List of Tables

# List of Figures

# Preface

S elf-esteem is considered by many to be a central component of personality that affects and is affected by almost any psychological difficulty. However, it is so interwoven in the personality that it is seldom the focus of psychotherapy. Most therapeutic models assume that treatment will indirectly modify the client's low self-esteem. The client's improved feeling about self comes, it is supposed, as a by-product of the therapy activity, not as a directly attended effort.

On the other hand, Jerome Frank (1981), in a major address on the common elements of successful psychotherapy, considered low self-esteem to be a nearly universal ingredient in the demoralization experienced by clients seeking psychotherapy. He asserted that the restoration of client morale (and therefore the improvement of self-esteem) is the sine qua non of successful treatment. In Frank's view, the restoration of morale depends more upon the quality of the therapeutic relationship than upon any specific treatment technique or the model of therapy involved.

The concepts presented in this book represent a radical departure from the expectation that self-esteem will improve simply as a by-product of symptom resolution or a good therapeutic relationship. Herein, we describe a therapeutic process that strategically shifts the balance of focus: making self-esteem the central issue of concern. One's overall evaluation of self, it is suggested, is the natural consequence of a person's tendency to consistently cope with or avoid that which one fears.

The therapeutic approach described in this book is deceptively simple. It does not teach self-affirmation or positive self-talk. Instead, it intervenes in the natural, raw moments from which self-evaluations are constructed by the individual. While the therapeutic relationship is essential, the renewed, vital sense of self is fashioned by the client, not by the force of the verbally persuasive therapist. We suggest that an enduring and deeply felt sense of self-approval is the inevitable consequence of learning to consistently cope with that which one tends to avoid. And, as a result, not only does self-esteem improve, but other psychological symptoms may disappear as well.

RICHARD L. BEDNAR
M. GAWAIN WELLS
SCOTT R. PETERSON

# Acknowledgments

S pecial thanks are extended to Melissa Peterson for her exceptional skill in typing, proofreading, and editing this manuscript. However, her real contribution to the development of this book is less obvious and more profound: She took upon herself many clinic responsibilities that were clearly beyond her job description so we would have more time to write. We truly appreciate her thoughtfulness and her skill.

Special thanks are also extended to Jay Behrman for his critical reviews. The value of his penetrating criticism is exceeded only by the quality of his discerning eye. Both of these people are valued friends and colleagues.

We are also grateful to the following sources for permission to reprint previously published material:

Pp. 22–23: Alfred Adler, *Superiority and Social Interest*, edited and translated by H. L. Ansbacher and R. R. Ansbacher. © 1964, 1970 Northwestern University Press.    P. 26: *George Herbert Mead on Social Psychology*, edited by A. Strauss. © 1964, University of Chicago.    Pp. 28–29: Gordon Allport, *Pattern and Growth in Personality*. © 1961 Holt, Rinehart & Winston. Rights have reverted to Robert B. Allport.    Pp. 30–31: Rollo May, *The Discovery of Being*. © 1983 W. W. Norton & Co.    Pp. 32–34: Carl R. Rogers, *Client-Centered Therapy*. © 1951 Houghton Mifflin Co.

P. 36: Ruth Wylie, *The Self-Concept: A Review of Methodological Considerations and Measuring Instruments* (Vol. 1, revised edition). © 1974 University of Nebraska Press.    P. 36: H. Markus and E. Wurf, "The Dynamic Self-Concept: A Social Psychological Perspective." Reproduced with permission from the *Annual Review of Psychology*, Vol. 38. © 1987 by Annual Reviews, Inc.    Pp. 40–41: B. R. Schlenker, "Identity and Self-Identification," in *The Self and Social Life*, edited by B. R. Schlenker. © 1985 McGraw-Hill.    P. 47: Stanley Coopersmith, *The Antecedents of Self-Esteem*. © 1967 W. H. Freeman & Co.    Pp. 48, 278: Excerpts from *Influences on Human Development*, Second Edition, by Urie Bronfenbrenner and Maureen Mahoney, © 1975 by The Dryden Press, a division of Holt, Rinehart and Winston, Inc., reprinted by permission of the publisher.

P. 50: Excerpt from *Self-Worth and School Learning* by Martin V. Covington and Richard G. Beery, © 1976 by Holt, Rinehart and Winston, Inc., reprinted by permission of the publisher.    P. 68: Carl R. Rogers, "A Theory of Therapy, Personality, and Interpersonal Relationships Developed in the Client-Centered Framework," in *Psychology: A Study of a Science, Vol. III, Formulations of the Person and the Social Context*, edited by S. Koch. © 1959, McGraw-Hill.    P. 92: Harry S. Sullivan, *Schizophrenia as a Human Process*. © 1962, W. W. Norton & Co.

# 1

# Self-Esteem: Paradoxes and Contradictions

E ven though relatively little is known about self-esteem, it is generally considered to be a highly favorable personal attribute, the consequences of which are assumed to be as robust as they are desirable. Books and chapters on mental hygiene and personality development consistently portray self-esteem as one of the premier elements in the highest levels of human functioning (Allport, 1961; Korchin, 1976). Its general importance to a full spectrum of effective human behaviors remains virtually uncontested. We are not aware of a single article in the psychological literature that has identified or discussed any undesirable consequences that are assumed to be a result of realistic and healthy levels of personal self-regard. Certainly, some have confused authentic self-esteem with such undesirable personal attributes as arrogance, self-centeredness, egotism, and an exaggerated sense of self-importance, or with other dysfunctional behavior, but these views are generally more emotive than substantive. They seldom warrant the attention of even the most elementary student interested in self-esteem.

Conversely, the absence of a healthy sense of self-appreciation seems to be one of the basic warning signs of a dysfunctional personality, and it is an assumed condition in virtually all contemporary models of disordered behavior. Clinical practice also suggests the same conclusion. Clinical populations commonly complain of low self-esteem, lack of self-approval, and lack of self-confidence. In cases where people have failed to acquire even the most modest

1

sense of personal self-approval, these complaints are often elevated to self-hatred and a pervasive sense of despair. However, it would be uncommon, if not impossible, to find people with high levels of personal self-esteem immobilized in a similar way.

The purpose of this book is to describe a new model of self-esteem in the hope of clarifying the origins and consequences of this important psychological attribute. The model we will be discussing had its conceptual origins in a special graduate seminar we taught several years ago. The purpose of the seminar was to assemble a small group of capable graduate students to spend a year considering two of the most fundamental questions mental health professionals might ask. Both questions focus on the "symbiotic" relationship between the diagnosis and treatment of emotional problems. These questions are:

*1. Are there psychological elements common to most emotional and behavioral problems?*

This question is part of the larger search for the psychological elements that may be common to most forms of emotional and behavioral disorders. The conceptual and practical benefits of being able to cluster an assortment of psychological symptoms together, on the basis of similar underlying elements, is undeniable. It could help clarify the complex foundations of psychopathology, psychotherapy, and personality development.

*2. If there are common elements that mediate the form and substance of different types of disordered behavior, can these underlying factors, rather than the diverse symptoms they produce, become the basis for understanding and treating psychological disturbances?*

A favorable answer to these two questions creates the possibility of being able to diagnose and treat emotional problems within a unified conceptual framework. Such an achievement would certainly be welcomed by many mental health professionals.[1]

During this seminar the participants debated research evidence, theoretical arguments, and the clinical lore relevant to these two questions. A variety of competing variables and arguments was considered. However, once the topic of self-esteem came up, it was almost always clear that low self-esteem was associated with virtually all types of emotional and behavioral problems, but it was hardly ever clear if it was a cause or a consequence of the attending psychological problems. Once we began to consider the possibility that low self-esteem could be both a cause and a consequence of disordered behavior, it gradually became clear that self-esteem could be a fundamental and productive consideration in both the etiology and treatment of many forms of dysfunctional behavior.

As we continued to explore the role of self-esteem in the development and remediation of behavior problems, we came to see its power and utility as a major explanatory construct. We gradually formalized our thinking into a new theoretical model of self-esteem. Our hope was to clarify the origins and consequences of this important attribute. As the model began to develop, its uniqueness also became apparent. On many important issues, it showed little allegiance to many of the traditional views and propositions about the origins of self-esteem. Additionally, the principles of psychological treatment that are a natural product of this model were also unusual for the same reason. They seemed to challenge many of the cherished views and values about some of the most basic ingredients assumed to be central to effective psychotherapy.

---

[1] The limited treatment applications that flow from our current diagnostic labels, as recorded in the *Diagnostic and Statistical Manual of Mental Disorders*, Third Edition-Revised (DSM-III-R), may well prove to be an unnecessary embarrassment to the applied mental health professions. Other diagnostic schemes are currently available (Millon, 1969) in which psychological symptoms are considered to be a direct extension of long-standing patterns of psychological coping and defense. And these patterns play a crucial role in defining disordered behavior and the appropriate goals and procedures for its treatment. We suspect that the most potent forms of psychological treatment will eventually evolve from the most incisive models of disordered behavior.

We have tried to avoid gratuitous praise or condemnation of the work of others in this area. Instead, we have attempted to emphasize and integrate ideas and propositions on the basis of conceptual merit. Obviously, that is a difficult task. Nevertheless, we hope our model can contribute to the gradual evolution of knowledge regarding (a) the psychological origins of high and low self-esteem, (b) some of the underlying dynamics of psychopathology, and (c) the principles of psychological intervention that are useful in the remediation of chronically low levels of self-esteem and some elements of disordered behavior, as well as in the enhancement of self-esteem.

Parenthetically, we define self-esteem as a subjective and enduring sense of realistic self-approval. It reflects how the individual views and values the self at the most fundamental levels of psychological experiencing. We have found that individuals, when asked, can observe and comment upon differentiated aspects of the self. A detailed inquiry into these different "parts" of the self yields a profile of emotions associated with the various roles in which the person operates. This information is basic to defining and understanding self-perceptions. But it is the affective experience associated with these events that defines the presence or absence of self-esteem. Fundamentally, then, self-esteem is an enduring and affective sense of personal value based on accurate self-perceptions.

## Self-Esteem and Success: A Major Paradox

From a commonsense point of view, trying to understand the origins of self-esteem involves several paradoxes and contradictions. *One of the most intriguing is why so many successful, competent people seem to be plagued with problems of chronic low self-esteem.* We will use several classic examples to illustrate this point.

The first is a statement from a 70-year-old man reflecting on his lifetime effort to better the world he lived in:

> My whole life has been a succession of disappointments. I can scarcely recollect a single instance of success in anything that I ever undertook. (Kennedy, 1956, p. 35)

The origins of this statement are not to be found in a life dominated by failure, nor was this person an object of pity and scorn to his contemporaries—nothing could be further from the truth. The writer was John Quincy Adams, who served with distinction as the sixth president of the United States, a senator, a congressman, a minister to major European countries, and a vital participant in many of the early and crucial events influencing the development of the nation. One cannot help but wonder how any person so entitled to an abiding sense of personal satisfaction after a distinguished life could be so plagued with self-disappointment. Somewhere behind the external achievements there must have been an internal filtering device that denied the successes and hoarded the failures, and then served them to John Quincy Adams as the fruits of his life's work.

The theme of this illustration is not limited to the elite. It is common to many segments of our society. Our other examples are far more typical and therefore more compelling. They seem to represent a ubiquitous psychological treadmill that can be as common to the talented high producer as it is to the typical outpatient clientele of middle-class America.

A young college graduate came to the startling realization that his low level of personal self-esteem was a major determinant in creating his current problems, and that it had shaped many of his other important life experiences. He wrote:

> For the past several years, I have felt that my life was meaningless. This was an ironic state of affairs considering all that I had accomplished. Friends and relatives were always lauding me for my good looks and intelligence. I was the first person on either side of my family to graduate from college, doing so with honors. I had a good job with an important accounting firm. I had plenty of dates. By all outward appearances, my life was very fulfilling. Yet I was miserable and felt increasingly depressed.
>
> Six months of psychotherapy had helped me to catch an occasional glimpse of the underlying cause of my unhappiness. It always seemed to involve low self-esteem or my disapproval of myself. Somehow, it seemed like I really did have a low opinion of myself, but I found that idea confusing because of all of the success in my life. Finally, I was able to put my finger

on the problem. Because I had such a low opinion of myself, I believed others would think of me the same way if they really got to know me. Because of this, I had been unwilling to expose myself to others as the person I really was. I took great pains to sidestep high-pressure situations, to gain the approval of others, and to avoid making decisions that might reveal things about myself that I didn't want others to know. I can see countless examples of this pattern in my life now that I have caught on to my style.

About 10 years ago, I agreed to hear missionary lessons from two young men representing a Christian church. I did so partly because I was interested in a particular girl who happened to be a member of that church. After the missionary lessons were completed, I agreed to be baptized a member. I shouldn't have. I was lying to myself. I had serious doubts about most of the basic concepts and beliefs of this church. I really joined so as not to disappoint the missionaries who had spent so much time with me, and because I hoped now to be more acceptable to the girl who had sparked my interest.

In college, I was interested in music, psychology, English, and physics. So what did I major in? Accounting! Why? Because accounting seemed like a difficult major—a good way to impress my friends. Also, being an accountant was prestigious and held the opportunity to make a lot of money. But prestige and money did not go a long way in making me happy, especially when I was working 8 to 10 hours a day at a job that bored me.

My unwillingness to let myself be known probably caused me the greatest difficulty in my relationships with the women I found the most attractive. My most recent relationship is a good example. After weeks of building up courage, I finally asked her out on a date. It was quickly obvious that she liked me as much as I liked her. I should have been elated, but instead I got scared about really making myself known to this woman. I put up a fake front designed to impress her. I was petrified of becoming too intimate or vulnerable. This led to behavior that was both hot and cold, as I kept testing her to see if I could let down my guard, be myself, and still be liked by her. When we broke up after 8 months, I was terribly lonely. I realize now that the relationship might have had a chance to have been meaningful on a long-term basis if I would have had the courage to risk presenting an honest picture of myself.

I am now amazed at how often I have chosen to avoid facing situations that would expose me to others. All of this because I don't want others to know me and dislike me the way I dislike myself.

Another former client wrote the following description of personal problems that originated in low levels of personal self-esteem:

Dragging Main Street with my friends in a '56 Ford convertible, we would occasionally damn some passerby with, "That guy is an accident looking for a place to happen."

More than a decade later, that statement, altered slightly, came floating back as I examined my feelings of beginning a career as a professor, a new PhD: I've been acting as though I'm a failure looking for a place to happen.

It seemed that whenever I began something new for which I had no experience, no "track record" of success, I expected this might be the place where I would fail. As a high school graduate, waiting for college to begin, I thought, This isn't going to be just like high school, where guys are here because they have to be here. These will be students who are here because they want an education. Can I measure up?

I went to college and found that it wasn't that much different. It was still a matter of completing assignments, taking tests, and writing papers. But, instead of recognizing and accepting that I had the ability, I tended to denigrate my expectations, deciding that there were a lot of goof-offs in college too. But in graduate school, that's where my true colors (inadequate bright yellow) would show.

When graduate school came along, it wasn't that much different: just more reading, more exams, and more papers. But where the sheep get separated from "us" goats was the graduate dissertation requirement—a piece of original research and a contribution to the scientific field. Well, I completed my dissertation, and it wasn't that tough. Did that mean I was that good, and a bona fide doctor of philosophy? No, of course not, it meant that I either fooled them or that the real test was just ahead. Almost anyone can be a student, but how about a faculty member at a university!

Another client provided this description of his reasons for being in therapy:

What am I doing here? I am 33 years old, married with 3 children, and a graduate of a good law school. I have a good position with my firm and a good salary. So why am I so tense and unable to enjoy any of this? And why am I getting psychological treatment?

Maybe it's because I don't know what I want to do for a living when I grow up. I am dragging myself to work every day, and most of the time I can't seem to concentrate. But I've got so much invested in it. Law is interesting to me. Besides, what else would I do if I quit?

When it comes right down to it, it seems like I didn't really choose to be a lawyer. Somehow it just happened. People would ask what I was going to be, and what do you do with a degree in English? So I said I was going to be a lawyer. That was cool and people thought I was hot stuff, so here I am being hot stuff. Except that I'm not a very good lawyer, and while the other guys are raking it in being trial lawyers, I stay back here doing research for the senior partners. My wife is envious of my classmates' salaries, but I'm just not the flashy, competitive type. Sometimes, I feel like I get dumped on by the more aggressive attorneys in the firm, but in the press of the situation, I can never think of what to say.

In each of these three examples, we can see the same thing: the trappings of external success coupled with internal distress. In each case, we are confronted with the same paradox. By what means do people learn to be so displeased with themselves when the world they live in is so eager to reward and approve of them?

## Ingredients of the Paradox

This is an intriguing paradox. Many of the traditional approaches to understanding the origins of self-esteem tend to emphasize social and interpersonal learning. Basically, these views suggest that individuals gradually acquire beliefs about themselves that are a reflection of the way they are treated by their social environment

(Bandura, 1986). In essence, people come to view and value themselves in much the same way they are viewed and valued by others. Of course, there are exceptions to this general orientation. Two notable ones include Rollo May's (1953) emphasis on personal awareness and self-alienation, and Carl Rogers's (1961) emphasis on self-congruence and perceptual accuracy. But even in these orientations, an unfavorable social environment is a crucial consideration. In both cases, it is the level of emotional acceptance in the social environment that fosters the conditions under which individuals become more or less self-accepting and self-congruent. We will review the contribution of all of these theoretical approaches in considerable detail in the next chapter.

For now, we only wish to emphasize that, according to these views, individuals with an abundance of approval and affection from their social environment, particularly from "significant others," are more likely to have high levels of self-esteem than are those coming from less favorable social learning environments. Sullivan (1962) was the first to formalize this view in his classic text *Schizophrenia as a Human Process*. One of his primary propositions was that the self-concept is made up largely of the reflected appraisals of significant others.

With these considerations in mind, the depth of the paradox becomes more apparent. Even the most successful people do not seem to develop any enduring immunity to problems of low self-esteem. Yet, most of our theoretical speculations suggest this should be otherwise. We need not limit our definition of success to business, finance, and high-status positions for this general statement to have a wide range of applicability. On the whole, it seems reasonable to suggest that a rigorous and objective assessment of the major life events of most people almost always shows that the absolute number of life successes exceeds the number of failures. In the course of a lifetime, most people manage to stay employed most of the time; have relationships in which they share both emotional and physical intimacy at least some of the time; provide support, sustenance, and direction for growing children or others they have responsibility for; keep their bills paid most of the time; and stay out of serious entanglements with the law. With just a moment's reflection, it becomes obvious that many of these life achievements are significant ones, requiring persistence, maturity, self-control, complex judgments, and the ability to endure short-term frustrations while long-term goals are pursued. Certainly there are exceptions to this general characterization, but, on the whole, the majority of people do seem to endure the trials of life relatively well yet fail to acquire a realistic sense of self-appreciation for their accomplishments. This is the paradox!

The question then is why, with 40 to 50 years of reasonably successful and responsible life experience completed, do so many people fail to acquire an enduring and realistic sense of self-appreciation? While some individuals do seem to have an easier time of it than do others, in an absolute sense, most people do experience more success in their lives than failure. In spite of this, many people fail to acquire a sense of meaningful and enduring personal self-appreciation that is proportional to their major successes in life. In some cases, it is probably fair to suggest that just the opposite is true. Self-doubts, a sense of personal inadequacy, and, in some cases, self-hatred prevail where self-approval would normally be expected. Without minimizing the difficulties of life all of us are required to contend with, it would seem more reasonable to find substantial numbers of people at midlife with a heightened sense of self-appreciation and approval. This would seem to be a more natural result of enduring and, perhaps, thriving in a society that can be competitive and hazardous at best. It seems paradoxical that such common and fundamental successes at life's primary tasks are not weighted more heavily in the equation that accounts for self-perceptions and self-approval.

## Insight Into the Paradox: Internal and External Factors

It should now be clear that we do not consider psychological factors external to the individual (social learning and environmental rewards) to be an adequate basis for understanding the origins of self-esteem. A broader conceptual foundation is needed. However, it would make little sense to deny or minimize the important role these social learning influences play in shaping our self-image. This is particularly true during early childhood, when the organism is so teachable and the shaping power of the social environment is so obvious. However, a theoretical position emphasizing only learning factors, which are external to the individual, does not seem to adequately account for the development of self-esteem. We see no necessity to rely solely on factors external to the organism to understand the origins of self-esteem for either children or adults.

There is ample evidence in the child development literature for the power of functionally autonomous reinforcement (Bandura, 1986). Anyone who has watched an infant take those first precarious steps across a room without falling cannot help but notice that the child does not need external reinforcement from parents to recognize and to be pleased with this accomplishment. The parents' pleasure in their child is equally obvious, but it is not the only source of reinforcement for the child. Thus, as we will suggest, any meaningful theory of self-esteem must take into account the individual's self-talk and self-thoughts spoken of in the early writings on the concept of the self (Allport, 1937; Hamachek, 1978; James, 1918).

Aside from having rather incomplete formulations of self-esteem, the traditional social learning approaches are also not much help to those unfortunate souls chronically plagued with low self-esteem. Even if we grant that these socially transmitted self-images might be more true than false, the reliance on external factors to understand the origins of self-esteem suffers from more serious concerns. If individuals must depend upon the affirmation from others in order to overcome low self-esteem, then part of a clinician's job is to teach the client to be a consummate performer, sensitive to the demands of the audience in order to win plaudits and "atta boys" from others. In our opinion, such a task is as impossible as it is undesirable.

Finally, common sense and clinical experience have led us to believe that high or low levels of personal self-esteem can be the result of events that have nothing to do with the way in which we are thought of by significant others. Children who are so lucky as to have affirming, affectionate, and loving parents should have unquestioning self-confidence. Conversely, children whose parents were harsh and critical should inexorably be victims who gradually internalize the criticisms as the given definition of themselves. Yet our clinical experience has taught us that this is not always the case. Some individuals coming from abusive and traumatic childhoods are remarkably intact, productive, and self-confident. Others, who come from apparently nurturing, supportive environments, may or may not be equally productive but suffer from debilitating self-doubt and low self-esteem. These observations suggest that more is involved in the development of high or low levels of self-esteem than just external social learning factors.

In summary, we consider the excessive reliance on external factors in understanding the origins of self-esteem to be ill-advised for the following reasons:

1. It does not accommodate the common observation that self-esteem does not necessarily vary as a function of numerous external factors such as loving parents, achieving positions of power and status, quality peer relationships, success in intimate relationships, or economic success.

2. It cannot explain the conspicuous absence of high levels of self-esteem in the general population, which probably includes many people who were raised in appropriately loving and nurturing social environments.

3. It denies the role of internal determinants of human behavior and psychological development, which common sense and simple introspection suggest to be valid considerations.

4. It is based on the implicit assumption that the development of self-esteem is a function of a favorable social environment that can be defined and that exerts uniform learning effects on different types of individuals.

## Overview

The model of self-esteem we are proposing will explain (a) the role of intrapsychic and interpersonal feedback in the development of self-esteem, and (b) the role of cognition, affect, and behavior in cultivating this important attribute. The model is based on assumptions about the role and influence of *interpersonal* and *intrapsychic* feedback. With regard to interpersonal feedback, we make the following assumptions:

> *1. Everyone should expect to receive regular amounts of negative feedback from the social environment, most of which is probably valid.*

*2. Most people receive and enjoy substantial amounts of authentic favorable social feedback but tend not to believe it.*

These two assumptions about interpersonal feedback have a number of striking implications for the development of self-esteem. One of the most important ones is the recognition that virtually everyone will experience and have to respond to interpersonal rejection. While we view rejection as a major activating catalyst for other psychological processes that are related to self-esteem, we do not suggest that rejection per se is a major cause of low self-esteem.

Instead, we suggest that individual response styles to rejection will involve varying degrees and mixtures of coping and defense. To the degree that a response style favors coping, it will increase the development of a realistic sense of personal identity. To the degree that a response style favors avoidance, it will increase one's tendency to try and gain the approval of others by *impression management*, that is, pretending to be what we believe is most acceptable to others. When people respond to rejection by impression management, they unwittingly create the conditions that will render most of the favorable feedback they receive untrustworthy, unbelievable, and psychologically impotent because of their internal awareness of their own facade. Even the most modest tendency to avoid the reality of rejection by making oneself more appealing to others by impression management can create the condition in which the individual cannot believe favorable feedback or questions the validity of unfavorable feedback. We explore the influence of these two conditions on the development of self-esteem in considerable depth.

The next two assumptions about intrapsychic feedback are equally striking:

*3. Self-evaluative processes are a psychological reality for most people.*

*4. Self-evaluations can provide a basis for continuous affective feedback from the self about the adequacy of the self.*

Ingredient in our discussion of internal feedback is the recognition that self-evaluations regularly accompany virtually any type of human experience. In essence, when there is consistency in one's tendency to cope or avoid conflict, there is a continuous basis for internal feedback from the self about the adequacy of the self. Avoidance motivated by fear and anxiety generates negative self-evaluations because of the inherently undesirable qualities of this behavior. Coping generates favorable self-evaluations because of the high quality of the psychological responses inherent in this behavior. Even though these self-evaluative processes go on at different levels of clarity and explicitness for different people, the effects are a psychological reality for most people. And it is the nature and quality of this internal, affective feedback that defines the nature of the organism to itself. High or low levels of self-esteem, then, are the result and the reflection of the internal, affective feedback the organism most commonly experiences.

Finally, we discuss the role of all of these factors hierarchically and developmentally, suggesting that levels of self-esteem are neither fixed in youth nor uniformly influenced by the same factors across the life span. We do suggest that internal self-evaluations play a more important role in determining the form and substance of self-esteem than do external evaluations— though both are clearly influential.

A brief overview of each of the remaining chapters is given below:

**Chapter 2—Conceptual themes: Overview and analysis.** This chapter provides a concise overview of the most prominent contributors to the conceptual and empirical development of the current concept of self-esteem, ranging from William James to Rollo May. The common themes and issues inherent in this body of literature are identified and discussed.

**Chapter 3—Avoidance and coping: Basic considerations.** This chapter discusses the role and function of avoidance in disordered behavior and coping in normal behavior. These concepts are considered in a cross-cultural context and are presented as building blocks for understanding the role of coping and avoidance in the development of high and low levels of self-esteem.

**Chapter 4—Internal and external feedback: Basic assumptions.** The role of feedback in human development is discussed in this chapter. Particular emphasis is placed on clarifying the difference between self-evalutive processes (internal feedback) and interpersonal feedback in the development of personal self-esteem. The psychological mechanisms and assumptions that influence the effects of both forms of feedback are also discussed.

**Chapter 5—Introduction to the model.** All of the major concepts introduced in the previous chapters are now integrated into a conceptual model of self-esteem. This model focuses on both the internal and external determinants of self-esteem and discusses the cognitive, affective, and behavioral considerations that are believed to influence the development of self-esteem. It is suggested that levels of self-esteem are neither fixed in youth nor uniformly influenced by the same factors across the life span.

**Chapter 6—Clinical applications: Remedial considerations in psychotherapy.** This chapter focuses on explaining and illustrating how the chronic patterns of avoidance that breed low levels of self-esteem can be permanently interrupted. Clinical illustrations and actual therapy dialogues are used to illustrate the application of the principles discussed in earlier chapters.

**Chapter 7—Developmental considerations in psychotherapy: Enhancing coping responses.** This chapter focuses on the means and methods for actually improving self-esteem. The patterns of coping that are essential to improved self-esteem are defined and illustrated. Numerous clinical illustrations and actual therapy dialogues are used to illustrate the application of the principles discussed in earlier chapters.

**Chapter 8—Unique qualities of the therapeutic relationship.** Because the model of self-esteem we are proposing departs from many of the traditional views about the origins of self-esteem, our conception of growth-inducing relationships is also different in several important respects. These differences are discussed and illustrated with examples.

**Chapter 9—Family relations and the development of self-esteem.** The fundamental ingredients in family relationships and child-rearing practices that are essential to the development of self-esteem are discussed. The importance of parental authenticity during stress and conflict is emphasized as a primary means of modeling the coping skills essential to the development of an enduring sense of personal well-being. Several myths about family relationships and child-rearing practices are also identified, discussed, and challenged.

# 2

# Conceptual Themes: Overview and Analysis

L ike any other model, the propositions in this book have their
conceptual ancestors: hypotheses about the nature of self-
esteem, its origins and development, and how to ameliorate low
self-esteem. This chapter's purpose is to consider early as well as
contemporary contributions that broadly mark the directions
taken in utilizing the construct.

The history of self-esteem as a concept began with writings of
some of the most well-known theorists in psychology, but early
theoretical efforts were followed by years in which the concept
was neglected as being unscientific and soft-headed. Gradually,
research began to accumulate, primarily oriented toward the measurement of self-esteem as a global, trait-like entity. Research attempts to measure self-esteem were resoundingly criticized at
irregular intervals by Wylie (1961, 1974, 1979). Finally, in the
present decade, a new generation of social psychologists has
claimed renewed utility of the concept through more refined measurement of specific aspects of the self-concept (see Markus &
Wurf, 1987).

This chapter reviews four major areas of literature on self-
esteem: (1) theoretical contributions, ranging from William James
to Carl Rogers; (2) conceptual developments, emphasizing contemporary efforts derived from research; (3) developmental writings, which focus on the antecedents of self-esteem; and (4) the
therapy literature for treatment of self-esteem problems. Inasmuch as the thrust of our concern is clinical, we emphasize the

applied elements in each of the formulations. Following each major section, we compare the authors' concepts to the proposed model. The review is by no means exhaustive, of course. Not only is the volume of literature too large to reasonably include in a book chapter, but often relevant concepts can be found under other labels, such as self-efficacy, self-evaluation, and self-concept.

# Theoretical Contributions

## Early Theorists

The concept of self-esteem per se is not discussed in depth but must be winnowed from related ideas about the self in the writings of early theorists such as William James, Alfred Adler, George Herbert Mead, and Gordon Allport. Similarly, because the focus is broad in these earlier writers, not much attention is given to questions of clinical concern or their development and remediation. Each thinker is considered briefly here to establish the "prime movers" of the concept.

**William James.** For James (1890), the self psychologically encompasses all of the attributes the individual would refer to as "part of me"—one's body, abilities, and reputation; even one's children, home, and possessions. If any of those component parts is diminished or enhanced, people respond as though they themselves were diminished or enhanced because they have indeed defined the part as the self. Thus, each person bases what James calls self-feeling or self-love on the successes and failures of what has been chosen as being the most true self. All the other equally possible selves not chosen become irrelevant to the individual's self-esteem.

> I, who for the time have staked my all on being a psychologist, am mortified if others know much more psychology than I. But I am contented to wallow in the grossest ignorance of Greek. My deficiencies there give me no sense of personal humiliation at all. Had I "pretensions" to be a linguist, it would have been just the reverse. . . . Our self-feeling in this world depends entirely on what we *back*

seem to decrease one's personal responsibility for the outcome of the self-esteem equation, creating instead a person distanced from the self.

*Commentary*—James makes no attempt to be a clinician describing means to overcome low self-esteem. He takes the position that people can be active in choosing and meeting their goals and are, therefore, capable of modifying their self-esteem. Without mention of environmental or parental influence, James describes the self as it exists in the adult. Hence, no comment can be made about his position on the developmental process of establishing self-esteem. Given James's successes/pretensions formula, however, one cannot help but wonder if he would assume that some pretensions or goals are universal among normal children, such as the desire to be loved and affirmed as valuable to their parents. Similarly, the goals to be affirmed by age-mates may be equally universal. Moreover, he doesn't speak to the critical and often terrifying moment of choosing to "back" one's self with a particular pretension. As clinicians, we have seen many clients who, having crashed on the shoals of unmet goals, now experience terrible anxiety about committing to seek new successes. The choice to avoid those goals, of course, exacts its own price upon their fragile self-esteem.

**Alfred Adler.** Adler was a practicing psychiatrist, more concerned with understanding abnormal behavior than other theorists considered here. His works are considered to be among the forerunners of social psychiatry, emphasizing the impact of family and society upon the individual. Indeed, Adler positioned the goals of cooperation (*social interest*) in work, community, and marriage as being central to the individual's mental health. Thus, even though Adlerian psychology is also known as Individual Psychology, it is not an *individualistic* psychology. His choice of the word was to emphasize a holistic understanding of the individual involved meaningfully with society, in contrast to Freud's and Jung's focus on unconscious determinants of behavior (Ansbacher & Ansbacher, 1956).

Adler was also a phenomenologist, believing that each person constructs his or her unique view of reality through what he called the *creative self*. This self strives to make sense of life, to meaningfully chart a course toward some final goal of completeness or perfection. Adler called the motivation of the creative self "striving for superiority" (a term that means self-actualization or self-fulfillment rather than narcissistic invulnerability).

Early in life the creative self chooses a *style of life*, a "window" through which it interprets events throughout life in order to reach its final goals. The individual's personal evaluations of reality are so subjectively compelling that he or she acts as if these were the only possible interpretations. If, through proper upbringing, one chooses a life-style in keeping with the innate human needs to belong, to be productive, and to be intimate, that person will be healthy. If one mistakenly chooses goals of domination, overweening dependency, isolation, and so forth, the search for a sense of completion and security will be in vain.

Adler was also responsible for the term *inferiority complex*. Feelings of inferiority represent the opposite side of striving for superiority; they arise early in life from the helplessness and imperfection of childhood. Thus, individuals are seen as seeking both to achieve actualization as well as to avoid the "minus situation," a sense of inferiority or incompleteness.

While all people normally struggle with feelings of inferiority at times, and these emotions may be appropriate motivators for achievement, the inferiority complex as such is qualitatively different. The inferiority complex is more pervasive and chronic, the consequence of abdicating the responsibility of living in accordance with social feeling. The individual becomes fearful and complaining, often evidencing physical symptoms of anxiety.

> To be a human being means to have inferiority feelings. One recognizes one's own powerlessness in the face of nature. But in the mentally healthy this inferiority feeling acts as a motive for productivity, as a motive for attempting to overcome obstacles, to maintain oneself in life. Only the oversized inferiority feeling, which is to be regarded as a failure in upbringing, burdens the character with oversensitivity, leads to egotistical self-considerations and self-reflections, lays foundations for neurosis with all its known symptoms which let life become a torture. (Adler, 1979, pp. 54–55)

The neurotic twist on striving for superiority that accompanies the inferiority complex is to use the symptoms to further, more permanently, avoid the responsibility to respond cooperatively. Now the individual is apt to say to the self and others, "Just imagine what I could have accomplished if it were not for my disturbance and these painful symptoms, caused by something (my heredity, my body, my education) for which I am not responsible."

Adler (1979) described the goal of treatment as being basically reeducative. The therapist must discern the client's mistaken choice in life-style, wherein the person strives for a socially useless goal of superiority. The therapist must help the client recognize the mistake and assist in increasing the "ability to cooperate," to accept and become involved in the elements of social interest. Therapy becomes a process of helping the client to belatedly mature.

*Commentary*—Adler does not mention the concept of self-esteem. Indeed, to the degree that self-esteem became a self-absorbing goal, he would consider it to be a source of neurosis. Perhaps a more appropriate Adlerian term would be *self-acceptance* ("the courage to be imperfect," to use a contemporary Adlerian slogan).

> The patient must be guided away from himself, toward productivity for others; he must be educated toward social interest; he must be led from his seclusion from the world, back to existence; he must be brought to the only correct insight, that he is as important for the community as anyone else; he must get to feel at home on this earth. (Adler, 1964, p. 200)

Thus, appropriate self-esteem entails a person's acceptance of the right to belong to humanity and a willingness to contribute to the social interest of the group.

Adler's work introduces a concept of considerable importance to the model to be presented—the issue of coping versus avoiding. That is, Adler described the essence of what we may term the low-self-esteem person as the individual who avoids the call to participate in the community's needs. Everyone must deal with feelings of inferiority, which come from being immature and observing others much more competent. Chronic avoidance of social interest produces the inferiority complex. The low-self-esteem person hides behind symptoms, fearing to give up narcissistic self-strivings for superiority.

**Charles H. Cooley.** Cooley's (1902) observations on the self take a decidedly more social approach than those of James, albeit a still more personal one than those of George Herbert Mead, whose work is an extension of Cooley's. To Cooley, the self has several aspects, the most importunate or pressing part of which is the social self. This social self, he says, arises from the individual's observations of how others respond to the self. That is, people learn to define themselves by their perceptions of the way others define them, the "looking-glass self."

> As we see our face, figure, and dress in the glass and are interested in them because they are ours, and pleased or otherwise with them according as they do or do not answer to what we should like them to be; so in imagination we perceive in another's mind some thought of our appearance, manners, aims, deeds, character, friends, and so on, and are variously affected by it. . . .
>
> This is evident from the fact that the character and weight of that other, in whose mind we see ourselves, makes all the difference with our feeling. We are ashamed to seem evasive in the presence of a straightforward man, cowardly in the presence of a brave one, gross in the eyes of a refined one, and so on. We always imagine, and in the imagining share the judgments of the other mind. (Cooley, 1902, p. 152)

While there are other selves in Cooley's theory, less mention is made of them. The social self is not only demanding, it is also the vehicle by which the internal sense of self develops and is refined. The child who is thrilled about some new achievement must show it to someone else. The other's response either further elates and enlarges the sense of self or, conversely, humiliates or enrages it, casting doubt on the self-perception of worth.

> We live on, cheerful, self-confident, conscious of helping make the world go round, until in some rude hour we learn that we do not stand so well as we thought we did, that

the image of us is tarnished. Perhaps we do something, quite naturally, that we find the social order is set against, or perhaps it is the ordinary course of our life that is not so well regarded as we supposed. At any rate, we find with a chill of terror that the world is cold and strange, and that our self-esteem, self-confidence, and hope, being chiefly founded upon opinions, attributed to others, go down in the crash. Our reason may tell us that we are no less worthy than we were before, but dread and doubt do not permit us to believe it. (Cooley, 1902, p. 216)

There are three steps in the momentary process by which the social self gathers its delightful or bitter food from the minds of others: (1) the individual's perception of how he or she must appear to the other person, (2) the individual's interpretation of how the other person evaluates him or her on the basis of that interpreted perception, and (3) the individual's personally experienced affective response to the perceived judgment. In other words, translated into a first-person scenario, the elements could be characterized as: "How do I appear to this person," "What does this person think about me (because of my appearance)," and "I feel (gratified or embarrassed or angry) toward myself because of this encounter." The interpretive nature of the described elements is critical. Here, for the clinician, the obvious likelihood arises that many, if not most, individuals project their own images of themselves onto the judging person(s) and then receive them back as "objective feedback," confirmatory proof of what each had thought about himself or herself all along. The stronger and more rigid a person's tendency to project feelings, the less likely that person is to accurately attend to the feedback coming from the other individual.

*Commentary*—At first glance, it would appear that Cooley views people as being basically reactive, responding helplessly to others' opinions of them. Cooley does view the development of self as proceeding socially but assumes that maturity brings greater self-control to monitor and direct one's own responses, making one less vulnerable to the effects of others' opinions. The mature individual is sensitive to the feelings of others but maintains the stability to choose one's own direction. Cooley does not describe how the internalization takes place.

Like James, Cooley is writing a descriptive, theoretical work. Little is said about changing or enhancing self-esteem. However, he asserts that people should search for a balance between valuing others' judgments and opinions and developing their own stable ways of thinking, which "cannot be upset by passing phases of praise or blame." How one is to approach the correct balance is not mentioned. But Cooley believes a judicious concern for the self (self-love) is appropriate. The more people understand themselves and prize their abilities, the more apt they are to risk performing in public, assuming that their assessment of themselves will be mirrored in the eyes of others.

**George Herbert Mead.** As a sociologist, Mead (1934) views the development of the self as most pertinent to the process of the individual's becoming an integrated part of a social group. His theory is concerned with the description of appropriate socialization, not self-esteem. As mentioned, Cooley's concept of the looking-glass self is extended in Mead's work. Language and society are essential elements in the development of the self because it is through interaction that individuals come to see themselves the way others see them. Significant others in the individual's life have a determining influence on self-esteem. The socialization process that teaches people values about all other aspects of the world applies to the ways in which they see themselves. Observing the actions and attitudes of parents and significant others, an individual gradually adopts them and internalizes them as one's own, as though one were an external object.

> That process to which I have just referred, of responding to one's self as another responds to it, taking part in one's own conversation with others, being aware of what one is saying and using that awareness of what one is saying to determine what one is going to say thereafter—that is a process with which we are all familiar. (Strauss, 1964, p. 205).

Without that socializing process, says Mead, social groups and communities could not function. Even children's games can be carried to some conclusion only because the attitudes of others about the rules of the game are accepted by all and, therefore, govern the activities. Individuals do not become complete selves until they can take the attitude of the groups they belong to as their own, including the attitude of the group toward themselves.

*Commentary*—Mead seems to adopt the most passive stance thus far reviewed about the individual's ability to autonomously determine personal self-esteem. He writes as if we come to look at ourselves as objects, without attachment or affective loading toward that person who is oneself.

The implications of Mead's theory are obvious: In order to have high self-esteem, individuals must have been held in high esteem by significant others. If, as children, they were ignored, rejected, or demeaned, they will view themselves as objects worthy of such spite. They will think of themselves with impatience, derision, and scorn. The therapeutic inference, of course, is that people must find significant others who will validate them, see them as worthwhile, and communicate praise and encouragement. Slowly, people should come to see themselves that way.

Although therapists might object to the pictured helplessness of the person so damaged, many subscribe to the posture it represents, wherein the therapist is reparenting the client as the substitute good parent the child never had. Indeed, the work of Truax and Carkhuff in the 1960s asserted that the essential conditions for therapeutic improvement were based on the relationship elements of unconditional positive regard, genuineness, and nonpossessive warmth (Truax & Carkhuff, 1967).

**Gordon Allport.** The growth of the awareness of a self proceeds along developmental learning lines, according to Allport (1961). From an early recognition of what is *me* and *not me* in the first year of life (a bodily awareness), a sense of continuity of identity over time in the second year, to a sense of self-esteem in the beginning of the third year, the child gradually adds parts to the sense of self. From ages 3 to 6, the concepts of self-image and extension of self (as seen in considering one's possessions a part of the self) come into focus. Here a child begins to learn what is expected of him or her to be considered a good or a bad person.

Cognitive maturation in adolescence produces a sense of self as a thinker, for the first time able to be conscious of the self and consider the effects of one's own thought. The ability to consolidate the aspects of self into an individual and cohesive identity is a major task of adolescence. The final task in the developmental maturation of the aspects of the self is a goal-directedness (what Allport calls "propriate striving"), a sense of purpose, knowing where one wants to go in life.

These several elements of the self Allport names the *proprium*, using a new label to encompass all the aspects a person learns about the object *my self*. These are the parts that the individual knows about the self. There remains the *knower*, that part which has observed and organized the propriate elements into the identity.

Allport's major contribution to the study of self-esteem is the recognition of the part played by psychological defenses. Harking back to James's formula regarding the ratio between aspirations and achievements, he notes that a surprising number of people experience strong feelings of inferiority. He points to a study indicating that only 12 percent of a group of college students do *not* know what it is to suffer the anxiety of inferiority feelings (McKee & Sherriffs, 1957). When one occasionally feels the disappointment of failure, the individual can shrug off the feelings or make adjustments in goals. If, on the other hand, the sense of failure happens frequently, the result is Adler's so-called inferiority complex, defined by Allport as "a strong and persistent tension arising from a somewhat morbid emotional attitude toward one's felt deficiency in his personal equipment" (Allport, 1961, p. 130).

At issue for the ultimate development of normal or abnormal personalities are the methods each individual uses to combat the experience of inferiority. Some will exert greater effort and practice, making the problem become a strength instead of a perceived weakness. Others will decide to pursue other goals. And still others will use psychological defenses such as rationalization or denial to avoid the pain of recognizing and facing the problem. The critical juncture for neurotic behavior occurs in the use or misuse of the psychological defenses.

> The processes making for normality and for abnormality are very different. Let us take an example. To *confront* the world and its problems is intrinsically a wholesome thing to do, since it brings about appropriate adjustment and mastery. To *escape* from the world is intrinsically a dangerous and diseased thing to do. Extreme escape is found in

the most severe forms of mental disorder, the psychoses. But now, you ask, do we not all do some escaping? Yes— and what is more, we may obtain recreation from it and find our daydreams eventually constructive. But such harmless and even beneficial results can come about *only if the dominant process is confrontation.* Left to itself, escapism spells abnormality. (Allport, 1961, p. 153)

> The mechanisms of ego-defense are sly devices by which we try to circumvent discomfort and anxiety. These self-protective strategies are common, but they do not by any means constitute the normal person's entire repertoire of adjustive actions. Often he faces up to his weaknesses and failings and proceeds to cope with them realistically. He meets his guilt, his fears, he blunders head on, and works out a way of life that fully and consciously takes them into account and makes of them building blocks for a more integrated personal edifice. The opposite of defense, then, is coping. The neurotic shows much defense, less coping. In the healthy personality coping ordinarily predominates. (Allport, 1961, p. 156)

*Commentary*—Allport's theory is very much an individual psychology, relying on the presumption of learning and choice to explain both the development of the self and the trajectory of the personality toward normality or abnormality. The press of society and interaction is barely mentioned. Parental influences are only alluded to. Of the authors considered thus far, Allport is the first to emphasize so clearly the importance of self-discipline, the courage to confront difficulties as the means toward health and greater self-esteem. As will be seen, his focus is a central issue addressed in the model to be presented.

**Rollo May.** In his consideration of *being* and *nonbeing*, May (1983) defines being as more than another name for self. It is one's "pattern of potentialities," one's sense of one's totality as a separate and unique person. Individuals are aware, some more dimly than others, of their being, and that relationship of awareness to expression of potentialities is the pivotal balance between mental health and neurosis. All people have a fundamental need to remain "centered" in themselves, aware of their being, accepting their right to be, and willing to tolerate the anxiety attendant upon its fragility.

Repression occurs when individuals choose to block off from awareness some part of their being. Yet, for May, at another level the individual still knows that the blockage exists and that one's being is denied expression or, perhaps more accurately, existence. Neurotic symptoms appear as a response to an attack upon the individual's sense of existence centered in the self. People adjust to protect their being from attack, but in doing so narrow the range of their behavior, accepting some portion of nonbeing. Neurotic individuals live in a shrunken world, rigidly clinging to symptoms, which both preserves their centeredness and sacrifices other aspects of their being. In our contemporary culture, many individuals suffer a neuroticism that comes from slavish conformity—outer-directed individuals who try so hard to please and identify with others that their own being is denied. The internal conflict between being and nonbeing creates anxiety, a uniquely human characteristic for May, which is different from any other emotion because it signals the individual's vulnerability to the many shades of nonbeing.

> The anxiety a person feels when someone he respects passes him on the street without speaking, for example, is not as intense as the fear he experiences when the dentist seizes the drill to attack a sensitive tooth. But the gnawing threat of the slight on the street may hound him all day long and torment his dreams at night, whereas the feeling of fear, though it was quantitatively greater, is gone for the time being as soon as he steps out of the dentist's chair. The difference is that the anxiety strikes at the central core of his self-esteem and his sense of value as a self, which is the most important aspect of his experience of himself as a being. (May, 1983, p. 110)

On the other hand, the presence of anxiety may also portend the freedom to fulfill a new potentiality. Recognizing the possibility of a new expression of the individual's being disrupts the self's security, calling into question other established patterns and beliefs about the self. Thus, the inherent risk entailed in change fosters a tendency to deny the potentiality, creating the conflict between being and nonbeing and the dread of anxiety.

Guilt, another singularly human emotion, is the inevitable consequence of denying one's potentialities. Thus, no one can successfully evade the responsibility to be, to become authentically oneself, without experiencing the anxiety and guilt associated with low self-esteem. The existential remedy to low self-esteem is clear. The individual must first become truly "self-conscious," open to the recognition of one's potentialities and willing to tolerate the anxiety entailed by the conflict it will generate. Finally, a person must have the "courage to be," living and accepting these potentialities.

> To the extent that my sense of existence is authentic, it is precisely *not* what others have told me I should be, but is the one Archimedes point I have to stand on from which to judge what parents and authorities demand. . . . The sense of being gives the person a basis for a self-esteem which is not merely the reflection of others' views about him. For if your self-esteem must rest in the long run on social validation, you have not self-esteem, but a more sophisticated form of social conformity. (May, 1983, p. 102)

May's explication of the conditions for self-esteem, embedded as they are in the search for being, emphasizes the central importance of those conditions in the person's psychological life. True self-esteem cannot obtain without authenticity, a person's willingness to express individuality in spite of the fact that others will undoubtedly exert pressure to change or deny it.

*Commentary*—May's work asserts the central importance of establishing autonomy to self-esteem. Psychological health requires individuality, listening to one's own being, and, therefore, aloneness. The person must repudiate or at least hold in suspicion any aspect of self that may have been defined by an outside source. However, it is also true for May that people need to venture from their centeredness in order to relate intimately to others. The critical question becomes how far can people risk their sense of being in order to participate with people about whom they care.

Although May doesn't describe either the process of the development of being or the appropriate position of parents' nurturing, their place is indirectly emphasized when he speaks of the task of the existential therapist. The essential first task of a therapist is to reach across the gap between his or her existence and that of the client, to create a communion wherein clients can begin to safely experience their own separate but unique existence.

**Carl R. Rogers.** The personality theory of Carl Rogers (1951) is an inductive summary, as it were, of his extensive experience as a psychotherapist. Developed gradually from his clinical observations and systematized into 19 propositions, Rogers views the condition of the self as being the pivotal factor in determining a person's emotional health. Like existential therapists, he views the essential condition for maladjustment to be a schism between what he calls the individual's own organismic valuing of events and the values that he or she consciously asserts. More will be said of that later.

Rogers was a phenomenologist, asserting that each person lives in a private and unique world of one's own perceptions, responding to the environment from the window of personal awareness. It is the individual's reality, the perceptual map one uses to choose actions and interpret others' responses. The developing infant gradually distinguishes between that part of this private world which is "me" and the portion which is "not me." Within the gradually developing sense of self, the child places a value, negative or positive, on those experiences deemed satisfying and enhancing or, conversely, threatening.

Because all people need acceptance, especially early in development, evaluation from others may violate the child's organismic valuing process. A prototypical example is the child who enjoys experiencing a bowel movement whenever and wherever he or she wishes. Yet the parents angrily communicate the message that the child is not loved and, therefore, in danger of being rejected for defecating at will. The resultant conflict may coerce the child into distrusting the internal sense of self, seeing it as dangerous and to be repudiated. Instead, the child may adopt or "introject" the values of the parents and define them as his or her own. For Rogers, introjects from parents or others are distorted symbolizations of experience and, therefore, can never match the sensed validity of direct experiencing.

It is here, it seems, that the individual begins on a pathway which he later describes as "I don't really know myself."

> The primary sensory and visceral reactions are ignored, or not permitted into consciousness, except in distorted form. The values which might be built upon them cannot be admitted to awareness. A concept of self based in part upon a distorted symbolization has taken their place. (Rogers, 1951, p. 501)

The perceived self grows out of the configuration of the directly experienced self and the distorted introjects. When a perception enters the consciousness that is distinctly at variance with the self as structured, the individual either denies its meaning or further distorts it. In that fashion, the self now channelizes or narrows the range of information and behaviors available to the person, confirming the structure of the self as one's definition of one's identity. If a substantial discrepancy exists between the person's organismic experiencing and the self-concept, tension and anxiety build as a result of the conflict between the organism's effort to satisfy its needs and the conscious self's attempt to remain unaware of those needs. The person may feel "like I'm coming undone."

How does psychological treatment help? Rogers's definition of the goal of therapy is the restructuring of the self. That restructuring process must be accomplished by the individual alone, of course, because the therapist's values would become another introject. The therapist's task is to create an atmosphere of acceptance and desire to understand. Therein, the counselor establishes a "safe place" for clients' to gradually permit themselves to explore their experience and compare their own sense of valuing as a process against the static codes of the introjected value system. As clients come to know "the real me," they can accept into awareness all the aspects of their organismic experiencing, respect and recognize their impulses, and consciously control their responding in a congruent manner. Clients will experience more spontaneity and yet also more accountability because all of their experiences are available to consciousness.

> The client finds that it is his own organism which supplies the evidence upon which value judgments may be made. He discovers that his own senses, his own physiological

equipment, can provide the data for making value judgments and for continuously revising them. No one needs to tell him that it is good to act in a freer and more spontaneous fashion, rather than in the rigid way to which he has been accustomed. He senses, he feels that it is satisfying and enhancing. Or when he acts in a defensive fashion, it is his own organism that feels the immediate and short-term satisfaction of being protected and that also senses the longer-range dissatisfaction of having to remain on guard. (Rogers, 1951, p. 523)

Rogers anticipates the reader's possible concern that total trust of one's organismic valuing process will lead to anarchy. Rogers's experience as a psychotherapist is that the opposite is true. Because people share many fundamental needs, he finds that each individual responds to a personal valuing process with a high degree of commonality. Each person, therefore, creates a unique and personal value system but one that is genuinely socialized.

*Commentary*—Like other writers whom we have considered, Rogers's thrust in understanding self-esteem is directed toward an individual's learning to know the self or perhaps, more accurately, learning to know the self that he or she is. Rogers differs in the sense that the self to be discovered is not the self's abilities or interests (the cognitive-achievement domain), but the person's values and even affective preferences. Rogers asserts that each person's most deeply held values are fundamentally beneficent and social. Adler similarly asserts that the biological substrate of all people is socially oriented but suggests that it must be nurtured and trained in order to make itself manifest. Rogers seems to suggest that the organismic valuing process is the only source necessary for calibration of values.

## Summary and Comparison

Let us consider how the early theories speak to the issues of self-esteem. How does a person develop high self-esteem? For James, the person chooses an identity, a self, and successfully matches accomplishment to hopes. People become what they have hoped they are. Self-esteem is dependent upon outcomes—setting goals and reaching them. For Adler, the person creates a style of life that fulfills the biological predicates of being human—feeling a belongingness and contributing to the social interest. The person becomes what personal evolution and appropriate parenting have prepared one to be. Self-esteem is dependent upon accepting imperfectness and still striving to complete the goals of a chosen style of life. For Cooley and Mead, the person is fortunate enough to have an environment that esteems one and the talents to win approbation. People come to see themselves approvingly because others see them approvingly. Self-esteem depends upon winning approbation from significant others. For Allport, the person develops an appropriate goal-directedness and responds to threat with healthy psychological defenses. The individual becomes psychologically healthy by coping with difficulties instead of avoiding them. For May, the person is willing to recognize all of one's being and respond congruently to that which is the self. One becomes oneself in spite of pressure to deny or distort aspects of being. Self-esteem depends upon the courage to allow all of oneself to exist. For Rogers, the person trusts the organismic valuing processes, choosing a life consistent with those deeply held values. Like May, Rogers suggests that high-self-esteem persons become themselves, not the introjects foisted upon them by others. Self-esteem depends upon the courage to become and remain authentic.

Our proposed model will be presented in its entirety in the next several chapters. However, it is useful to briefly compare it to the theories described above. We assert that self-esteem in the adult is an internal process that focuses upon the inherently self-affirming or self-negating evaluations that obtain inexorably from observing oneself respond to psychological threat. While it is important to be approved of, we suggest that fundamentally self-esteem is not dependent upon winning approbation, nor does it require the existence of an articulated self dependent upon congruent responding. We suggest that the essential construction of self-esteem occurs in the process of exercising coping or, conversely, avoidance responses, not in their outcome as judged by meeting goals.

Now we turn to self-esteem propositions that have emerged from contemporary research in social psychology.

## Recent Conceptual Developments

Until recently, the study of self-esteem as a focus for research has yielded disappointingly small fruit. Ruth Wylie (1961, 1974, 1979) comprehensively reviewed the measurement of self-esteem and its relationship to theory. She concluded:

> Internal inconsistency apparently characterizes all personality theories which emphasize constructs concerning the self, although the vagueness of their statements often makes it impossible to identify inconsistencies with certainty. On this score alone, none of these theories, as presently formulated, can be called wholly scientific. Probably these inconsistencies are partly responsible for the poor state of measurement and research design in this area. (1974, p. 322)

Contemporary reviews, however, have asserted that research in self-concept is finally coming of age. Markus and Wurf (1987) claim the progress has come about through a decision to abandon the attempt to study self-esteem as a global, unidimensional entity. Measurement of the self-concept is becoming increasingly viewed as being influenced both by the self-motives being served as well as the press of the immediate social situation. Researchers have also chosen to examine more fine-grained behaviors. Thus, the self is seen as

> . . . a dynamic interpretive structure that mediates most significant *intrapersonal* processes (including information processing, affect, and motivation), and a wide variety of *interpersonal* processes (including social perception; choice of situation, partner, and interaction strategy; and reaction to feedback). (Markus & Wurf, 1987, p. 300)

### Disparity Models

As illustrated earlier in the book, one of the most intriguing theoretical questions for the clinician is, "How is it that so many apparently successful people privately experience such negative self-esteem?" As suggested above, we propose that the answer lies in the individual's choosing to avoid difficult situations rather than coping with them and doing so in a manner that is, at some level, unacceptable to the self. The individual's self-evaluations are, therefore, negative in spite of the possibly laudatory judgments of significant people in one's life.

Other authors have suggested the importance of disparity to explain negative self-esteem. Higgins and his associates (Higgins, 1983; Higgins, Klein, & Strauman, 1985) hypothesized three classes of self-conceptions: The "actual" self (the doer or performer of tasks), the "ideal" self (representing the attributes that in fantasy the person would like to possess as an ideal conception), and the "ought" self (representing characteristics that the person reasonably expects to achieve). Discrepancy between classes of self produces discomfort. Thus, Higgins et al. (1985) found that depression was correlated with disparities between the actual and ideal selves, while anxiety was more likely to be associated with disparities between the actual and ought selves. It is assumed that chronic disparities of either kind yield a pervasive sense of negative self-esteem.

Rosenberg's (1979) major study of adolescent self-esteem posits a similar classification of selves: the extant self (as one privately views oneself), the desired self (as one would like to be), and the presenting self (the self one attempts to disclose to others). It must be remembered, Rosenberg cautions, no one knows the "real" self, but each individual creates and interprets images of the self. There is no way to know who we really are. People must impose a construction on their acts without ever truly being able to verify their assumptions. Still, many people attempt to get verification of their worth from others.

Within the extant self, Rosenberg differentiates between self-confidence and self-esteem. Self-confidence is closely related to Bandura's (1977) concept of self-efficacy—the expectation of successfully meeting challenges and overcoming obstacles, and a general sense of control of self and the environment. Self-esteem is more an affective sense of accepting one's self and feeling self-worth. Thus, self-confidence may contribute to self-esteem, but the two are not synonymous. A person may expect to succeed at any task and still not accept such accomplishments as *counting,* of being worthy of self-respect.

Like Higgins's (1983) conceptions of the self described above, Rosenberg describes the desired self as having an idealized component and a "committed" component, which is that part of the desired self that we really think we can become. A third component is the moral self, which is more or less a set of standards and values to which the individual feels obligated rather than an actual image. Its particular importance in self-esteem is the condemnation that follows violation of one's standards. The experience of self-condemnation seems to represent more direct damage to self-esteem than other failures. Rosenberg cites the example of the soldier who commits suicide because he fled under fire. Ironically, he kills himself *as punishment for being afraid of being killed.*

The importance of the presenting self, or self as shown to others, appears in the attempts people make to manage the impressions they create. Herein, the theoretical issue of disparity conflict becomes particularly meaningful. The moral self may be discrepant from the image the individual privately holds and may, therefore, conflict with other components of the self-concept. It may view one's attempt to impress others as putting on an act and, therefore, as duplicitous and shameful. Moreover, because any positive feedback one receives is attributed derisively to acting ability, a person cannot believe what may be sincere praise. A second possibility is that the extant self may view one's pretensions as committing one's self to a performance standard of which the person privately may not feel confident. This self-doubt vitiates the individual's commitment and concentration when there is performance pressure.

Another alternative observed by clinicians is that of an individual who is sufficiently insecure in the verification process of the extant self that one constantly seeks verification from others. This person may be in the vulnerable position of having to convince others about having certain characteristics in order to convince the self about having them. The individual lives in the constant apprehension of not knowing who the self is and that the image just confirmed by one person may be invalidated by another.

Greenwald and Breckler (1985) propose a developmental sequence by which four facets of the self emerge, viewing the process as analogous to Loevinger's (1976) theories of ego development. The *diffuse* self is actually a preself, a self oriented only to survival and pleasure needs. It is not a true self because it does not represent an object of knowledge. That is, the diffuse self occurs before the child has sufficient self-consciousness to form a concept of self. The *public* self gradually develops out of the realization that many pleasures come from pleasing powerful others. It is sensitive to evaluation from others, seeking to win approval and social verification of worth. The public self provides a forum for the development of values and a gradual definition of self apart from public evaluation, forming the *private* self. The self now has an inner audience for evaluation, creating more sensitivity to its own attitudes and affective states. A final self, the *collective* self, forms as the individual identifies with and internalizes the goals of the reference group. The individual's goals now transcend being concerned about pleasing others or meeting personal needs for achievement; they are focused on advancing the tasks of the group.

For Greenwald and Breckler, the existence of private and public selves suggests the likelihood of private and public self-esteem. Negative self-esteem can occur at any level when failures occur in the face of expected success. However, the additional possibility arises that the goals of the individual's private and public selves conflict, yielding a new source for self-dissatisfaction. In the presence of important others, people may seek to meet needs of social accreditation that, in the privacy of a later hour, they may repudiate as unworthy of the private self's need for achievement.

## Situated Identities Versus General Identity

Schlenker (1985) views a central activity of the self to be the identification of self's characteristics and abilities. Comprehending one's identity is integral to self-regulation, making self-judgments about potential success or failure in endeavors, or evaluating accomplishments. Schlenker defines the individual's identity as one's comprehensive theory of oneself, identical to the self-concept. However, there are frequently times when a person may be placed in a social circumstance wherein environmental pressures force a "situated identity," an identity of the moment. This identity may or may not match the characteristics of the generalized identity.

Discrepancies between the situated identity and generalized identity may occur when the individual attempts to construe information about the self in what is perceived as a more acceptable image or when others influence the person to adopt a distorted identity that meets their desires. Conflict occurs when the individual attempts to create a particular impression of self to one's audience that contradicts the self-as-audience. If the discrepancy continues over time, the conflict between the situated identity and the generalized identity threatens other desired images of the self-concept, particularly one's sense of integrity.

Other events may foster low self-esteem. Failure, which may or may not be the responsibility of the individual, or the consistently negative behavior of others may create an identity image that is worse than the one desired. Again, if the discrepancy persists, such as one might find in a denigrating occupational relationship or a difficult marriage, the situated identity negatively affects the generalized identity over time, producing negative self-reactions and, perhaps, serious personal problems.

Another characteristic of the self-defining identity is the assessment of likelihood of success in reaching goals. If individuals anticipate success, they are apt to concentrate on the task and persist in the face of obstacles, thereby facilitating performance. On the other hand, if individuals assesses their chances of success as being poor, they will avoid the task if possible or give up when they experience difficulty. Schlenker's conclusions about the effect upon the individual who anticipates failure but cannot escape the situation are a fascinating description for the clinician:

> When actual withdrawal is blocked, people become frozen or locked in assessments of self, situation, audience, and the problem. Their minds race with thoughts about the unreachable goal and their inability to attain it; they become self-preoccupied and self-focused, continually reexamining their limitations. The combination of cognitive withdrawal from the difficult situation (e.g., fantasizing about more preferred activities, outcomes, and being anywhere but where one is at the moment) and self-preoccupation produces distraction and further debilitates social

performance. Information processing declines in effectiveness, reducing sensitivity to ongoing events, and self-monitoring and self-control worsen. . . . . People whose personality characteristics and life situations continually expose them to problems in constructing and maintaining desired identities become chronically anxious, fearing the worst in any particular situation and avoiding interpersonal interactions as much as possible, producing a spiral into loneliness. (Schlenker, 1985, pp. 88–89)

*Commentary*—As suggested earlier, the above models view self-esteem as a component part in the construction of the self. The disparity between different selves or identities is thought to be a major source of low self-esteem. In contrast to the historical theorists, current authors view the selves as being more personalized and capable of conflict. That is, James and Cooley both described different selves but seemed to consider them as simply contributing different sources of information to the total self-concept. Each of the current authors regards the selves as separate entities of the *me*, which, when in conflict, create discomfort and self-denigration by the executive ego, *I*.

Like Allport, Greenwald and Breckler posit a developmental process, but again they consider the public, private, and collective selves as more complete and personalized than Allport does. Self-esteem for them would seem to hinge on the maturation process, and the particular successes/pretensions tasks would vary correspondingly. Thus, one would expect that while a person is currently in a public-self stage, popularity and praise would be most important for high self-esteem. Later, the importance of praise would wane in favor of private approval for integrity, for instance. Still, the disparity or conflict between the goals of the separate selves is seen as the primary seedbed for low self-esteem.

## Self-Concept as a Self-Theory

Epstein (1973, 1979a, 1979b), another contemporary theorist, focuses on the hypothesized activities of the executive ego, *I*. He proposes that one can gain a meaningful understanding of the self-concept by conceiving of it as a self-theory. The *I* attempts to make sense of the *me*'s abilities and interests as it interfaces with its world to achieve certain ends.

> It is a theory that the individual has unwittingly constructed about himself as an experiencing, functioning individual, and it is part of a broader theory which he holds with respect to his entire range of significant experience. . . . Like most theories, the self-theory is a conceptual tool for accomplishing a purpose. The most fundamental purpose of the self-theory is to *optimize the pleasure/pain balance of the individual over a course of a lifetime.* Two other basic functions, not unrelated to the first, are to *facilitate the maintenance of self-esteem,* and to *organize the data of experience in a manner than can be coped with effectively.* (Epstein, 1973, p. 407)

While Epstein recognizes the commonalities between his conceptualization and George Kelley's (1955) self-as-a-scientist theory, Epstein proposes that the role of emotion is much more central to the functioning of self-theory than that accorded it by Kelley. Indeed, many of the problems attendant upon negative self-esteem are seen as distortions that occur as a result of stress and anxiety. Because no theory is completely valid, the utility of the self-theory depends upon its approximation to reality and its ability to self-correct in the face of disconfirming evidence.

As a child develops, his or her self-theory is initially easily overwhelmed by emotions. Over time, however, the individual's cognitive capacities increasingly affect and modulate the power of emotion. Epstein assumes that the individual experiences exhilaration when the self-theory expands by assimilating new information or resolving inner conflict. The experience becomes a motivator to continue to explore and expand the individual's conceptual system.

As might be expected, anxiety occurs when new information is not currently assimilable. This conflict motivates the person either to search more strenuously for resolution or to defend against the anxiety by creating defenses to protect the system. When, because of overwhelming stress to the system, the individual shuts the self off from corrective experiences, the self-theory becomes restricted and less valid, leading inexorably to the defeat of the basic purposes of the theory. Self-esteem is damaged, the individual is exposed to more painful experiences, and the incoming data are distorted, preventing self-correction of the theory. For Epstein, the result is neurosis or, in extreme cases, psychotic retreat from reality.

Chronically low self-esteem provides an interesting paradox in Epstein's model. Given that one of the major purposes of the self-theory is to enhance self-esteem, why do some people act in ways that appear to deliberately destroy self-esteem? Epstein suggests that chronically low self-esteem is preferable to individuals than precipitous disconfirming experiences, which cause a sudden drop in self-esteem. Expecting further assaults upon self-esteem, these people devalue themselves, opting for the dull ache of low self- esteem rather than the sharp pain that comes of hoping for more success, only to be dashed against the shoals of what they assume to be harsh reality.

*Commentary*—Epstein has restored the maintenance of self-esteem as a central function of the self's activities. His emphasis, however, is less on the congruence of selves or match between aspirations and achievements than it is focused on the individual's sense of control. Having confidence in predicting and then meeting one's expectations of the self is the source of high self-esteem. Low self-esteem results from inaccurate or distorted perceptions, which create confusion and distrust of one's capabilities. Moreover, he provides an explanation of the psychological economy of the self-hating individual and why such a person actively chooses self-denigration. His description of the resistance and anxiety attendant upon a low-self-esteem person's believing good things about the self sounds a resonant chord with the psychotherapist.

## Summary and Comparison

The more recent conceptualizations have emerged in response to the inconsistent findings of self-concept research, wherein the self is postulated as a unitary, global construct. Compartmentalization of the self into several "selves" that may disapprove of one another creates a cognitive mechanism whereby negative self-esteem may be experienced. Similarly, Schlenker utilizes a cognitive evaluation process by which the self assesses the possibility of success. When the expectation of success is low but the opportunity for escape is blocked, the affective consequences of the threatening situation include injured self-feeling. Epstein takes the cognitive process one step further, creating a self whose task it is to construct an accurate theory of itself. In the press of anxiety, this scientific self may reach inaccurate conclusions, which are ineffective in reaching the goals of maximizing pleasure and preserving self-esteem. Collectively, it appears that this group of studies speaks more to low or negative self-esteem than to the conditions for high self-esteem. Moreover, the generic solution to the question of how low self-esteem is created requires a two-stage cognitive evaluation process: (1) different selves or identities within the person create cognitive or cognitive-affective conflict, and (2) the disparity or conflict engenders a self-evaluation that is negative.

By contrast, the proposed model requires no such complex cognitions. We propose that the process of simply observing oneself repeatedly avoid a conflict situation inherently communicates to the self a cognitive-affective message of some admixture of shame, fear, helplessness, and sense of inadequacy.

To this point, the literature reviewed has considered the nature of adult self-esteem. Indeed, as suggested earlier, many of the conceptualizations of self-esteem would require adult cognitive capacity to perform the operations attendant upon the theory. The immaturity of the developing child has been included peripherally at best.

We have found that, although no authors attempt to construct the inner world of the child's self-esteem, several writers have studied the environmental characteristics that foster or inhibit its development. We turn now to their work.

## Developmental Considerations

As expected, the child's parents are considered to be the central players on the stage of enhancing or denigrating the child's sense of self; however, it will be seen that some psychologists hold the school environment to be an equally potent contributor.

For most theorists considering the self-concept, there seems to be a generic expectation about the development of the positive or negative quality of self-evaluation: Parents reward or punish the child's attempts to grow and define the self. Gradually the child internalizes the expectations of parents or significant others, judging the self by the same standards. As the child matures, the disparate parts of the self coalesce into an identity with expectations of its own about success and failure (which influence its outcome). As self-definition proceeds, the self-concept becomes more resistant to change, protecting itself to maintain consistency. Some of the authors reviewed below have not examined in any great depth the actual course of self-esteem development; instead, their focus has been on this question: What are the characteristics of those significant others who foster negative or positive self-esteem?

**Stanley Coopersmith.** Coopersmith's (1967) *Antecedents of Self-Esteem*, certainly the best-known work in this area, suggests four major factors that contribute to the development of self-esteem: (1) the value that the child perceives others have toward the self—expressed in affection, praise, and concerned attention; (2) the child's experience with successes—the status or position one perceives oneself to hold in the environment; (3) the child's individual definition of success or failure—the aspirations and demands one places upon oneself determine what constitutes success; and (4) the child's style of dealing with negative feedback or criticism. Since all people must experience devaluating events, the child's capacity to respond in ways that are not self-denigrating is significant. The central role of parents in each of the factors is obvious.

Coopersmith's (1969) evaluation of parents of high-self-esteem children suggests the importance of three general conditions in the home. First, the parents communicate clearly their *acceptance* of the children, as suggested above. The children know that they *belong* in the family, that they are prized and valued members. Second, parents communicate *well-defined limits* and *high expectations for performance.* The children recognize expectations for mature behavior and their parents' confidence in their ability. And, third, parents *respect* the children's individuality, allowing them *latitude* to be different and unique within the general boundaries established. Contrary to the expectation of other writers, Coopersmith finds high self-esteem and creativity are more likely to follow from well-structured environments, with limits and demands, than from open-ended, exploratory settings. He suggests that appropriately paced demands for greater competence foster improved capacity, that children will recognize their own growth, and that they will take pride (a stronger sense of competence and worth) in their accomplishments.

Parents' own experienced competence and self-esteem are also significant factors. The child observes the parents' confidence, their approach to challenge, and their method for dealing with difficulties or disappointment. The child may observe them evaluate their good points as well as deficiencies in the face of criticism, learning how they operate to define an event as a challenge rather than a threat. Children's positive expectations of themselves are much more likely to be fulfilled if they have observed their parents model those attributes.

Coopersmith finds that, when parents communicate the qualities of acceptance, clearly defined limits, and respect for individuality, their children are more apt to be self-motivated. He hypothesizes that the children become confident enough in their own judgment that their self-rewards are more important than the external sanctions of others.

In addition to data regarding parental characteristics, Coopersmith describes other salient attributes of children with positive and negative self-esteem. For instance, he finds that popularity is unrelated to self-esteem; that is, while popularity does predict people's ability to present themselves as poised and confident, favorable attitudes about the self are not strongly affected. Self-judgment of worthiness apparently requires more internally defined qualities, even in children.

Individuals with high self-esteem trust their judgment and decisions, thereby enabling them to pursue personal directions that differ from the group. Coopersmith finds children with more self-trust are more aware of their own opinions and more willing to express their convictions in the face of opposition. By contrast, children who are insecure in their assessment of their abilities tend to be cautious, unwilling to enter controversy or expose themselves to criticism. Coopersmith hypothesizes that low-self-esteem children are self-critical and, therefore, expect the same criticism from others, accepting negative statements about themselves from others as true, being congruent with their own observations.

> The judgments, being internal, cannot be evaded and hence serve as constant reminders of inferiority. They result in an omnipresent malaise marked by preoccupation with the self and attention to shortcomings and deficiencies. This preoccupation is masochistic in its consequences if not in intent. By dwelling upon their ineptitude and insufficiencies, those low in self-esteem are exacerbating their point of greatest sensibility, and at the same time reducing their opportunity for obtaining successes. (Coopersmith, 1967, p. 69)

An assumptive link between the individual's self-doubts and parental practices is the child's experiencing of what Coopersmith calls *power* in relationships. Children sense their own power in the respect given to their opinions and rights. Thus, parents who recognize their children's individuality, giving them greater opportunity to choose their own direction, foster the children's confidence, "inoculating" them to resist pressure to conform without their own approval. Coopersmith defines the resultant characteristic as *courage*—"the attitudinal posture an individual adopts to attain or maintain actions consistent with his beliefs" (1967, p. 56).

**Diana Baumrind.** Baumrind (1963, 1966, 1971, 1975) did not study self-esteem as such; her search was for *competence* in children. Observing the behaviors of preschool children over a three-month period, Baumrind identifies three groups of children who differ in their self-reliance, self-control, happiness, and ability to respond appropriately to adults as well as peers. She then observes the behaviors of the children's parents to ascertain the parental characteristics of the competent children.

Baumrind (1975) designates the resultant patterns of parental control as *authoritative, authoritarian,* and *permissive.* Those parents whom she describes as authoritative are the parents of children most apt to be competent. The parents are warm, rational, and attentive to the child's expressed needs. They are also controlling and demanding, expressing high expectations for achievement. According to Baumrind, *"These parents balanced much warmth with high control, and high demands with clear communication about what was required of the child"* (1975, p. 275).

Citing characteristics similar to those noted by Coopersmith, Baumrind describes authoritative parents as respecting the child's independent decisions but being firm about a position they have taken. Demands upon the child are accompanied by reasons.

Children who are relatively more discontented, withdrawn, and distrustful experience the parenting style Baumrind classifies as authoritarian. These parents apparently value obedience and respect above any other virtues: respect for authority, respect for work, and respect for order and tradition. Authoritarian parents are found to be more detached but controlling, with little interest in explaining their reasoning to their children. While they stress responsible behavior, Baumrind observes that they do not model responsibility to the same degree as the authoritative parents. More concerned with their own ideas and standards, they sometimes neglect the child's interests and welfare.

The parents of the least mature children are described by Baumrind as permissive. These parents are relatively warm (although less so than the authoritative parents) but lax in discipline, making only weak demands for maturity upon the child. Lacking the attention and training for independence, the children of permissive parents behave immaturely, dependently, and demandingly. They are least prepared to interact or play cooperatively with peers. As a result of her research, Baumrind takes issue with the oft-used concept of unconditional love as being the essence of good modern parenting.

> The parent who expresses love unconditionally is encouraging the child to be selfish and demanding while she herself is not. Thus, she reinforces exactly the behavior which she does not approve of—greedy, demanding, inconsiderate behavior. . . . I believe that a parent expresses her love most fully when she demands of the child that he become his best, and in the early years helps him to act in accordance with *her* image of the noble, the beautiful, and the

best, as an initial model upon which he can create (in the adolescent years) his own ideal. (1975, p. 278)

*Commentary*—The work of Coopersmith and that of Baumrind are remarkably similar in their findings regarding the correlation between high self-esteem in parents and competence in their children. The qualities of emotional warmth, high expectations for achievement, and respect for individuality parallel the themes of earlier writers, emphasizing two major dimensions of self-esteem: acceptance and individuality. In addition, their separate studies point to the importance of parental modeling, both of their own self-esteem and of their approach to problems. Thus, parents affect the child both directly, in their expression of acceptance and discipline, and indirectly, when they demonstrate to the child the behaviors that build esteem.

A parent reading Baumrind and then Carl Rogers for implications about child-rearing would, of course, find a fundamental philosophical conflict. Baumrind particularly warns parents that the lack of control and absence of demand for responsible behavior connoted by unconditional love will foster immature and confused children. Rogers, on the other hand, reports that individuals who experience what he might call the intrusiveness suggested by Baumrind will become constricted and confused children. There is no easy resolution of the conflict; the controversy represents a centuries-old value choice between philosophers—Rousseau's trust of the individual's innate benevolence versus Locke's emphasis on the necessity of training for citizenship.

**Martin Covington and Richard Beery.** In a small book, *Self-Worth and School Learning,* Covington and Beery (1976) assert that there are institutional pressures toward low self-esteem so ubiquitous throughout American education as to be unnoticed. Schools have become institutions of evaluation where an individual's worth is measured by achievement, not institutions of learning. Constant evaluation makes children excessively fearful of making mistakes, seeing school grades as a test of one's worth, while worth is synonymous with ability. Surveys indicate that older students devalue success that comes through hard work, while success achieved solely on the basis of ability is more highly regarded. Indeed, a comparison between Japanese and American students found that Japanese students believed effort was the most important characteristic to guarantee success, while American students chose ability as the best predictor. It is little wonder, then, that self-esteem becomes so bound to the concept of ability. In classrooms where examinations and grades are seen as evidence of ability, students daily face threat to their self-esteem. Covington and Beery observe:

> Out of such anguish and frustration a fateful decision is often made, unwittingly and without regard for the consequences. In essence, the student may reason that if he cannot be sure of succeeding, then at least he can protect his dignity by avoiding the experience of failure, with its implications for demoting his belief in his ability. (p. 7)

Although there are several identifiable strategies for avoiding failure, the ironic outcome is that usually students must act in ways that eventually foster overt failure in their struggle to avoid the feelings of failure. They may procrastinate, or blame relationships with teachers, or insist that they don't care about the outcome—all in the search for a means to protect themselves from finding out that they may not have the requisite ability. Thus failure-avoiding students continue to harbor doubts about their ability, experience anxiety in any evaluation situation, and usually need additional assurances of success before risking the effort. The authors insist that the sheer number of threatening evaluation experiences in school may make the institution as powerful a force in shaping self-esteem as that of parents.

Covington and Beery note a sometimes hidden variation of failure-avoiding (and low-self-esteem) individuals in school, the *overstrivers*. These students seem to be driven to perform, are unable to enjoy their successes, and react immoderately to any signal of failure. The authors note that frequently these students set strict, unforgiving self-standards that are almost impossible to achieve, often criticizing themselves unmercifully for mistakes. Why would people needlessly punish themselves so continually?

The authors suggest that self-criticism becomes a symbolic expiation for the sin of being less than perfect. Thus, the self-punishment is followed by a sense of relief, reducing anxiety and guilt, which has a reinforcing value for the individual. The behavior is, of course, a vicious circle, setting up more opportunities for failure, anxiety, self-punishment, and so forth. The root cause, fear of negative evaluation, remains intact.

Students who, by dint of early experiences, believe in their ability choose an orientation of striving for success. Presumably they approach new challenges with greater confidence and less anxiety (and therefore greater ability to concentrate), and they persevere longer when faced with obstacles. Their successes teach these students to see themselves as equal to most school tasks. More importantly, when occasional failure does occur, their interpretation of the event is that they did not exert enough effort. Thus, failure does not represent a threat, in that their ability is not impugned in the failure.

Success strivers may receive plaudits from others, but the intrinsic reinforcement that comes from stretching to meet new goals is most powerful. Moreover, for Covington and Beery, these people's acquaintance with success inoculates them against the damage that they might experience when limits are finally reached. Success strivers are better equipped to accept their limits gracefully without devaluing themselves. They then can maintain their aspirations for success in other endeavors.

*Commentary*—Covington and Beery's assertions may be particularly trenchant in light of both theoretical and research findings described earlier. James' basic successes/pretensions formula assumes that people can choose the areas in which they commit themselves to performance. In school, those alternatives are severely narrowed by curriculum demands. Moreover, Schlenker (1985) describes the self-defining process as one in which the individual is continually assessing the likelihood of success. If, for whatever reason, children have experienced failure in school evaluations, they will be likely to assess their future chances as poor—and threatening. They will attempt to withdraw or by other means defend themselves against the anticipated humiliation, usually setting in motion the events that will later guarantee further failure.

## Summary and Comparison

The proposed model is essentially directed toward adult self-esteem, assuming as it does that the individual has the cognitive ability to observe the self; hence little comparison can be made directly to the model from the child-rearing-and-self-esteem literature. Chapter 9 of this book, however, provides an examination of the implications of the model for child-rearing. Our more limited work in the developmental processes for self-esteem corroborates the importance of the findings of Coopersmith and of Baumrind. We suggest, however, that their findings have not been taken far enough, and that the relative emphasis of nurturance, performance expectations, and respect for individuality should shift to match the developmental needs of the child. In addition, we suggest that a frequent parental error may be that children are socialized developmentally only to Loevinger's "public self" stage, leaving them unprepared for appropriate individuation.

Thus far, we have considered the historical beginnings of a theory of self-esteem, more recent derivations from social psychological research, and environmental antecedents in childhood. The final section of the chapter reviews therapeutic efforts to promote self-esteem or treat problems of low self-esteem.

# Therapeutic Remediation of Low Self-Esteem

Apart from the applications suggested by the theorists reviewed earlier (Rogers, 1951; May, 1983), a search of the literature for treatment of low self-esteem finds a dearth of relevant, focused comment. There are, however, some articles that speak directly to the treatment of low self-esteem, including a major thrust by Bandura (1977) in the related concept of self-efficacy. We next review those articles.

Bandura (1977) noted the growth of cognitive behavioral therapy and the emerging theoretical importance of cognitive processes in behavior change. Expectations about one's self and one's efficacy in performing particular tasks become a primary mediator affecting outcome. Bandura suggests that individuals ask themselves two questions as they approach any performance challenge: What behavior will it require to accomplish this task? and

Do I have the ability to perform those behaviors? People's percep-tions regarding their own effectiveness will affect whether they will even attempt the task or, having begun, persist when diffi-culties arise.

People fear and tend to avoid threatening situations they be-lieve exceed their coping skills, whereas they get involved in activ-ities and behave with assurance when they judge themselves capable of handling situations that would otherwise be intimidat-ing.

> Not only can perceived self-efficacy have directive influ-ence on choice of activities and settings, but, through ex-pectations of eventual success, it can affect coping efforts once they are initiated. . . . The stronger the perceived self-efficacy, the more active the efforts. Those who persist in subjectively threatening activities that are in fact rela-tively safe will gain corrective experiences that reinforce their sense of efficacy, thereby eventually eliminating their defensive behavior. Those who cease their coping efforts prematurely will retain their self-debilitating expectations and fears for a long time. (Bandura, 1977, p. 194)

The relationship of perceived self-efficacy to self-esteem is ob-vious. The self-evaluative processes that follow the challenge of any difficult task, interpersonal or object-oriented, are the funda-mental contributors to the construction of self-esteem.

Bandura's analysis of the impact of therapy on perceived self-efficacy suggests four sources of influence: performance accomplishments, vicarious experience, verbal persuasion, and emotional arousal.

Performance accomplishments entail treatments that provide for enactive responding, such as performance exposure, partici-pant modeling, performance desensitization, or self-instructed performance. The task of the therapist is to construct experiences for clients in such a way that they will experience successfully coping with the challenge. The accumulation of personal mastery experiences not only affects self-efficacy expectations for that task but also can be generalized to other challenging situations. For Bandura, treatments that promote behavioral accomplishments are the most effective means of promoting feelings of self-efficacy.

Vicarious experience methods, involving both live and symbolic modeling, are also a source of treatment. Herein, the assumed cognition is a social comparison designed to persuade the client that if the model can do it, so can the client. Moreover, the model provides information relevant to the outcome expectancy in that the client observes what behavior is required to achieve the goal.

Verbal persuasion methods encompass the bulk of extant therapies. Here, the task of the therapist is to convince clients verbally that they can cope successfully with challenges that have overwhelmed them in the past. Clients are to change their perceived self-efficacy because the therapist "believes" in them or encourages them to modify their self-evaluations in the direction of greater efficacy. While Bandura marshals evidence to suggest that verbal persuasion is a rather weak and transitory intervention, he does find that people who are persuaded to believe they have the capability to meet their particular challenges will initiate new attempts at mastery and mobilize greater effort to succeed.

Emotional arousal methods, as seen in symbolic desensitization, relaxation training, and so forth, entail altering the physiological arousal states of the individuals facing performance challenge. Herein, the practitioner assumes that heightened anxiety not only debilitates performance but also affects the individual's perception of efficacy. The clients' developing skill in controlling negative arousal states should permit them to enter threatening situations with greater presence of mind, as well as provide them with an experience in mastery that can be generalized to other challenges.

*Commentary*—Although Bandura's theory is an important addition to the performance component of self-esteem, perceived self-efficacy remains only a portion of the total concept of self-esteem. Too many theorists as well as clinicians have observed the essential contribution of a sense of relatedness and belonging to positive self-esteem to negate it. People need acceptance as well as achievement to feel good about themselves. Moreover, Bandura's methods speak especially well to specific fears. More diffuse anxieties or skill deficits are less amenable to creating performance accomplishments.

As mentioned, few other writers have specifically addressed the problem of treating low self-esteem. Those who have done so either have posited its importance in treatment for particular disorders or have conducted experimental studies that are so brief as to be suspect. Friedenberg and Gillis (1977, 1980) tested the hypothesis that feelings of self-esteem are attitudinal and, therefore, susceptible to attitude change attempts. Their experimental test of a direct persuasive attempt by a warm, high-credibility speaker showed improvements in expressed self-esteem over 2 weeks' time. Gauthier, Pellerin, and Renaud (1983) evaluated two different cognitive strategies designed to foster greater self-esteem. One group used cognitive restructuring, in which individuals were trained to recognize self-derogatory ideas and modify them with more accurate and affirming thoughts. A second group was trained to focus on and review positive aspects about themselves. Results showed that each group benefited approximately equally from the procedure in comparison to controls. Gains were maintained over a 4-week follow-up.

Daly and Burton (1983) evaluated low-self-esteem individuals on the Irrational Beliefs Test (IBT), a measure derived from Ellis's (1962) Rational-Emotive Therapy (RET). While no clinical attempt was made to alter self-esteem, the authors did find a significant negative correlation between low self-esteem and irrational beliefs. Specific irrational belief factors that were better predictors of low self-esteem were (1) demand for approval, suggesting the overwhelming importance of acceptance in the low-self-esteem individual; (2) high self-expectations, the problem of irrationally setting rigid and unattainable standards; (3) anxious overconcern, highlighting an intensive and fruitless tendency to worry; and (4) problem avoidance, illustrating the self-defeating proclivity to avoid confronting and coping with stresses.

*Commentary*—Although sparse and perhaps too limited in time and scope to reach definitive conclusions, the literature points to the utility of several approaches to modify problems of low self-esteem. Perhaps the most common is simply the accepting, supporting relationship established as a foundation of most therapeutic schools of thought. For Rogers, it is the primary ingredient in successful treatment. The notion of acceptance has been encountered many times throughout this review; so also has developing and encouraging individuality, which is another issue often a matter of focus in therapy settings. Here the client learns to deal with the threat of rejection and overcome what may be the irrational fear of declaring oneself. Rollo May's existential therapy concepts are particularly sensitive to the process of individuation.

Finally, the self-efficacy work of Albert Bandura provides an excellent example of the behavioral approach. Without resorting to deeper, more dynamic explanations, his thrust is to build self-confidence by the straightforward teaching of real skills. Clients experience higher self-esteem because they know the important tasks to accomplish goals, and they have experienced performing them or similar behaviors.

## Summary and Discussion

Although the limited number of studies focusing on the treatment of low self-esteem prevents a detailed comparison, their findings are promising. Bandura's work represents a major thrust in social learning, and the smaller studies suggest the utility of a cognitive-behavioral approach. It is important to note, however, that the proposed model is both more similar and dissimilar to Bandura's work than it might appear. In the later chapters on clinical implementation, it will be seen that the therapist deliberately creates an enactive, in vivo experience in avoidance and coping within the therapy session. The presenting symptom events are utilized to set the stage for clients to "catch" themselves avoiding or coping. The therapist assists clients to focus on the consequent self-evaluative process as they encounter it. In that sense the model coincides with Bandura's work, emphasizing the benefits of enactive learning as opposed to the more traditional verbal persuasion process in therapy.

On the other hand, we suggest that the self-evaluative process is less similar to self-talk approaches entailed by cognitive-behavioral therapy. The therapist makes no attempt to identify irrational thoughts; indeed, we assume the accuracy of the client's self-evaluative process.

## Unanswered Questions

Throughout the review we have attempted to present the concepts of the major authors in the self-esteem literature. And, while the chapter's major purpose is to compare the propositions of the model to the relevant theory and research, we hope it serves as well to acquaint the reader with the field in general. In that hope we present here questions that have not been addressed in the study of self-esteem:

1. William James and others suggest that people choose the endeavors in life on which they base their self-esteem (what they back themselves to be). The centrality of particular life domains is individually chosen. This activity, then, allows for a reciprocal interaction between people's interests, the encouragements they receive from significant others, and their native abilities in "choosing" themselves. Yet, to read the humanists Rollo May and Carl Rogers, one has the sense that the individual *discovers* a self that is already there as opposed to *choosing* or *developing* a self, gradually filling the life space called the self with choices. Although Adler allows for a phenomenological creative self, his thesis is that one achieves the most fulfilled self by aligning oneself with the biologically given template of the requirements of social interest. These writers may not agree, of course, with the extrapolation; however, developmental researchers studying temperament or heritability of personality, such as the longitudinal studies of Thomas and Chess (1977), might agree at least that the range of choices of whom we back ourselves to be is limited by some biological proclivities. Thus the theoretical question is: *Is one's fulfilled self discovered, biologically given, or chosen?*

2. Another theoretical question emerges on the issues of attachment and individuation, spoken to briefly in earlier comments. Cooley and Mead emphasize the importance of acceptance and belonging in the development of self-esteem. That is, we learn to prize ourselves as being worthy of respect only if significant others prize and validate us. Rogers views the primary task of the therapist as that of establishing an accepting atmosphere in which clients discover themselves. The underside of the argument is that rejection is a universal fear, *the* malevolent force that destroys self-esteem. Both Rogers and May view the process of becoming separated from the self as one in which the fear of

rejection provokes the individual to muffle or deny one's own authentic expression. The remedy, explicitly stated by Rollo May, and certainly implied by Rogers, is to abandon the need for acceptance in favor of individuation. Therefore, the second theoretical question is: *In developing self-esteem, what is the appropriate balance between receiving acceptance and establishing individuality? In other words, is the path to high self-esteem one in which individuals grow up needing acceptance as well as individuality but gradually must give up the need to receive acceptance from anyone besides themselves?*

3. Receiving negative feedback is intertwined with the fear of rejection and is presumably a universal experience. Covington and Beery (1976) found that success-striving students were more likely to respond to negative evaluations as an indication of insufficient effort. Failure-avoiding students experienced negative feedback with considerably more anxiety as evidence of lack of ability. Several of the more recent researchers, including Coopersmith, Epstein, and Schlenker, similarly have remarked about the potent effect of the attributions attending the receipt of negative feedback. Thus, a significant concern for the clinician attempting to ameliorate low self-esteem is: *What set of experiences can the therapist provide or foster that will effectively "inoculate" the client against the debilitation of negative feedback?*

4. While feedback and its interpretation is a vital part of long-term self-feeling, an individual's experience of anxiety and threat in a situation demanding performance is almost surely the initiation point of the events that lead to self-evaluation. Several of the authors reviewed have suggested that the pivotal question for self-esteem in the immediacy of that moment is, "Will the individual react with a coping response or resort to a defensive avoiding behavior?" Allport and Adler wrote that the predomination of coping over avoidance was the essence of psychological health. Rollo May views the courage to express one's being in the face of threat as the goal of existential therapy. And Epstein considered the anxious press of performance demand to be the most likely factor to distort one's self-theory. For the theorist as well as the clinician, then, the question is: *How critical to self-esteem is the coping/avoidance conflict, and if coping is essential, how does the therapist foster habitual choosing of coping responses in the client?*

Chapter

# 3

# Avoidance and Coping: Basic Considerations

**W**e will begin our discussion of avoidance and coping by describing an experiential learning exercise we frequently use at professional training workshops on the development of self-esteem. We originally designed this exercise to quickly and clearly illustrate the role and power of what we consider the most influential elements affecting self-esteem. We encourage the reader to vicariously participate in the psychological activities we describe.

## Workshop Training Exercise

We generally start this exercise by having 8 to 12 participants lie on the floor in a circle and put on a comfortable blindfold. We have them increase their level of relaxation by some traditional deep-breathing exercises that last about 5 minutes. We then proceed as follows:

### Phase I: Avoidance

1. We ask the participants to recall a specific, chronic problem they tend to *avoid* facing. Once the problem has been clearly identified, the participants are asked to recreate the problem situation as clearly and vividly as possible. This includes images of the people involved, the feelings expressed, arguments that take place, the participants' avoidance behavior, and all of their unexpressed

thoughts and feelings. (Note that in our directions we make no suggestion about the type of events that might be avoided, how long ago they may have happened, or what avoidance might mean; all of these meanings are provided by the individual participants.)

2. After the participants have recreated a specific problem event in its entirety, they are asked to mentally relive this event as if they were watching a movie. We ask that they carefully observe the behavior of all individuals in the event, particularly their own. (Again, note that we ask all participants to observe *carefully* without making any suggestions about what behavior might be important or why.)

3. With these preliminaries completed, the participants are asked to identify the three adjectives that most accurately describe *how they feel about themselves* for their behavior in this specific event. It is particularly important that the participants understand we are *not* asking how they feel about the event, the consequences of the event, or their own general feelings during the event. We are asking them to identify their thoughts and feelings *about themselves* for their behavior during the event. After the participants have had about 2 or 3 minutes to reflect on our question, they write the adjectives on a 3" × 5" card.

## Phase II: Coping

1. Without any discussion of the exercise, the participants put on their blindfolds, lie down on the floor again, and repeat the original deep-breathing exercises. We then ask them to recreate the same problem situation, but this time we ask them to respond as if they were the kind of person they would like to be in this specific situation. (Note that again we make no suggestions about what or how they might want to be; more important, we make no suggestions that the outcome of this situation will change or improve if they represent themselves as the type of person they want to be.)

2. We then ask the participants to recreate the event just as they did before, carefully observing their own behavior as well as the behavior of all others involved in the problem. When this is completed, they identify the adjectives that best describe how they feel *about themselves* for their behavior in this specific problem situation.

3. The participants write down the adjectives they have selected, and these are all turned in to the workshop leaders.

## Phase III: Results

Generally, there is an unusually high level of agreement among different participants in the specific words they select to describe their thoughts and feelings about themselves in the "avoidance" and "coping" phases of this exercise. The level of agreement is even higher when we look for the level of conceptual equivalence conveyed by different words. In the avoidance phase, the words appearing most frequently are (a) *wimp*, (b) *weak*, and (c) *coward*. These words appear approximately 70 percent of the time. A variety of other adjectives also appears, but a simple semantic analysis of these terms suggests that most of them are variations on the general theme of personal weakness.

The same type of consensus emerges from the coping phase of this exercise. The thematic message conveyed is altered dramatically, however. The adjectives appearing most frequently are (a) *strong*, (b) *courageous*, and (c) *brave*. Again, the other terms frequently submitted are consistent with a general theme of personal strength or adequacy. Very seldom do workshop participants select adjectives with a favorable self-evaluation for the avoidance phase or with an unfavorable connotation for the coping phase of the exercise.

## Interpretive Speculations

After using this exercise in more than 20 training workshops, we began to wonder what the consistency of these results might mean. On the one hand, if this exercise is considered to be nothing more than an entertaining gimmick to liven up a workshop, there would be little point in examining the resultant phenomenon too closely or too frequently. If, however, these results reflect the central dynamics in the development of self-esteem, our training exercise may be a reflection of some fundamental determinants of self-esteem. The potential implications that flow from these results could be far-reaching if they are valid. But their validity can be established only by persuasion and logic.

Certainly, a harsh critic could, and really should, point out that the phenomenon we have identified could easily be an artifact of the training workshop procedures, resulting from cues perceived by the participants as to our expectations about this exercise. This would be a difficult criticism to refute. Situational demand characteristics and the role of expectations in influencing perceptions and actual behavior are well documented (Kazdin, 1980). Because of our own intellectual investment in the point of view we are developing, we are not immune to these intellectual contaminants and must therefore guard against them.

On the other hand, this exercise was derived from a new model of self-esteem that is based on more than 40 years of cumulative clinical experience, during which time the authors have attempted to carefully observe the role of self-esteem in the development and remediation of various forms of psychopathology. And while we are fully aware of, and appreciate, the crucial difference between the reliability of deliberate clinical observations and rigorous empirical data, we appreciate equally the fact that careful observation is the first step in truly good science (Bednar, Burlingame, & Masters, 1988). Ironically, it is also probably the most neglected phase in the mental health sciences.

We wish to suggest, then, at least tentatively, that our training exercise does represent a fairly realistic psychological microcosm in which some of the essential elements and dynamics involved in self-esteem come into sharp focus. We ask the reader to consider the following:

1. After a wide variety of relatively successful individuals are asked to identify how they feel about themselves for avoiding a problem situation, they tend to see themselves as weak and inadequate.

This finding is a little unusual. Most puzzling is the convergence toward unfavorable self-evaluations. Few participants, if any, have ever recognized the value of avoiding some problem situations. When problems are insoluble, and many are, avoidance can be a very adaptive and appropriate response. It seems a little strange that this point of view is not held by many of the participants who have been doing the avoiding! In light of the accompanying negative self-evaluations, perhaps avoidance, irrespective of its intrinsic merit in some situations, is a psychologically unsatisfying response because of what it symbolizes.

2. When a wide variety of relatively successful people are asked how they would feel about themselves if they could cope with the problem situation they usually avoided, the overwhelming majority see themselves as strong and courageous. Again, we must ask why. What is it about facing problem situations that are usually avoided that seems to generate favorable self-evaluations?

Once again we find an interesting paradox. Admittedly, facing a difficult problem situation does require courage. But it also involves fear, anxiety, stress, risk, uncertainty, and sometimes failure. That is why we started wondering why *courageous* emerged as the most frequently cited adjective to describe the self in the face of so many other competing variables that are decidedly less favorable. Certainly courage represents the most socially desirable answer, but if social desirability were such a dominant influence, why did the same people think of themselves as weak and cowardly when they avoided the problem situations in the first scenario? Obviously, other more socially desirable answers were readily available if that is what the participants wanted. Eventually, we started considering an intriguing possibility: that is, the very act of coping with problems that are usually avoided might provide an intrinsically satisfying psychological experience.

Our hunch that avoidance may be the basis for many negative self-evaluations whereas coping may provide the basis for a good deal of self-approval is not limited to the workshop exercise we have described. Most experienced clinicians have noticed the consistency with which pathologically dependent persons start to experience pride and pleasure as they become more independent. This tends to be true even when that newly acquired independence brings greater burdens of personal responsibility. Similarly, the neurotically underachieving student almost always feels a sense of pride and personal approval for improved performance, even though that performance requires higher levels of commitment, concentration, and inconvenience. And in the clinical cases with the most remarkable levels of client change and self-approval, the clients have almost always learned to cope successfully with the very psychological events they have most avoided in the past.

All of these observations have led us to ask several questions:

1. By what psychological processes can individuals come to think of themselves as weak or cowardly for *avoiding* certain types of psychological events?

2. By what psychological processes can individuals come to think of themselves as brave or courageous for *coping* with problem situations they might easily avoid?

3. Is it possible that styles of psychological coping and avoidance are crucial factors in the development of high or low levels of personal self-esteem?

It may be that *what* people do (content and achievements) does not affect the development of self-esteem nearly as much as *how* (process and style) people conduct their lives. This is potentially an important observation for understanding self-esteem in an achievement-oriented society such as ours, in which personal integrity and principles must often be compromised in the pursuit of achievement and success.

Our answers to these three questions provide the crucial elements for the model of self-esteem we will be proposing, and each of them will be discussed more fully throughout the book. Our immediate task, however, is to discuss some of the fundamental considerations involved in the concepts of avoidance and coping.

## Avoidance and Abnormal Behavior

Three questions will guide our discussion of psychological avoidance:

1. What is psychological avoidance?

2. What function does avoidance serve for the personality?

3. Does avoidance influence self-perceptions and self-evaluations?

### What Is Psychological Avoidance?

The concept of avoidance has played a central role in general psychological theory. This is particularly true in the areas of psychopathology, psychotherapy, concepts of normality and abnormality, and personality development. We cannot discuss all of the concepts relevant to psychological avoidance because of their diversity and complexity; that would be a different book. We can, however, identify the general elements common to psychological avoidance in different conceptual systems for understanding the etiology and treatment of disordered behavior. To do this, we will adopt a framework suggested by Gordon Allport (1962) to organize psychological theories on the basis of fundamental similarities. He suggested that most theories are based on one of the following three images of human beings:

1. Humans as reactive beings (behavioral).
2. Humans as reactive beings in depth (psychodynamic).
3. Humans in the process of becoming (humanistic-existential).

Each of these groupings of psychological theory is based on radically different assumptions about the nature of human beings and the preferred methods of clinical intervention.

**Humans as reactive beings.** This school of thought is anchored to a deterministic view of man in which past conditioning (learning) determines the future. The human being is considered to be one more creature of nature whose behavior, when properly studied, becomes predictable by general laws. The basic vocabulary of this point of view includes such staple psychological terms as *reinforcement, conditioning, drive reduction, stimulus,* and *environmental determinism.* In recent years, this point of view has expanded to accommodate cognitive-behavioral approaches such as those of Beck et al. (1979), Meichenbaum (1977), and Mahoney and Thoresen (1985).

The concept of avoidance has played a prominent role in behavioral formulations of disordered behavior and its treatment (Rimm & Masters, 1979). These theories explicate the laws of learning by which irrational or exaggerated fears and anxieties are acquired, generalized, and eliminated. Most of these views suggest that once irrational fears are acquired, these fears and all of the events with which they become associated are avoided by the client. Supposedly, avoidance of the feared stimulus (object, event, thought, situation, or feeling) becomes a means of preventing the unpleasant experience of fear or anxiety. Successful treatment generally involves the use of a wide variety of treatment techniques, most of which involve introducing a client to the feared stimulus at low levels of psychological distress or anxiety.

The ultimate goal, of course, is the elimination of the need to avoid the feared stimulus.

From a learning point of view, then, avoidance is a learned, maladaptive response. It is a response that can be quickly learned and reinforced when it is the means by which stress and anxiety are successfully avoided. Nevertheless, it is a self-defeating behavior pattern because it prevents the individual from reapproaching the feared stimulus and learning that such fears are exaggerated and irrational. From a learning point of view, avoidance is a psychological attribute that one would not wish to possess to any significant degree.

**Humans as reactive beings in depth.** This psychodynamic tradition is based on an image of man that has been well publicized in the last half-century. Its influence is readily apparent in all of the major mental health professions. Surprisingly, relatively few seem to understand the fundamental similarities between this point of view and traditional behaviorism. Both share a deterministic view: that is, the present and future are determined by the past. In both there is a conspicuous absence of interest in or concern about proactive human behavior. And both minimize the significance of conscious mental activity as a means of understanding the etiology and treatment of emotional disorders. The distinguishing feature of psychodynamic theories is their emphasis on intrapsychic determinants of behavior. It is a form of intrapsychic determinism rather than environmental conditioning. The most widely recognized terms that emerge from these orientations to describe intrapsychic events include *repression, regression, abreaction, resistance,* and *reaction formation.*

Freud (1924/1961) was the first to formalize a theory of neurosis in which avoidance of anxiety played a central role. Among other things, Freud suggested that the core conditions of neurosis are fear and anxiety. The client attempts to avoid these fears by the use of varied and elaborate defense mechanisms, all of which are in the service of the ego to deny, distort, repress, displace, sublimate, or disguise the feared event as a means of avoiding intrapsychic conflicts.

Successful treatment of disordered behavior is accomplished by bringing previously hidden, unconscious conflicts into consciousness, where they do not have to be so fastidiously avoided with various protective strategies. Awareness and insight are the primary means of cure. Both of these conditions imply an absence of avoidance and defensiveness. Fundamentally, then, avoidance plays essentially the same role in psychodynamic formulations of disordered behavior and its treatment as it does in the behavioral approaches: It is the means by which individuals attempt to excuse themselves from facing unpleasant psychological events.

**Humans in the process of becoming.** The humanistic-existential movement in psychology has explored an extremely wide range of human experience, far too broad be reviewed here in any detail. There are, however, underlying similarities in this array of viewpoints upon which we can comment. The most distinguishing feature of this movement is its optimistic view of man, in which *personal identity, self-direction, personal growth, individual accountability,* and *free will* are dominant considerations. The self-concept, or one's image of oneself, is obviously central to any point of view concerned with qualities such as identity, growth, choice, and self-determination. All of these activities presuppose the existence of a self that guides and directs the activities of the individual in a purposeful and self-fulfilling manner.

Even though humanistic-existential systems are radically different from all other conceptual systems we have discussed, the discussion of avoidance in humanistic-existential systems is virtually indistinguishable from that in the other systems. According to most self-theories, psychological stress is the result of perceived incongruity between actual life experience and the self-concept (Rogers, 1959). For instance, a typically outstanding student who does poorly on an exam would have to deal with the incongruity between this performance and his or her usual self-concept as a high scholastic achiever. Such incongruity is the primary source of psychological anxiety, which can threaten the integrity of the self-structure. Defensive behavior develops as the person attempts to prevent the anxiety from occurring by distorting the perception of real events so they are more congruent with the existing self-concept. Unfortunately, many of the terms used to describe the dynamics of human behavior can be difficult to understand because of their vague definitions. To more clearly illustrate defensive avoidance, we will summarize an example originally provided by Carl Rogers (1959).

> Let us consider for a moment the general range of the defensive behaviors from the simplest variety, common to all of us, to the more extreme and crippling varieties. Take first of all, rationalization ("I didn't really make that mistake, it was this way . . ."). Such excuses involve a perception of behavior distorted in such a way as to make it congruent with our concept of self (as a person who doesn't make mistakes). Fantasy is another example ("I am a beautiful princess, and all men adore me"). Because the actual experience is threatening to the concept of self (as an adequate person, in this example), this experience is denied, and a new symbolic world is created which enhances the self, but completely avoids any recognition of the actual experience. (p. 228)

As with the other conceptual systems we have discussed, the essence of psychological treatment in this system is to provide a means by which the client can abandon self-defeating avoidance behavior (in this case perceptual distortion) and face events more realistically, with less fear and anxiety. The primary treatment consideration associated with self-theories is to enhance the development of an accurate self-concept by means of personal self-exploration in a climate of psychological safety.

**Clinical illustration.** Perhaps the meaning and function of psychological avoidance are most succinctly revealed in a letter from a former client that vividly describes his intellectual insights into the purpose and extent of his own patterns of psychological avoidance:

> For the past two days I have sat in the library reading your new text, at times filled with laughter at the insights revealed to me about myself and at times on the brink of tears for feeling that a terrible burden was being lifted from my shoulders. During my therapy I kept looking for one underlying aspect common to all of my problems (dislike of job, fear of girls, lack of meaning in life, and so forth) and never really latched onto it until now. I think you underestimated the extent to which my avoidance pervaded all aspects of my life and overestimated my understanding of the "game" I was engaged in. Finally, I see what you were getting at when you asked whether I approved or

disapproved of my actions, or how I felt at the end of a session about my behavior during the session. I remember how you would try to get me to answer a simple "yes" or "no," and I would manipulate the terms of the question so that I could answer either yes or no and thereby keep you from ascertaining anything about me.

At the bottom of the whole thing was the fact that I did not want to accept things about myself, so I put up this tremendous impression to fool myself and others about who and what I really was. This style was so consistent that I in fact became totally alienated from myself, or, as I put it, I was "looking out at the world as if from the inside of a box." The whole thing snowballed to the point where my apparent choices did not make me happy and I didn't know why. I think we eventually called it "selling myself out."

My college major is a good example. Chemistry seemed like a prestigious thing to do, and in my mind it was one of the toughest majors. So I tried to prove to myself and others that I was smart and would be successful. Honestly, I think of myself as average or below. I hated my major and I hate my current job. Everyone seems to have sensed it but me.

My dismay over masturbation is because the sexual impulse reminded me that I needed female companionship, which was too big of a step because I would have to expose myself. The easiest alternative was to get rid of the desire, which made me feel not only cowardly but hopeless about ever having the courage to establish a relationship.

There is more to the letter, but this example provides a highly personal account of precisely the same point the major theoreticians are making about the role of avoidance in disordered behavior.

**Summary.** We have seen, then, the essential similarity of the role psychological avoidance plays in different conceptual systems for understanding the etiology and treatment of disordered behavior. In spite of vast differences in basic assumptions, explanatory constructs, and clinical intervention methods, all of these systems consider avoidance to be a protective strategy that may or may not be voluntary. Furthermore, in all of these schools of thought, the very psychological defenses that are employed to avoid unpleasant events are frequently the major symptoms of disordered behavior as well as the objects of psychological treatment. In light of all these considerations, it does not seem extravagant to suggest that the concept of psychological avoidance is a staple ingredient in the major psychological formulations of disordered behavior.

## What Psychological Function Does Avoidance Serve?

To answer this question is more difficult than it may first appear. Any answer must ultimately be an extension of our current definitions of both normal and abnormal behavior. Though many of us may wish it were otherwise, the mental health professions are far from having robust conceptual models of normal and abnormal behavior. This unhappy state of affairs is hardly surprising given the absence of conceptually adequate definitions of either normal or abnormal behavior. However, our lack of achievement in this area is not because of lack of interest or effort. Attempts to define and differentiate normal and abnormal behavior have been the subject of intense debate in the psychological literature for at least 60 years (Korchin, 1976). And while we cannot review the issues involved in this topic in any depth, we do want to identify the major issues, particularly those that will help us understand the psychological function avoidance may serve.

At the crux of this knotty problem are four central questions:

1. What are psychological disturbances, and how can their presence be reliably ascertained?

2. What is psychological health, and how can its presence be reliably ascertained?

3. Are there essential differences between psychological health and disturbance, and can these differences be reliably ascertained?

4. Are the attributes that define and differentiate psychological health and abnormality culture bound, or can they be applied on a cross-cultural basis?

These are not easy questions to answer. Particularly difficult are questions three and four. Question three is difficult because it requires not only a definition of normality and abnormality but also the crucial variables that will differentiate these two conditions. Question four is even more difficult because now not only must discriminating variables be identified, but these variables must also be applicable across cultural boundaries. We recognize that there are no definitive answers to these crucial questions in the immediate future, but several fruitful possibilities do exist. Surprisingly, the one consideration that seems to hold a great deal of promise for both defining abnormality and differentiating it from psychological health is avoidance.

**Avoidance: A necessary element in abnormality.** Differences of opinion about what constitutes abnormality are far from random or arbitrary. Rather, they seem to be a systematic extension of fundamental social values about what constitutes personal well-being. For example, in the affluent and psychologically minded areas of North America, this might include the ability to care for others in intimate relationships, cultivating clear thinking and personal self-direction, or developing a sense of personal identity and personal responsibility. This view assumes that striving for and attaining highly valued, socially desirable attributes is the essence of what it is to be normal (Linton, 1956).

On the other hand, cultural relativists (e.g., Benedict, 1934) have argued that ideals are pertinent only to particular cultural groups and that there are no values or ideals that transcend cultural boundaries. Accordingly, they suggest that the problem of defining normality or abnormality cannot be solved by studying behavior, which varies widely from culture to culture, and just as important, from subculture to subculture. They suggest our understanding of normal and abnormal behavior can best be served by directing our attention to the underlying motivations of behavior.

Wegrocki's (1939) views are a good illustration of this stance. His basic thesis rests on two assumptions. The first is that abnormality cannot be considered to be any behavior that some group considers aberrant. The second is that it cannot be defined in terms of conformity to social standards, values, or expectations; all of these are contaminated by arbitrary cultural considerations, the relevance of which to basic models of human behavior is obviously suspect. However, abnormality can be understood in terms of underlying motivation. Wegrocki points out that virtually any form of human behavior can be considered either normal or abnormal, depending on the function the behavior serves "in the total economy of the personality." Specifically, he suggests that the quintessence of abnormality is *the tendency to choose a type of reaction that represents an attempt to escape from a conflict-producing situation.* He develops this thesis with a series of cross-cultural analyses of different behavior patterns. These include:

1. The Dobuans of Papua, who are characterized by what we would consider to be an unusual and unnatural degree of fear and suspicion.

2. The Plains Indians, with their religiously colored visual and auditory hallucinations.

3. The Yogis and their trance states.

4. The frequent inclusion of homosexuality as an accepted practice in the religion or social structure of different cultures.

Each of these examples represents behavior patterns that are considered perfectly normal in the culture in which they occur, but they would be highly abnormal in Western culture. He then cites examples that would be considered normal in Western societies but abnormal in other cultures. These include:

1. The Zuni Indians believe that the individual with undisguised initiative and greater drive than other people is probably a witch and should therefore be hung up by the thumbs.

2. The Northwest Coast Indians would consider Americans more than a little odd because of our disposition to acquire material possessions. For these Indians, the possession of property is secondary to the prestige they acquire when they freely give away all of their possessions in what is called a *potlatch* ceremony.

In the analysis of each of these behavior patterns, the primary point remains the same: to illustrate how deceptive it is to try to understand the meaning of normality or abnormality without taking into account the underlying motivation that lies behind any behavior pattern. The following example illustrates Wegrocki's most basic assumption as it relates to what Western civilization would call paranoid delusions, which are in fact quite normal in the culture of the Northwest Coast Indian. He writes:

> . . . the Haida Chief [is a person] in whom the "delusions" of reference and grandeur are externally imposed patterns. A Northwest Coast Indian, if given the opportunity for a naturalistic investigation of the situations that provoke his

"paranoid" reactions—as, for example, through an education—could unlearn his previous emotional habits or at
least modify them. He is capable of insight; the true paranoiac is usually beyond it. The latter, if he kills the person
who he thinks is persecuting him, only temporarily re-
solves his difficulty; the Indian chief who kills another
family "to avenge the insult of his wife's death" achieves
a permanent affective equilibration with regard to that incident. His prestige restored, he once more enjoys his self-
respect. The Haida defends imagined assaults against his
personal integrity only when some violent extra-personal
event occurs. The paranoid psychotic defends himself
against imagined assaults even though there is no objective evidence of any.

The point that the writer would then emphasize is that
the delusions of the psychotic and the delusions of the
Northwest Coast Indian cannot by any means be equated.
Mechanisms like the conviction of grandeur are abnormal,
not by virtue of unique, abnormal qualia, but by virtue of
their *function in the total economy of the personality*. The
true paranoiac reaction represents a *choice of the abnormal;*
the reaction of the Haida chief represents no such choice—
there is but one path for him to follow. If one of the chief's
men showed paranoid symptoms by proclaiming that *he*
really was the chief of the tribe and that his lawful place
was being usurped, the institutionalization of paranoid
symptoms within the culture would not, I am sure, prevent
the rest of the tribe from thinking him abnormal. (Wegrocki, 1939, pp. 169-170)

The essence of this point of view is that abnormality cannot
be defined by any specific pattern of behavior irrespective of its
content or form. Any behavior that is culturally determined and
reinforced simply cannot be considered abnormal in the true
sense of the word. The judgment of abnormality is reserved for
avoidance behavior that is motivated by fear, anxiety, or an in-
stinct to protect the self from intolerable conflicts. Accordingly,
behavior per se is not the index against which normality or abnormality can be judged. Rather, as we noted earlier, it is the function
any specific behavior serves for the individual that reveals its normality or abnormality. *One of the quintessential qualities of abnormality is avoidance—avoidance motivated by fear and anxiety.*

Please note that this conception is remarkably similar to the general conception of abnormality inherent in most of the major models of human behavior reviewed earlier in this chapter. It now becomes more obvious why avoidance is such a central proposition in our most basic formulations of disordered behavior. It is one of a very few concepts in psychological theory the underlying function of which seems to be commonly and almost consensually understood and accepted from a variety of different perspectives. Granted, different theorists have explained the dynamics of avoidance in different and imaginative language. But the underlying function of avoidance is virtually always the same: to defend and protect the individual from unpleasant or unwelcome psychological experiences. It is a process we engage in that allows us to cling to our childish ideals by not facing those unpleasant psychological realities that can expose the fraud and faults in our idealistic self-conceptions. There are, of course, other definitions of avoidance, but our use of the term is restricted to its generic meaning as a defense mechanism common to most disordered behavior.

Avoidance differs from coping in many important ways. Certainly it is a more primitive response to psychological threat than is coping. It is nothing more than an attempt to evade the threat and, we suppose, pretend the conflict doesn't exist before it is understood or resolved. In its most basic form, it is a type of denial. The purpose of the denial is obvious enough: to excuse the individual from the unpleasantness of the threat. But herein lies a paradox of major proportions (McCall, 1975). The moment we choose avoidance over coping, we openly and undeniably announce to ourselves (and any others who care to observe) that we have detected impulses within that are so unacceptable that they cannot be faced realistically. It is as though we try to say to ourselves that this is too unpleasant to be true and then proceed to act as though it were not. However, there must be some recognition of the possibility of truth; otherwise there would be no threat that would mobilize the defenses. The threat must be at least partially recognized before it can even arouse defensive instincts. Ironically, then, the very attempt to deny the threat can verify its existence. Obviously the prospects for personal growth are virtually nonexistent when the individual's response to threat is *to deny that which it has already glimpsed to be true.*

**Clinical illustration.** The following example of fear-motivated avoidance is a good illustration of the principle we are discussing.

A 34-year-old in-house writer for a large corporation was attempting to expand his career on a free-lance basis. He had already completed several small, independent projects but had yet to become involved in anything that would truly test his talent and skills, which were abundant. He had recently submitted a proposal to write a documentary screenplay for a major motion picture studio. The studio accepted his proposal without recommending any changes. This was a significant professional opportunity, but more to the point, one that would require the utmost of his abilities. The prospect of having to produce materials that would be reviewed by established experts that would reveal what he was capable, or incapable, of doing proved to be incapacitating.

This behavior was not entirely puzzling to him. In fact, he responded to this challenge just as he had to numerous other opportunities to establish himself professionally. He was well aware that his fear of this experience was tied to his fear of failure, in this case the fear that his best efforts would be found lacking. In spite of this person's ambition and hunger for success, his attempts at productive work were continually interrupted by television, eating, and other inconsequential activities that he would attempt to construe as important and necessary. Even though he had been endowed with considerable creative and intellectual talents, they remained essentially unused because of the person's fear that his talents would be found inadequate in an authentic test. To this day, the manuscript remains only partially completed. That portion is excellent and the studio remains eager for him to complete his assigned task. It will probably never be completed. By only partially completing the task, the person has again demonstrated the adequacy of his talents to himself in such a way that it cannot be refuted by others.

As you might suspect, a life of mediocre accomplishments and personal dissatisfaction is the only realistic outcome for this person as long as he continues to avoid facing his irrational fear of failure.

## Does Avoidance Influence Self-Perceptions?

The importance of this question will probably become obvious if it is asked in generic terms. Considered in this light, the question is really asking if a person's behavior (which in our view includes thinking, feeling, and overt actions) influences self-perceptions. The answer, of course, must be a resounding *yes*. If one's most intimate knowledge and daily experience with the self do not have a profound effect on self-perceptions, we can't imagine what else would. Our attention, then, almost automatically shifts to trying to understand how patterns of avoidance influence self-perceptions. We will discuss this problem more fully in a later chapter. For now we only wish to preview the two major points on how patterns of avoidance can influence self-perceptions. First, it is doubtful that most people can remain completely oblivious of their tendency to avoid some types of conflict situations. Second, the self-evaluations that accompany patterns of avoidance are almost always negative because of the inadequacies inherent in avoidance responses. In light of both of these considerations, we will suggest that patterns of avoidance are a staple ingredient in the psychological mixture that brews chronically low levels of personal self-esteem.

**Summary.** Our discussion of psychological avoidance has emphasized three primary points. First, the concept of avoidance is implicit in most of the major formulations of disordered behavior. Even though different theories are based on different assumptions and models of man, there is almost universal agreement that the psychological function of avoidance is to provide an escape from unpleasant psychological events.

Second, one of the quintessential qualities of abnormal behavior is a tendency to choose a type of reaction that represents an attempt to escape from psychological conflict to avoid the fear and anxiety associated with the conflict. Accordingly, we have suggested that the problem of defining normality or abnormality cannot be approached by studying any specific and overt patterns of behavior, which vary widely from culture to culture and, just as important, from subculture to subculture. Instead, we have proposed, as have others, that our understanding of both normal and abnormal behavior can be best served by directing our attention to the underlying function the behavior is serving for the personality.

And third, the psychological processes involved in avoidance are qualitatively different from those involved in coping. Avoidance is basically a form of denial and escape that requires distortions of thinking and perception. These processes virtually preclude the possibility of personal growth and development because of the inadequacies inherent in these responses.

## Psychological Coping and Normal Behavior

We now turn our attention to the process of psychological coping and its effects on the development of normal behavior. Our discussion will focus on the two basic questions listed below:

1. What is coping?
2. What are the underlying psychological attributes necessary to sustain a process of psychological coping?

In our discussion of psychological coping and the development of normal behavior, it is important to remember that behind most conceptions of normality we can usually expect to find a variety of ideological assumptions and values that are assumed to reflect the essential elements of personal well-being. We are now ready to discuss what we consider these most basic ingredients to be. This is a more difficult problem than defining abnormality and, regrettably, one that has received far less scholarly consideration. Numerous essays do exist on the topic (Lynn, 1959; Shoben, 1957; Seeman, 1959). In spite of the quality of these fine essays, it is difficult to find a unifying conceptual thread to bind these diverse views together. We must start our discussion of normality by frankly acknowledging that we know far more about the deviant, the diseased, and the disordered than we do about normal persons. This unhappy state of affairs obligates us to be even more tentative in our speculations and more modest in our hopes for conceptual clarity.

Our views of normality will be guided, at least initially, by our views on abnormality. Let us explain and illustrate. We have already suggested that the essence of disordered behavior is (a) psychological fear and anxiety (b) that leads to avoidance of conflict situations. The antithesis of avoidance would be coping, which is essentially a realistic facing-up to threatening situations. We suggest that just as avoidance is the essence of abnormality, the ability to successfully face psychological threat is the essence of normality. This is not meant to imply that the absence of avoidance constitutes normality. We have higher conceptual aspirations than simply defining normality as the absence of abnormality. Circular reasoning of this type would do little to enhance our understanding of the fundamentals of normality; more important, it would be conceptually misleading.

We will suggest that the ability to successfully cope with psychological threat implies the presence of other psychological attributes (e.g., risk taking, personal responsibility). We consider the process of realistically facing and resolving threatening situations to be essential to personal growth, development, and change. This process is the cardinal, distinguishing feature of normality. To understand normality requires an understanding of the process of coping.

## What Is Coping?

Coping involves a candid and realistic facing-up to threatening situations. This usually requires personal introspection, personal honesty, and a willingness to openly acknowledge imperfections in the self. Even though candid self-evaluation can create high levels of subjective distress, this is not an unreasonable ingredient for a concept of coping that is associated with personal growth and development. We have not read a single sentence that would suggest that the healthiest personalities can be excused from psychological threat and anxiety. Actually, most psychological theories would suggest just the opposite. The healthier the personality, the more anxiety-laden conflicts it can face without being overly influenced by the threat inherent in difficult situations. The anxiety can be felt, but it can also be tolerated without evasive action.

It seems reasonable to suggest, then, that psychological threat is a reality for all of us. Furthermore, its presence implies the existence of some inadequacies in the personality that can either be coped with or avoided. When these inadequacies are faced with candor, they become a unique source of personal growth tailored to each specific individual. This is the path of psychological insight and reality testing, which are crucial considerations in personal growth and development.

An illustration of coping may help illustrate the fundamental differences between this growth-producing attribute and avoidance. Our example is factual, continuing the life of the free-lance writer we have already introduced. This event takes place about 10 months after our first example. He has now successfully completed 6 months of individual psychotherapy and is involved in group therapy on a weekly basis.

> As a result of the understanding and insight our client acquired in therapy about his pattern of avoidance, he re-enrolled in the graduate program he had previously discontinued. He needed only to complete his thesis, but in the face of this specific crucial task, he again started to show the familiar signs of avoidance. A pivotal therapy session occurred when he brought this topic up in a group meeting. He requested assistance from the group members to help him, in his words, "to gain the necessary insight" he needed to motivate him to complete his thesis. The group listened to his story patiently and attentively, as was their custom. When he had finished, they thoughtfully pondered his problem. With unprecedented unanimity, the group members confronted him with the obvious reality that *he didn't seem to really want to complete his thesis, and they were puzzled about why he pretended he did.* In spite of his protestations to the contrary, the group continually and unanimously maintained that they would feel more comfortable with him if he stopped making excuses for what was obvious to everybody—he didn't really want to finish his thesis, and he was probably afraid to try. Frustrated and discouraged, he told the group they had been of no help to him and that he felt let down by them.
>
> At this point the group leader intervened with what proved to be a poignant moment in this man's life. He said, "It sounds as though you're your own man with this one. No one here seems able to provide you with the help you seem to need, though we wish we could. And you don't seem able to get past this barrier on your own. Perhaps it's time to accept the possibility you simply won't be able to finish your thesis."
>
> With that comment, all rationalizations ceased, as did the client's attempts to find reassurance from the words of others. In

the absence of these defenses, his acute personal disapproval of self for not even trying began to surface and far exceeded his fear of attempting the task and failing. Not even trying to scale the symbolic wall before him said something about him he found frightening and fundamentally unacceptable. He had no further recourse but to squarely face the fact that he felt deeply inadequate to the task. Upon closer examination, he de- cided that if he could not complete his thesis, he probably couldn't complete anything else of importance, either. He now understood and accepted that reality—but more important, he took responsibility for his own failures. His thesis now turned into the explicit test of his adequacy that it had always been implicitly. But now, with his resources mobilized and the meaning of the test clear, he declined the invitation he usually accepted: that is, denying his feelings of inadequacy and avoid- ing any test of his adequacy. It became important to him to see what kind of work he could actually produce.

Group members applauded his honesty and indicated that if it turned out he couldn't finish his thesis, at least he should "go down fighting the whole way." If he didn't, they would be disappointed in him. They would rather see him give his maximum effort and fail than see him "get by" with another partial effort. Interestingly, no one reassured him that if he tried he would succeed.

His efforts were well rewarded. He completed his thesis and was given more than the usual number of compliments by the faculty. Far more important, he had taken the first major step in removing his incapacitating fear of failure. The small confidence in himself he had acquired was well earned. He is now at a much closer approximation to the free-lance writer he always wanted to be, and with a little luck he may become a successful writer. Though his accomplishments are still few, his sense of personal well-being has increased measurably and is fairly obvious to those who know him. We suspect that his improved state of well-being is not a result of his modest success, though that was undoubtedly helpful. Rather, it was a result of the self-respect he feels for coping with a major personal conflict instead of avoiding it. As a result of that process, he has acquired some realistic reasons to believe that he can trust his talents and abilities when they are most needed. He has also come to understand the per- sonal cost of his tendency to avoid rather than face personal conflict. These two elements constitute major ingredients in a new definition of self the influence of which will probably be undeniable in many future events.

We hope this example has illustrated how coping with threatening situations rather than avoiding them is the means by which individuals can create unique personal learning experiences that teach about the self and its diverse abilities, liabilities, and needs. According to our view, the most accurate self-knowledge is acquired when one tests oneself in real situations. Please note that we did not say this is the only means by which individuals can acquire self-knowledge, but we do suggest it is generally the most accurate. Knowledge about the self, when properly acquired, becomes the basis for individuals to orchestrate their lives into a meaningful, satisfying, and self-directed experience for which they readily accept personal responsibility. We will say more about how self-knowledge is "properly" acquired later. Until then, we ask the reader to note that our definition of coping and normality refers more to a process that regulates realistic learning about the self than it does to any specific psychological quality, attribute, or achievement. Coping, then, is a growth-oriented process in which personal development is the inevitable result of facing, understanding, and resolving conflict situations. It is also a process that involves psychological ingredients fundamentally different from those involved in avoidance. The two most important ones are *psychological risk taking* and *personal responsibility.*

## Coping: Essential Attributes and Consequences

Just as avoidance is indicative of highly sensitive inadequacies in the personality, the ability to successfully cope is a measure of personal adequacy. Individuals who, when confronted with conflict situations, allow themselves to experience the anxiety inherent in these situations and elect to realistically face and resolve the conflict are on the threshold of a powerful personal learning experience. It is hard to imagine how it could be otherwise. Psychological learning is the inevitable result of facing conflict openly, realistically, and nondefensively. The quality, duration, and depth of this learning, however, is most likely to be mediated by two other important psychological attributes: psychological risk taking and personal responsibility. Both of these attributes play a crucial role in our concept of coping and the development of personal self-esteem. Let us explain and illustrate.

**Psychological risk taking.**[1] The notion of psychological risk is difficult to conceptualize. It is a phenomenon where knowledge by acquaintance may be superior to knowledge by description, probably because psychological risk is such an idiosyncratic experience. It does, however, seem to have certain common properties. It involves the possibility of psychological injury or loss. Some easily recognized risks include the possible loss of self-esteem, injury to one's reputation, loss of approval from others, greater vulnerability, increased anxiety, increased subjective distress as one moves closer to facing unpleasant impulses and emotions, and open rejection by others. Different psychological theories vary in their explanations for these experiences, and they argue about the causes and their meaning. Recognition and acceptance of these experiences, however, is universal.

In general, psychological risk taking involves at least two components that are central to our views on psychological avoidance and coping. One is intrapsychic; the other is interpersonal. There is no reason to suppose that risk taking is necessarily limited to these two areas. However, there can be little question that a great deal of what is called psychological risk takes place within these two domains.

Intrapsychic risk refers to increased exposure to and awareness of unacceptable or feared thoughts and feelings. It is the risk of *knowing*. It can result from introspection, confrontation, or loosening of defensive barricades. The risk is to find out about oneself, to face the possibility that one's greatest fears are in fact true, or even partly true (e.g., "I am unlovable," "My anger is uncontrollable," and so forth). The more immediate and intense the feelings associated with any intrapsychic event of this kind, the greater the psychological risk that is experienced as the person attempts to cope with rather than avoid the feared event.

---

[1] Much of the material included in the Psychological Risk Taking and Personal Responsibility sections was developed by Dr. Richard L. Bednar and Dr. Theodore J. Kaul in an unpublished manuscript entitled "Group Psychotherapy: A Comparative Review and Analysis."

Interpersonal risk is similar in kind but stimulated by different events. It is the risk of *being known*. It involves interpersonal perceptions, interpersonal rejection, and having one's psychological secrets exposed to others. Interpersonal risk taking involves increased exposure to and awareness of interpersonal fears. While these two types of risk taking involve fear of different events, the severity of psychological risk is mediated by the immediacy and intensity of emotions associated with the particular psychological event.

These two areas of psychological risk taking are the most important ones in our discussion of coping and defense. They represent the areas in which learning about the self and the development of self-esteem are most central. Obviously, the presence of any enduring disposition to avoid reasonable and appropriate risks in these two areas diminishes the prospect of intrapsychic and interpersonal learning when threat is involved. We might even go so far as to suggest that the greater the risk the personality can tolerate, the more important the psychological learning that can take place. Inherent in this formulation, however, is the inescapable conclusion that coping, as we have defined it, involves personal risk taking, and by implication, personal discomfort. We suggest that the ability or disposition to take psychological risks is a learned attribute that can be enhanced and cultivated.

The role of risk taking in personal growth is illustrated by the following example.

One of the members in the therapy group we have already mentioned (with regard to our free-lance writer) was a quiet person. Her personal history was one from which risk taking was noticeably absent. Only on the rarest occasions would this woman talk about her personal feelings or views. Neither would she engage in conversation that was personally revealing. Her marriage, though far from being satisfying, was acceptable. But as might be expected, few problem areas were discussed openly, and many sensitive areas were avoided systematically. On the surface, it appeared that this woman had developed a "don't-rock-the-boat" style. Underneath the exterior was a person who worried a lot, experienced a great deal of self-consciousness, and felt as though life was proving to be more displeasing than it really needed to be.

Needless to say, she was not well prepared to deal with the personal and interpersonal intensity that can develop in group psychotherapy. This was a high-functioning group, which only served to heighten her ambivalence about participation. On the one hand, it was fairly obvious that meaningful participation could pay high dividends. The benefits derived by some group members were obvious. On the other hand, the modus operandi of the group was at a level of emotional intensity and immediacy that served only to further frighten her. She was stuck at a major crossroads. She wanted to participate, but her fear and anxiety seemed to be an insurmountable obstacle. After a particular session had ended, she remained to talk with the group leader to explain her dilemma, which the therapist was already well aware of. He quickly stopped her and asked if she would be willing to start the next group session with the conversation she wanted to have with him now. She reluctantly agreed.

At the next group meeting, she bravely initiated her conversation with the group leader. He immediately stopped her and asked if she would be willing to start by telling the group members what it felt like to talk in front of the group. She nervously but bravely responded. She indicated that she had dreaded this meeting all week, her mouth was dry, and she felt a lot of fear and anxiety. She couldn't explain why she was afraid, but it was clear to her that she was. She was actually very articulate in her description.

When she was through talking, the group leader asked if there were other group members who had similar experiences in the group, or if there were members whose participation continued to be limited because of similar feelings. Much to this woman's surprise, over half the group members felt just as she did. She had been so sure she was the only one! In the conversation that followed, this woman and most of the group got to explore their fears of really being known and of knowing others in depth. It was a particularly poignant experience for this woman. She found out that she was not the only one with such basic fears, but more important, she found out what it was like to be closer to people as a result of authentic sharing based on simple honesty with self and others. It came as quite a revelation to her. She had many preconceived notions about meaningful relationships' being based on personal perfection and desirability more than on simple authenticity. Her behavior in the group gradually changed as she became more and more willing to make herself really known to others. As she became more comfortable with herself, she also became more comfortable knowing others, and being known by them. *None of this could have occurred without someone's taking the psychological risks involved in courageously facing the unknown.* As usual, the greatest benefits in this situation were derived by the person who took the greatest risks. With the help of her therapists, this woman was able to create a personal learning situation that was perfectly matched to her particular and idiosyncratic concerns.

**Personal responsibility.** In psychological circles, personal responsibility generally refers to behavior that is considered to be psychologically responsible. Responsibility to family, society, or nation is seldom discussed. If discussed, it is usually only to clarify the assumption that seems implicit in other presentations: that is, that personally responsible behavior will lead to socially responsible actions, that one will necessarily follow the other. It is an interesting assumption, but it is not held in all cultures.

Although the concept of personal responsibility is discussed in different terms, two common elements do seem to emerge. The first element common to most conceptions of personal responsibility is the personal attribution of causality or control. Most forms of psychological treatment share the goal of increasing their clients' level of personal responsibility and control over their lives. No approach attempts to persuade its clients that they are responsible for the weather, famines, or the existence of evil. But virtually all treatment approaches, in their own way, attempt to increase clients' willingness to see themselves either as causal agents or at least as being able to exert more control in their own lives. This is accomplished by encouraging clients to accept the consequences of their own thoughts and actions. They are shown how their thoughts and emotions can affect their actions and how their actions influence the actions of others. They are continually encouraged to achieve more symmetry between what they wish to have happen to them and what actually happens.

Second, most discussions of personal responsibility imply or express the view that it involves accurate self-perceptions. High levels of personal responsibility are suggested by insight; non-defensive recognition of impulses, emotions, or thoughts; completely experiencing oneself; and perhaps leading a self-directed life-style. Increasingly accurate perceptions and knowledge about the self are at or near the top of the hierarchy of considerations involved in our discussion of normality and coping.

It should be obvious that high levels of personal responsibility are generally indicative of normality, coping skills, and manageable levels of psychological stress and anxiety. It would be an understatement to call this a pleasing and highly desirable trait. This is not meant to imply a tension-free existence. Our existential colleagues have carefully taught us about the anguish involved in personal choices under these conditions (May, Angel, & Ellenberger, 1958). But, functionally, it is more than that. It is a process in which individuals hold themselves accountable for much of what does or does not happen in their lives. The debate about their being or not being causative agents in their own lives has ended. They are! The crucial question is now, "What do I need to do differently so other things will be different in my life?" Once this is understood, it becomes a powerful incentive to cope efficiently and effectively. It is the means by which individuals can avoid pain, disappointment, and remorse in their lives. It is the most reliable means for improving the quality of one's existence. "After all, if I am the cause, I can also be the cure."

High levels of personal responsibility are illustrated in the following two examples. The first example is based on a client in psychotherapy, the second on a psychologically mature friend we have known for a number of years.

A client had been in therapy for about 3 weeks because of deeply conflicted feelings about his father. The client was 26, married, with no children. In previous sessions, the client reported many favorable perceptions and experiences with his father. All of these seemed to be the result of having a father who was genuinely preoccupied with his family's well-being, being a good friend and provider to all, valuing family participation more than professional opportunity, and always being available to provide assistance when needed. In this particular session, the client was talking about his conflicted feelings about spending the Labor Day holiday on a family picnic his father had arranged as opposed to getting away with his wife for two days. It was clear this young man preferred to go away with his wife, but felt as though that would be unfair and disloyal to his family in general and to his father in particular.

After carefully listening to the client's remarks, the therapist said, "You seem to have difficulty accepting your feelings of resentment toward your father for smothering you." The client recoiled briskly. Obviously, the therapist's comment was on target but premature. The client wasn't willing or ready to face such negative feelings in such a sensitive area. The therapist asked the client to close his eyes for five minutes, turn inward, and without saying anything, work toward identifying his feelings toward his father at that moment.

Much to the therapist's surprise, the client opened his eyes and announced, "I really do resent him. I didn't realize how much." Though this client found these feelings puzzling, unacceptable, and problematic, they were now his. From then on, the client was able to explore openly what it was about *himself* that made it difficult to become emancipated from his somewhat overbearing father. Though the idea of resenting his father still does not sit well with this client, he makes no attempts to deny this reality to himself.

Our second example is unusual. It is a true story of a no-nonsense, middle-aged man who was being recruited for a prestigious professional position. After the usual preliminary screening was completed on both sides, an interview was arranged. This is what actually happened.

At the end of two days of interviews, group meetings, meals, and professional presentations, the applicant met with the president and his two vice presidents for a farewell luncheon. During this meeting, the president indicated that all had been most favorably impressed and that they wanted to offer him a position. An unusually generous salary was included in the offer. In a totally unpretentious way, the candidate responded to the offer by saying that he appreciated the generous offer, the thoughtful and courteous way he was treated during the visit, and their approval of him as a professional person. However, he felt as though he would be uncomfortable in the position and must decline. Puzzled, the chief administrators pressed him to clarify the reasons they might lose this outstanding candidate. The candidate asked in what depth and at what level of honesty they really wanted to know about his reservations. They insisted on absolute candor. For over six hours, they discussed the company with regard to deficits in moral values, personal integrity, work habits, and simple honesty. The candidate basically informed them that he would find it personally embarrassing to be affiliated with them on a professional basis irrespective of salary or apparent prestige. The company officials so appreciated his views and candor that they offered him a consultantship that would focus exclusively on the development of moral integrity in the organization. This offer was undoubtedly the result of the candidate's impressive ability to present himself as the most obvious exprssion of his own moral views and values.

**Risk and responsibility: Important differences.** The concepts of personal risk and responsibility are similar in several ways. They can refer to similar or highly related psychological events in some instances, making it difficult to differentiate the two clearly. In spite of these potential sources of confusion, several points help demarcate the boundaries of these two important concepts and the functions they serve.

A fundamental difference between personal risk and responsibility is contained in their core definitions. Risk taking refers to increased awareness of and exposure to feared psychological events, whereas personal responsibility refers to a willingness to attribute the cause and consequences of one's own behavior to the self. Whereas risk taking is most easily recognized by a willingness to expose oneself to feared situations without a clear understanding of how these events might affect the self, personal responsibility refers to a willingness to acknowledge one's psychological experiences as a direct reflection and extension of the self. In this sense, personal responsibility is a form of psychological ownership: a recognition of the reality that one's thoughts, feelings, and behavior reflect who or what one is.

## Summary

Our discussion of psychological coping and normality has emphasized its underlying attributes, which we consider to be psychological risk taking and personal responsibility. We have suggested that these qualities are the foundation upon which a lifetime of continual growth and development is based.

We have also suggested that the psychological processes involved in avoidance are qualitatively different from those involved in coping. We have suggested that avoidance is based on psychological processes that deny or distort unpleasant psychological realities. We cannot think of any enduring benefits to be derived by consistently avoiding conflict situations as a way of containing fear and anxiety. On the other hand, we have portrayed coping as the means by which one can acquire an accurate understanding of self and perhaps others. Coping involves facing conflict realistically, learning how to tolerate the distress inherent in these situations, and gradually modifying the personality through personal conflict resolution. We have continually emphasized the favorable social and psychological connotation of coping and conflict resolution. The underlying attributes that mediate personal growth and development are socially valued and, in addition, may stand scrutiny in an absolute sense as well.

Our discussion of psychological coping and defense is central to the model of self-esteem we will be discussing. It raises two fundamental questions basic to our model of self-esteem:

1. Is it reasonable to assume that a person with a deeply ingrained tendency either to cope or avoid conflict is, or could be, completely *oblivious* of that fact?

2. Is it reasonable to assume that self-perceptions *will not* be influenced by one's tendency to cope or avoid conflict?

These questions provide the basis for much of our discussion in the next chapter.

# 4

# Internal and External Feedback: Basic Assumptions

## The Importance of Feedback

Our model of self-esteem is based on four underlying assumptions, each of which involves *feedback* about personal and interpersonal acceptability. Because feedback is a term that is commonly used and misused in a wide variety of disciplines, it may be useful to clarify some of the most fundamental elements of this important concept. It was originally postulated as a regulatory mechanism in biological systems by Walter Cannon (1939) in his principle of homeostasis. Since then, it has gradually found application in systems theory, information theory, and cybernetics. Norbert Wiener (1948), a cyberneticist, defined feedback as the control of a machine on the basis of actual rather than expected performance, which required sensory units for such performance monitoring.

The crucial elements in the concept of feedback are: (a) it provides a particularly relevant type of information (feedback) intended to monitor, define, and correct undesirable deviations, (b) the source of the feedback can be either internal or external to the system being monitored, (c) feedback can vary from highly intermittent to continuous, and (d) feedback can vary in its potency to correct deviations. In brief, feedback is a special type of information that can describe, evaluate, or influence performance: in our case, human behavior. This complex concept occupies a central role in several major theoretical approaches to personality development, psychotherapy, and psychopathology.

Although he used different terminology, Harry S. Sullivan (1962) was among the first theorists to systematically discuss the role of feedback in personality development. In his classic text, *Schizophrenia as a Human Process,* information about the self from others (interpersonal feedback) plays a preeminent role in personality development. Sullivan maintained that:

> There is within the personality a system of experience to which we apply the terms, the ego, or the self. This is built up of all the factors of experience that we have in which significant other people "respond" to us. In other words, *our self is made up of the reflections of our personality that we have encountered, mirrored in those with whom we deal* [emphasis added]. (1962, pp. 249-250)

Sullivan further maintained that interpersonal processes in general, and interpersonal feedback in particular, play a major role in the development and treatment of disordered behavior. The essence of his view is that feedback from others shapes the formation of the self-concept. If one receives responses from significant others that are essentially negative, this is incorporated into the self-image. The perception and interpretation of many future events is determined by that self-image.

Carl Rogers (1951) and George Herbert Mead (1934) have expressed essentially the same view of personality development, though the specific semantics of their presentations vary somewhat. Rogers (1951), for example, has suggested that feedback is a means of assisting the client to establish congruence between the self and the real world. This is accomplished by the therapist's empathically understanding the client's experiential world. The therapist can reflect back to the client perceptions that are intended to increase awareness. Regardless of variations in descriptions, Rogers, Mead, and Sullivan emphasized the role of interpersonal processes in the formation, maintenance, and alteration of personality.

In addition to theoretical speculation, there is a growing body of research literature that further suggests the potency of interpersonal feedback as a primary source of psychological influence

(Stockton & Moran, 1982). Yalom (1985) has reported a good example of this type of research. He found that the most significant event for clients in group treatment was the expression of strong positive or negative comments to other group members.

In more general terms, interpersonal feedback is considered to be one of the premier curative factors in group therapy (Bednar & Lawlis, 1971; Bednar & Kaul, 1978; Kaul & Bednar, 1986). Despite the apparent success of the use of feedback in clinical settings, an empirical understanding of the phenomenon is still rather incomplete in two fundamental respects:

1. There is a lack of clarity about what psychological feedback actually is and is not.

2. It is unclear under what conditions and with what type of client feedback can or should be used.

Nevertheless, some general principles about the therapeutic use of interpersonal feedback are emerging in the psychological literature. The most consistent research findings suggest that (a) most people prefer positive to negative feedback, (b) negative feedback is most likely to be accepted by high-self-esteem individuals, or if it is preceded by positive feedback, and (c) most people find it easier to deliver positive rather than negative feedback (Kaul & Bednar, 1986). The generality of these findings is not at all clear because of the usual methodological problems that accompany a young science.

## Underlying Assumptions

The four basic assumptions in our model of self-esteem involve the delivery of positive and negative feedback about personal or interpersonal acceptability. Each assumption considers feedback from different sources (internal and external) as well as its probable consequences. The first two assumptions focus on feedback originating in the social environment. In these cases the self-evaluations of *others* are the primary source of the feedback. Assumption #1 explains how and why virtually all individuals receive fairly regular and substantial doses of negative feedback from their social environment. (Ironically, we suggest that most of this feedback is valid, at least from one perspective.) Assumption #2 identifies and explains the dynamics behind the common observation that negative interpersonal feedback tends to be more believable than positive interpersonal feedback.

The remaining two assumptions are based on internal sources of feedback. In these cases, the self-evaluations of the *individual* are the primary sources of the feedback. Assumption #3 suggests that self-evaluations can and usually do take place. This is important in that it makes explicit what most of us implicitly recognize and experience: that we notice, monitor, and evaluate what we do. Assumption #4 suggests that our self-evaluative thoughts provide continuous internal feedback about the adequacy of the self. Each of these four assumptions will be described and illustrated with care, inasmuch as their validity is the most important consideration in our model of self-esteem.

# External Feedback

## Assumption #1

*People should expect to receive regular amounts of negative feedback from their social environment, most of which is probably valid.* This may appear to be an unusual assumption—if not unusual, then certainly pessimistic for those constantly hoping for the approval of others. Nevertheless, the following considerations suggest that this assumption may well be the most reasonable of the four.

**Individual differences and social acceptability.** The field of psychology probably knows more about individual differences than any other single topic (Tyler, 1978). If this appears to be an overstatement, we can retreat to a more modest position and point out that "differences between people" is one of the very few topics that has been the subject of extensive data collection for 50 years or more. As a result, we know that people differ from each other along almost every conceivable dimension. In the area of personal appearance, we have all noticed the consistency with which people differ in height, weight, and girth. The same is true in less obvious areas, such as special aptitudes for learning, aggressiveness, temperament, and frustration tolerance. Our best evidence (Kolb & Wishaw, 1985) also suggests that the scope and magnitude of these individual differences extend into the biological substrata of human behavior and include such basic factors as brain morphology, sympathetic and parasympathetic reactivity, and neural capacity. The evidence that people consistently differ from each other in (a) physical appearance, (b) performance, (c) aptitudes and talents, (d) personality attributes, and (e) biological and neurological characteristics is simply undeniable.

But what does all of this have to do with personal and interpersonal acceptability? If we consider these facts in conjunction with the social nature of human beings, the answer becomes more obvious. Almost all human activities take place in a social context. We tend to associate together in groups such as churches, neighborhoods, fraternal organizations, families, professional associations, political parties, and employment organizations. Some groups are formed to satisfy our need for interpersonal relationships and togetherness. Others are formed to foster achievement and accomplishment. Still others exist for the benefit of the disabled and bereaved. Each group has its own membership requirements, which may include level of education, designated talents, and special interests. Each has its own norms and approves or disapproves of members according to the degree to which they (1) comply with group requirements and expectations, and (2) enhance the goals for which the group was formed. Group members tend to be recognized and rewarded for their allegiance and contribution to group goals and values.

Because of the number and diversity of admission requirements and role expectations for different groups, and because of the divergent nature of human beings, it is simply illogical to expect any one individual to be equally adept at satisfying the varied demands of all groups in which membership is either required or desired. Consequently, we will always be unacceptable to some groups and some people. More importantly, our acceptability to the various groups to which we do belong will vary depending on our contribution to the group's goals and values. It is important to notice that group acceptance or rejection is not necessarily attached to any higher set of standards or values; it is usually based on simple compliance with group norms and values. Whether these more restrictive norms and values are desirable is seldom considered in the broader context of social values and their consequences. For example, creativity in some circles is a highly desired and valued trait. This is most likely to be true in areas where conventional thinking is unlikely to produce answers to unorthodox problems. Under these conditions, creativity will be appreciated and encouraged. Blessed is the group member who, through genetics or social learning, is disposed to view problems and their solutions in divergent and unorthodox ways. Heaven help this same person, however, in a public education system. Research in the 1960s and 1970s (Hetherington & Parke, 1986) has left little doubt that busy schoolteachers with large classes tend to ignore, punish, and reject creative students, who are not inclined to respond to classroom instruction in a conventional and convergent way.

Other examples would reveal the same underlying process. Our personal acceptability in the social circle we belong to, either by choice or by chance, is far from unconditional. It depends on the degree to which we are equipped to contribute to the goals and purposes the group values. We suggest this process to be as true of the small family that values and teaches personal responsibility to its children as it is of large corporations that value profits and require productivity of their employees.

**Ambiguous social evaluations.** Most of the difficulties that can be expected in finding an appropriate match between group values and individual talents could be avoided if individuals would seek companionship only from the groups to which they are most suited. Three considerations prevent this, however. The first is that this would require individuals to react to rejection comfortably and move on in search of more accepting peers. This seldom happens, particularly in the formative years, when our reference groups are a major source of self-validation. Rejection from these significant groups can hardly be expected to be taken indifferently. Additionally, we know of no reason to suggest that rejection by our primary reference groups at any time should be responded to indifferently. Such indifference is usually a denial of the strong emotion that is typically evoked by rejection.

Second, membership in many groups is not volitional, and the prospects for moving on to greener pastures are nonexistent. Examples of this include membership in families, and to a lesser extent, employment status.

Third, and clearly the most important, a majority of the appraisals we receive from significant groups or individuals are not entirely rejecting. Rather, they are messages in which disappointment is veiled by expressions of hope that we might do better next time. A loving mother's eagerness to assist her daughter with her first home-cooked meal can also imply an inability to do it alone. Similarly, a friendly reminder of a deadline also suggests that we might forget. And if a teacher singles us out to compliment us on our academic work with the suggestion we apply ourselves more diligently, haven't we also been told that our performance is less than desirable? Praise also cuts two ways. A parent's delight with a child's latest achievement also creates the possibility of being disappointed next time. Because most of these evaluations are veiled, they seldom permanently damage the self, but they do alert it to the negative possibilities of what might be said. Rejection is implied; rarely is it stated explicitly. And comments about one's assertiveness as appropriate in some situations may also be a reminder of the importance of knowing and keeping one's place.

These are the messages of real life. They are descriptive evaluations having undesirable qualities or lacking desirable ones. Some of these messages are explicit, but more often they are implicit. Others are almost completely veiled, detectable only by, for example, the strain of a throat being cleared.

Much of what is pertinent to the development of self-esteem, and for that matter, the larger question of abnormality, depends on the manner in which we respond to these thinly disguised criticisms from our social environment. The two most basic responses to these "mixed" messages are to cope with or avoid the conflicts inherent in these messages.

**Responding to mixed messages.** To cope with these veiled criticisms would require the individual to actively seek explicit clarification of the views, feelings, and perceptions behind the messages. This would remove ambiguity and replace it with clarity and precision of language. It would make explicit what message was intended, either intentionally or unintentionally. It would require the messenger to behave at a high level of personal responsibility. All of this involves a high level of personal risk taking. It creates the possibility of finding out that one is seen as inept, lazy, impulsive, dull, or whatever else the self fears finding out.

It also requires a high level of personal introspection and reality testing to see if perceptions by others are fundamentally true of the self. And if they are true, we must also decide how *we* feel about them compared to the reference group. It is entirely possible that being called lazy by a group of obsessive overachievers is not really such a bad thing, or that being called dull by intellectual snobs is a pleasant compliment if properly understood. The most likely consequences of coping are to (1) integrate the perceptions of others into a more accurate self-image if those perceptions are valid, or (2) excuse oneself from the coercive influence of others' perceptions if their evaluations and values are not in harmony with the perceptions and values of the individual.

Avoidance of these complex and threatening issues is the easier course to follow. All we must now do is avoid critical questions and deny any responsibility for our personal views and feelings. As we do this, it becomes easier to mold our behavior so that it is more acceptable and pleasing to the wishes of our reference group. Pretending is the easiest solution. If we appear to be pleasant when we are angry, cooperative when we are belligerent, and entertained when we are bored, there will be few occasions for others to find fault with us. Efforts in the direction of conformity are usually rewarded quickly as our chameleon exterior takes on the colors of those around us. The results of avoidance are (1) an increase in our skill at *impression management*, which is the ability to appear to be what others want us to be, and (2) a gradual decrease in our sense of personal identity and self.

**Summary.** Contained in Assumption #1 are two essential features in our model of self-esteem. The first is the recognition that, because of the undeniable individual differences among humans, there exists the certainty that all of us will have to deal with rejection. We are not saying that this disapproval is a major source of low self-esteem. Rather, it is a catalyst that activates other psychological processes that influence the development of self-esteem. Second, individual response styles to this rejection will involve varying degrees and mixtures of coping and avoidance. To the degree that a response style favors coping, it will increase the development of a realistic sense of personal identity, self-evaluation, and personal growth. To the degree that a response style favors avoidance, it will increase one's tendency to manage impressions as a means of gaining the approval of others. This inevitably, and even necessarily, contributes to a fundamental alienation of the self and its authentic thoughts, feelings, impulses, and strivings.

## Assumption #2

*Most people receive and enjoy substantial amounts of authentic favorable social feedback, but they tend not to believe it.* In our discussion of the inevitability of rejection, under our first assumption, we were able to base many of our observations about individual differences and group sanctions on some commonly recognized facts from the social and behavioral sciences. We were glad for the conceptual guidance provided by an existent body of knowledge. Such information helps minimize extravagant speculation; more importantly, this accumulated knowledge actually helps shape the development of new explanatory constructs and assumptions.

Assumptions are generally considered the most useful when they appear to be logical extensions of a relatively well-established body of knowledge (Kazdin, 1980). Of course, this is not always the case. But in our discussion of self-esteem it seems most applicable because this topic is only in the formative stages of knowledge development.

Regrettably, the development of our second assumption was not influenced by, and cannot be based on, reliable supplementary information as the first one was. Clinical experience, shared observations, and a fair amount of consensual agreement among our colleagues is the basis for this assumption. Again, however, we wish to remind the reader that careful observation is the first step in truly good science (Bednar, Burlingame, & Masters, 1988; Kazdin, 1980). While recognizing the limitations of persuasion by clinical example, we will explain and illustrate our second assumption.

Western society is far from stingy when it comes to giving favorable feedback to others. Compliments almost always attend the appearance of new clothes, cars, furniture, and other material possessions. Our public-relations-minded society requires managers to compliment and reward quality performance in its employees. Improvement is often just as important as outstanding performance, so compliments are hardly limited to the gifted few. Certainly some of this favorable feedback is not authentic and is appropriately disregarded. But much of it is completely authentic and is still disregarded. Two examples will illustrate this point.

About 10 years ago I remember reading a very impressive term paper by a first-year student in a clinical psychology training program. I was so impressed by the paper that the first time I saw that student in the hall I stopped and talked with her. It was a short and simple conversation. I told her I had read her paper carefully and was very impressed. I mentioned several of the specific points in the paper that made it so exceptional in my view. I also explained what qualities set this particular paper apart from other first-year papers. It was a brief but pleasant conversation. I delivered a well-deserved compliment and forgot about it. Several weeks later this student came to my office and wanted to talk. It was a difficult conversation for her. She wanted to know what I *really* thought about her academic talents!

Our second example represents an experience we have found to be quite common to psychotherapy groups.

One of the most common and puzzling experiences in small groups generally takes place the first time group members clearly request direct feedback about how they are seen by other group members. This usually occurs early in the life of the group, and the requests tend to be rather simple and straightforward. Usually, such a request can be taken at face value; the group members are curious about the type of first impression they make. Seldom is the request made in such a way that would suggest the need for a carefully reasoned and documented character analysis or sweeping value judgment regarding the worth of the individual. It tends simply to be a request for feedback about first impressions.

Nevertheless, such a request almost always generates an inordinate level of anxiety, avoidance, and a misunderstanding of the literal meaning of the request. Seldom do group members show a willingness to share their first impressions of the group members, though such impressions are clearly present. Put most simply, adults tend to be very apprehensive about the prospect of telling others how they really see them. Eventually, and usually with a great deal of tension, someone will start sharing his or her impressions with group members. Gradually, more and more group members get involved in sharing interpersonal perceptions. The initial tension starts to subside, and individuals begin asking more specific questions about how they are seen by others. Once this takes place, an interesting thing happens. If the feedback is generally favorable, people listen attentively and appreciatively. But once the favorable feedback ends, they say something like "Go ahead and tell me about the negative things—I can take it." The implication is that the real truth has been withheld, or worse, the favorable feedback was just a means of "getting ready" for the real truth. Ironically, if the initial feedback is unfavorable, seldom, if ever, have we seen clients ask for feedback about their more desirable qualities.

These are only two of many clinical or social examples we could use to illustrate the degree to which favorable feedback seems to be less believable than unfavorable feedback. This observation raises an interesting question. Why is it that so many people are willing to accept negative feedback from others, which may or may not be valid, while they tend to reject positive feedback, even when it is valid?

The answer lies in our disposition to impression management: to make ourselves appear more acceptable to our peers when we get messages that we are not. Many different fears can be involved in our eagerness to avoid rejection by others. But all of these fears share a common property—they are all immediate and highly motivating psychological states. In social situations, one of the most frequent expressions of fear of rejection is approval-seeking; that is, presenting oneself to others in a way that is congruent with the expectations, values, and dominant interests of others. Earlier in this chapter we defined this as impression management. The specific term, however, is not as important as the function this process serves. It is a method of gaining approval by being that which pleases others.

Unfortunately, this process can have two devastating and self-defeating components. The first is rather obvious and has already been discussed in detail earlier in this chapter. That is, the more persons act in ways dictated by external sources, the more alienated they may become from themselves. Far more important, however, are the destructive effects of impression management on new social learning. If people continually present themselves to others in ways that are artificially designed to be pleasing, then any interpersonal feedback about their pleasing qualities will be a reflection of the facade they have presented rather than the enduring qualities of the personality.

Because most people cannot remain entirely oblivious of their impression management tendencies at all times, they are also aware that much of the feedback they receive is not believable because it is based on the facade they have presented. The effects of such feedback are minimal inasmuch as the limitations on the credibility of the feedback are perfectly understood by the impression manager. This principle is clearly portrayed by common statements such as "If you really knew me you wouldn't think I was such a good friend," or "We'll see what you think of me when you really get to know me." Such statements portray the rejection of favorable interpersonal feedback because of impression management designed to hide other attributes, which are assumed to be less desirable. Similarly, a common curative factor assumed to be operating in most forms of psychotherapy, irrespective of specific treatment techniques, is the endurance of an interpersonal relationship with the therapist, who "knows all" (absence of impression management) and voluntarily stays in the relationship.

An interesting paradox about impression management now becomes obvious. The more individuals engage in it as a means of gaining approval and acceptance, the less likely they are to believe and accept the favorable feedback they desperately seek. In general terms, it appears that *the greater the impression management, the less believable the favorable feedback.*

**Summary.** Collectively, then, external feedback is of primary importance for the development of self-esteem in two ways. First, it is the source of abundant unfavorable feedback that is reasonably authentic and potent. And second, if people avoid facing reality by impression management, they create the conditions that render most of the favorable feedback they receive untrustworthy, unbelievable, and psychologically impotent. In fact, most of the feedback from our social environment does not foster good coping skills because of the social pressure to deny the self and conform to social expectations.

# Internal Feedback

In psychological circles, feedback is usually thought of as an interpersonal phenomenon. We seldom hear about feedback as an intrapersonal event, and when we do, it is generally referred to as *self-talk* by most behavioral scientists. We will suggest that intrapersonal feedback, or internal feedback, is both a common and influential psychological event for most people. We will attempt to identify and describe this phenomenon in considerable detail and differentiate it from the traditional concept of self-talk. The following three questions will guide our discussion:

1. What are self-evaluations?

2. How are self-evaluative processes different from the various conceptions of self-talk that have become so influential recently (Beck, Rush, Shaw, & Emery, 1979; Meichenbaum, 1977)?

3. What role do self-evaluations play in the development of self-esteem?

## Assumption #3

*Self-evaluations are a psychological reality for most people.* We will suggest that self-evaluative processes play a pivotal role in the development and maintenance of either high or low levels of personal self-esteem. As will become clear later, however, we see little structural or substantive similarity between traditional formulations of self-talk and our conception of self-evaluative processes. We will clarify these important differences later in our discussion. Our thesis is that most people are continually engaged in a process of noticing, monitoring, thinking about, and evaluating their behavior and performance. We suggest that these self-evaluations are the primary basis for feelings of personal approval and disapproval *because they frequently reflect the degree to which a person has developed a response style that favors either coping or avoidance.*

## What Are Self-Evaluative Processes?

Self-evaluative processes involve two basic ingredients: cognitive awareness and affective experiencing. Throughout the book, and in all of our examples, it is important to note that all self-evaluations are cognitive-affective events. Both components are equally important and will be explained in greater detail later in this section. We will illustrate self-evaluative processes with an example, and then discuss the role of cognitive awareness and affective experiencing in self-evaluative processes.

> Several years ago our department hired a young new assistant professor. She was a talented researcher and therapist with a promising future, but her current teaching skills left something to be desired, as did her teacher ratings. We became good friends and talked often. Whenever these conversations touched on her anxiety about teaching, which was often, she would almost always start the conversation with a statement such as "I am doing better," "The last class was horrible," or "I don't think I was cut out to be a teacher." All of these statements are uncamouflaged self-evaluations about performance.

A moment's reflection will reveal that self-evaluations of this type are common to most of us. But not all self-evaluations focus on such obvious and observable behavior, however. For example,

> I once had a client who had developed an interpersonal style designed to minimize interpersonal conflict. She did this by consistently trying to be as acceptable and pleasing to others as possible. This is not a particularly unusual style; it is commonly referred to in psychological circles as that of a "pleaser and placater." As this client became more aware of her avoidant

behavior and the function it served for her, she started exploring the feelings she had about herself for being a pleaser at all costs. She thought of herself as weak for needing the approval of others so desperately. She also thought it was inappropriate for an adult to pretend to be something she was not as a means of buying approval from others. As a result of these self-evaluations, her personal feelings about herself were negative and intense. She hated herself for being unable to stand alone, or, as she put it, "to be true to myself." It is important to note that these self-evaluations were anchored to fairly accurate perceptions of her behavior and the function it served.

**Cognitive awareness and self-evaluative processes.** As we said earlier, cognitive awareness and affective experiencing are major components of self-evaluation. We have no reason to believe that these two attributes are equally distributed in the population. Rather, it seems much more likely to suppose that they are learned attributes, with some people being much more adept than others in either or both areas. *But we have absolutely no reason to believe that people can be completely unaware of their behavior and the function it serves or the self-evaluations that accompany that behavior.* This could be a controversial point in the minds of some, particularly those who favor an analytic point of view, with its emphasis on repression and denial. We will not even attempt to resolve the question of how complete repression can be. For the purposes of our discussion, however, it is sufficient to point out that even Freud (1915/1937) suggested that repression could not be absolute. Hidden impulse, at a minimum, would find expression in one form or another. Additionally, we wish to remind the reader that anxiety-producing conflicts, no matter how deeply repressed, must be recognized before they can be responded to defensively. Again, we see the possibility that awareness of behavior and its meaning is a psychological reality for most people. Certainly, vast differences in the clarity and precision of this awareness can be expected. But these differences are probably more a question of explicitness than of existence. For some, there can be a high degree of clarity and explicitness in their personal awareness and self-evaluations. For others, the same phenomenon takes place, but at a level of clarity that could only be called vague.

The important point is our assumption that self-evaluative processes are a psychological reality for most people, and when necessary, these self-evaluations can be made more clear and explicit by appropriate methods of observation and inquiry.

For example, it would be unreasonable to expect the woman who was a pleaser in our earlier example to be able to accurately and succinctly label the role and function of her behavior without assistance. However, she would probably not find it difficult to describe the way she acted around people she wanted to like her if she were asked such a question. It is equally doubtful that she would find it very difficult to speculate about the reasons she acted that way. And once behavior styles have been identified and described with reasonable clarity, the self-evaluations that accompany these behavior patterns can become obvious to both the client and therapist. In principle, then, we are suggesting that virtually all self-evaluations can be made reasonably clear and explicit with appropriate methods of observation and inquiry. We will say more about this process in Chapter 6.

**Affective experiencing and self-evaluative processes.** Although cognitive awareness is an essential component of self-evaluation, it is not the most important one. It is imperative that self-evaluative processes not be confused with detached, analytical, or purely cognitive activities. Our conception of self-evaluation is too emotionally robust to be accommodated by such a limited definition. We assume that virtually any human experience will have some affective valence attached to it. Some of these emotions may be more obvious or intense than others, but these are variations in degree, not existence. People regularly notice what they do (cognitions), how they feel (affect), and how they feel about what they are doing (cognitive-affective).

Self-evaluative processes are ultimately anchored to what clients cognitively see and affectively experience about themselves as a result of their own most authentic motives and behavior. It is as though individuals are participant-observers of their own lives. This allows individuals to observe their own tendencies to avoid or cope with psychological threat. A coping response, in which the person actively seeks resolution to psychological conflict in spite of fear and anxiety, is a fundamentally self-affirming experience. The favorable, and sometimes intense, affective evaluation that follows is the inevitable consequence of the adaptive behavior. The converse is equally true of an avoidant response. No matter how strategic a retreat from pathological anxiety may appear, it will still evoke a virtually reflexive negative affective evaluation. Self-evaluations are close relatives of primary processes and need little, if any, secondary interpretation.

For example, pleasers and placaters are (or can become) aware of the underlying meaning and motives of their behavior, and they have an affective response (evaluative) to their perceptions. In this case, the lack of psychological integrity implicit in the act of avoiding rejection by pretending to be that which is more pleasing to others can be (1) accurately perceived by the individual at some level of awareness, and (2) the source of considerable affective displeasure for the undesirable psychological qualities inherent in the motives and behavior. We are suggesting a high and continuous level of correspondence between the level of psychological integrity inherent in some response patterns and the affective evaluation it generates.

**Brief commentary on self-evaluative processes.** At the highest levels of cognitive awareness and affective experiencing, self-evaluations are anchored to identifiable patterns of behavior and motives. Please note that we are not talking about specific events or situations. We are referring to "behavioral styles" or "trait dispositions" that transcend events and endure time. We are talking about patterns of motives and behavior that are identifiable and describable.

And these patterns of behavior will contain varying degrees and mixtures of one's enduring tendency to avoid or cope with anxiety-producing conflict. We suggest that self-evaluations tend to be consistently negative in the presence of patterns of avoidance simply because avoidance patterns are so unflattering. We further suggest that people are, or can become, aware of their avoidance patterns and the personal inadequacies implicit in avoidance strategies. Those perceptions, or psychological realities, are the basis for the negative self-evaluations. They are at least partially reality bound.

Conversely, favorable self-evaluations are the inevitable result of coping. Inherent in coping responses are higher levels of risk taking, personal responsibility, and human growth, which are more satisfying psychological responses to anxiety and conflicts. This could result from social learning factors, which are rather obvious in our society, or from more intrinsic rewards inherent in the process of coping. In either case, more favorable self-evaluations tend to accompany coping than avoidance because coping is in fact a more favorable response.

This entire process may occur at lower levels of clarity and explicitness than we have described. When self-evaluations are not clearly attached to identifiable patterns and motives, they are simply more difficult to understand. They are more general and free-floating. Similarly, when self-evaluations remain vague, it is more difficult to understand feelings of despair and poor self-regard. But, in either case, feelings of approval or disapproval probably accompany coping or avoidance even though people differ in the clarity and explicitness with which this process is seen and understood.

This does not mean, however, that we are suggesting some mystical process that is difficult to understand. Just the opposite is true. We have found very few clients who have had difficulty identifying, describing, and labeling their most important behavior patterns and the self-evaluations that accompany them. It seems to depend entirely on the desire of the therapist to ask clients to identify and describe selected behavior patterns and the self-evaluations they generate. We will say more about the methods of observation and interviewing essential to this task in Chapter 6.

## Self-Evaluative Processes and Self-Talk: Important Differences

We see few similarities between our conception of self-evaluative processes and the major conceptions of self-talk.

**Accurate perceptions or social learning?** We have already indicated that self-evaluative processes are based on a continuous process of noticing, monitoring, thinking about, and directly experiencing the affective consequences of one's enduring patterns of behavior. Our definition of behavior refers to more than observable behavioral acts; it also includes internal events such as thoughts and feelings. Traditional conceptions of self-talk rely almost exclusively on the cognitive elements of personal awareness and evaluation. According to these views, human emotions and behavior are an expression of the attitudes and beliefs we acquire about ourselves in a social context. Typically, these attitudes are most obvious in the specific sentences people use when they talk to themselves about themselves.

For example, if students did poorly on an exam, they might say something to themselves such as, "I did poorly on this exam. Boy, am I a dunce." The result would be negative feelings about themselves. Examination of the self-talk involved in this scenario reveals what most cognitive-behavioral therapists would call irrational beliefs in their sentences, which are the proximate cause of their newly acquired psychic distress. The first irrational belief is that they are dunces because they did poorly on the exam. This would be considered irrational because it is an overgeneralized statement. In reality, doing poorly on an exam does not make one a dunce. Few would dispute that fact. Accordingly, eliminating irrational and self-accusatory sentences from self-talk can also eliminate the cause of the negative feelings.

The second irrational belief in this case is more implicit but just as influential and irrational. It is the belief that it is horrible to do poorly on an exam. If a cognitive-behavioral therapist were to examine this irrational belief, a dialogue between therapist and client would probably sound something like this:

| | |
|---|---|
| Therapist: | You seem a little down-in-the-mouth today. Care to talk about it? |
| Client: | It's *horrible*, Doc! I just found out this morning that I failed my chemistry exam. |
| Therapist: | You say you failed your exam, and it's horrible! |
| Client: | Look, Doc, if I can't pass a simple exam like that one, what'll it be like when I have to take the final? I may as well start packing right now. What's the use? |
| Therapist: | It sounds to me as though you believe failing that one exam is a major catastrophe. |
| Client: | Well, that's exactly what it is—a *major* catastrophe. |
| Therapist: | Okay, Jim, you are telling me how horrible and catastrophic it is that you failed that test, right? Now, I |

|            | want you to pay careful attention to how you're feeling at this moment. Can you tell me what you're feeling? |
|------------|---|
| Client:    | I feel like the door to my future just slammed shut. I feel—well, hopeless is the best word I can think of. |
| Therapist: | So, you failed an exam, you tell yourself it's horrible, and you feel hopeless. Can you see how labeling that event as horrible causes you to feel hopeless? |
| Client:    | But it really seems that way to me. |
| Therapist: | Have you ever done poorly on a test before? |
| Client:    | Well, sure I have, a few times. But this seems so much worse. |
| Therapist: | Can you recall how you felt during those times? |
| Client:    | Well, I guess I felt a lot like I do now. |
| Therapist: | So it probably seemed horrible then, too. But here you are. You've graduated from high school, been accepted into a fine university, and successfully completed two semesters. That doesn't seem so horrible to me. |
| Client:    | Well, when you look at it that way, it doesn't seem quite so bad. |
| Therapist: | And that's precisely the point. As you look at it differently, you'll have different feelings. Now, rather than labeling your test failure as horrible, let's explore some more rational ways of viewing it and see what happens to your feelings. |

In essence, then, cognitive-behavioral approaches emphasize the irrationality of human thinking and personal beliefs in the development of emotional distress. All of these approaches share the assumption that the irrational beliefs revealed in self-talk are without foundation: They are simply acquired beliefs that are best disregarded. Additionally, most of these approaches view self-talk as a psychological trigger that activates useless negative feelings that eventually come to serve as inhibitors to human behavior and performance. Consistent with these views is the assumption that negative feelings and emotional inhibitors can be most expeditiously removed by identifying and eliminating irrational beliefs, values, attitudes, and sentences from self-talk.

Self-evaluations, on the other hand, are based on an entirely different set of assumptions and psychological processes. In the first place, they are not considered to be acquired, irrational beliefs. Rather, they are assumed to be at least partially valid self-perceptions. And these perceptions have their origins in one of the most fundamental levels of psychological experiencing. They are based on a cognitive awareness of self and the direct affective experience that accompanies that awareness. The most fundamental differences between self-talk and self-evaluative processes should now be more apparent. In the first place, self-evaluations are based on what we consider to be at least partially valid self-perceptions. They are not simply learned, irrational beliefs that are central to the various definitions of self-talk. Second, self-evaluative processes are based on the best elements of cognitive and affective dimensions of human experience, whereas self-talk is primarily a cognitive event. And because the affect in self-evaluations is intimately tied to enduring patterns of behavior, these emotions are generic to the individual and can be quite intense and durable.

## Self-Evaluations and Self-Esteem

We maintain that high levels of self-esteem are the product of a response style that favors coping over avoidance. When this is the case, conflicts are faced, understood, and resolved, resulting in self-confidence, personal approval, and feelings of personal well-being. Patterns of excessive avoidance breed just the opposite results. The very act of avoidance, by denial and distortion, precludes any feeling of adequacy. Therefore, the tendency to cope or avoid virtually dictates the positive or negative nature of personal psychological experience.

Finally, it is of utmost importance to note that self-evaluative processes and the levels of self-esteem they create are based on the *process* of coping and avoidance, not the *outcomes* they produce. A rather amusing example of this comes from one of the writer's clients who was acutely self-conscious about his inability to sing.

The client avoided any occasion where his lack of vocal talent might be evidenced. Sufficiently exasperated, he resolved to confront his fear once and for all. He did so by responding to an ad in a music trade paper announcing auditions for a professional singer. The client entered the crowded audition hall, stood before the director, producer, and dozens of other auditioning singers, and sang "My Country 'Tis of Thee" without accompaniment. The director smiled, the producer shook his head, and there were several audible coughs and laughs from the onlookers. The client said "thank you" and walked out of the room. The outcome is obvious. The client did not make the callback list, and there was ample negative feedback to verify what he already knew about his singing skills.

However, there were other outcomes that were less discernible. In undertaking this action, the client (1) understood the risks involved in auditioning (potential embarrassment, ridicule), (2) openly acknowledged and accepted those risks, and (3) made his best effort at performing, never denying the possibility of a negative outcome. Although his worst fears were realized in some respects, his ability to approach this long-avoided task produced personal pleasure and self-approval for not letting his fears entirely dictate his behavior. To this day, he tells this story with pride, humor, and fondness.

## Assumption #4

*Self-evaluative processes can provide a basis for continuous affective feedback from the self about the adequacy of the self.* It is time to discuss the role of personal emotions in the development of self-esteem. As will quickly become obvious, we consider emotions to be the crowning element in the development of either high or low levels of self-esteem. As we discussed earlier, cognitive activity is important to our model because it provides a means to identify and clarify the role and function various behavior patterns serve. In this respect, cognitions are in the service of increasing psychic clarity and understanding. But cognitions per se are not affect laden. Their power to motivate and influence human behavior is limited compared to the power of aroused affect. And in our model, self-esteem is not a thought but a subjective and enduring state of realistic self-approval. It is a feeling people experience about themselves. The same thing is true of low self-esteem. We must attempt to explain where these feelings come from!

In our view, in a corrective therapeutic encounter clients directly experience their own affect in its full intensity. The fact that emotions can be discussed and understood cognitively does not necessarily alter the nature of the feelings or their influence. And the self-evaluative processes we have already discussed provide the conduit for accessing client emotions that are most relevant to the therapeutic process. We will illustrate this point with two clinical examples. The first is a patient suffering from paranoid schizophrenia who was in treatment for 7 years. The second is a typical client treated on an outpatient basis. We have included the former to help illustrate this proposition because it represents one of the most difficult clinical situations we can imagine. In each of these examples, we hope to demonstrate the rapidity with which self-evaluative processes, and the feelings they represent, can influence the behavior of the individual. We will start with the schizophrenic client.

This particular client was a young woman with exceptional intellectual talents. She was first diagnosed as a paranoid schizophrenic approximately 9 years earlier. She had frequent psychotic breaks, which could only be partially controlled with phenothiazines. However, she was able to remain unhospitalized as long as she met with her therapist weekly. On those occasions when her therapist was out of town for more than a week she would invariably be hospitalized. She had been in treatment with the same therapist for over 5 years when this particular example occurred. During this time, the client had maintained what must be considered a remarkably good therapeutic relationship, given her diagnosis.

In this particular session, the client arrived and took her customary seat. She was slightly more quiet than usual and obviously preoccupied. After an appropriate silence, the therapist asked if she thought she should be talking about the thoughts and feelings she seemed to be avoiding. She indicated that she didn't know. The therapist then asked how she felt about herself for her avoidance during a therapy session. After an extraordinarily long silence, the client said that she *should* talk about it, but that she was afraid. Her therapist asked her to try to identify what she needed to do during the session so she could approve of herself when it was over. She thought about it and hesitantly started talking about the increasing tensions in her marriage and the growing prospect that her husband might leave her. The prospect of being alone terrified her, mostly because of the implications of her mental health problems. In spite of the distressing content she was discussing, the client gradually became more responsive to herself and her therapist. When the session was over, the therapist asked if she was leaving the session approving of what she did during the hour. She said yes. Moreover, she wished she could handle other issues in her life in the same way without the assistance of her therapist.

In this example, we see three areas of self-evaluation and their emotional consequences. The first is the client's personal disapproval for avoiding the issues about which she was most concerned. This disapproval was manifested verbally and by her dysphoric mood and withdrawal. The second area of self-evaluation was her personal approval for facing the issue during the therapy session. This was manifested verbally and by her improved mood and behavior. The effects of this approval seem to have transcended the stress associated with the topic being discussed. The third area of self-evaluation was her disapproval for needing the therapist to help her face problems rather than avoid them.

On the whole, however, this client experienced substantially more self-approval during this hour than disapproval, and the session ended with the therapist fairly confident she would not need to be hospitalized during the week or call for additional sessions. In the therapist's mind, her attempts at coping with a difficult life issue produced more personal self-approval than could be obtained by hiding from these unpleasant realities. We find that attempts by the client to cope with difficult psychic issues almost always engender more internal self-approving affect than is necessary to successfully cope with the stress involved. This tends to be true irrespective of the stress and fear associated with some topics, no matter how fragile the client. We suggest that this client found hope in a fairly desperate situation because of the immediate self-approval she *felt* as a result of coping with this difficult situation for the better part of an hour. While we cannot be absolutely sure this is the case, it is obvious that her improved mental status was *not* the result of an improved marriage, diminished fears about being left alone, external reassurance, or significant progress toward resolution of a personal problem!

Our second example is more typical.

> This client was a middle-aged, upper-middle-class businessman. A number of therapy hours had already been devoted to examining his tendency to avoid interpersonal conflicts. This client found it less distressing to simply accommodate the needs and wishes of others than to get into interpersonal confrontations. Regrettably, however, this strategy was as effective at diminishing his self-respect as it was for avoiding conflict. He suffered moderately severe depression, and considered himself to be a coward and hypocrite. In reality, he resented others' demands on him and his inability to resist them. The client finally arrived at the point of understanding that his own personal approval required that he represent himself more honestly in his dealings with others whether this would lead to conflict or not. He promptly went to those with whom he had unresolved issues and expressed his feelings more openly and honestly than usual. While these people were mildly surprised at his feelings, it was hardly a noticeable event in their lives. Even though these behavioral changes made no obvious or appreciable difference in how this man was seen or treated by others, he reported feeling "like a new man." He took great pride in his accomplishments, vowed not to be dishonest in his dealings with others for any reason, and found himself feeling remarkably better.

In both of these examples, we see the possibility of significant personal improvement because of the self-approval experienced by clients in their attempts to cope with problems they typically avoided.

This entire proposition is based on the assumption that self-evaluative processes can be continuous, and their affective consequences are immediate. This is particularly true when there are deliberate shifts from avoidance to coping in an attempt to face what is usually avoided. It is important to note that improved self-evaluations and the self-approving feelings they create are more the result of attempting to cope than of achieving any specific outcome. In many cases, even an unfavorable outcome will not negate the psychological benefits of attempting to cope. The effects of the very act of avoidance or coping are assumed to be more potent, consequential, and influential than most of the outcomes either act will produce.

The prominent role of emotions in our formulation of self-esteem should now be obvious. Ultimately, the development of self-esteem is directly anchored to what clients actually experience affectively *about* themselves as a result of their own behavior. Coping breeds a pleasant and rewarding affective experience. And if the organism has an enduring tendency to cope rather than avoid, the organism's internal, self-evaluative feedback loop will produce favorable affective feedback for the organism. *And it is the nature and quality of this internal, affective feedback that defines the nature of the organism to itself.* High or low self-esteem, then, is the result and the reflection of the internal, affective feedback the organism most commonly experiences.

## Summary

We have described a process of internal self-evaluation that we suggest is a central element in the development of either high or low levels of personal self-esteem. In essence, when there is consistency in one's tendency to cope or avoid conflict, there is a continuous basis for internal feedback from the self about the adequacy of the self. Avoidance breeds negative self-evaluative processes, feelings, and perceptions because of the inherently undesirable qualities of this behavior. Coping is associated with favorable self-evaluative processes, feelings, and perceptions because of the high psychological quality of the elements associated with this response. In each case, these perceptions are assumed to be at least partially valid and a direct reflection of the actual attributes involved in coping and avoidance. Even though these self-evaluative processes go on at different levels of clarity and explicitness for different people, their effects are a psychological reality for most people. Finally, we have suggested that internal self-evaluations play a more important role in determining the form and substance of human behavior than external evaluation does, though both are clearly influential.

# 5

# Introduction to the Model

We are now ready to combine the prior concepts we have discussed with our four assumptions about feedback into a series of propositions to explain the origins and dynamics of high and low levels of personal self-esteem. We will discuss these propositions sequentially and then illustrate the assumed interrelationships among them.

## Origins and Dynamics of Personal Self-Esteem

*1. Self-esteem is a dynamic attribute.* We do not consider self-esteem to be necessarily fixed at any point in the life span. We think it can be either static or dynamic, depending on the changing behavior dispositions of the individual across the life span. Rigid behavior patterns characterized by a tendency to consistently avoid conflict are not likely to be associated with improved self-esteem. This is not because self-esteem is invariant but because the behavior patterns that most readily influence the development of self-esteem are fixed. We believe that feelings of personal worth are highly responsive to authentic, consistent feedback from either the social environment or self-evaluations. Favorable internal feedback is more potent, with longer-lasting benefits, than is social approval for reasons we have already discussed. Similarly, negative feedback from either source can prove to be devastating. In either situation, however, feelings of personal approval are responsive to the evaluative thoughts of self and others.

We submit, then, that a sense of self-appreciation is primarily a reflection of one's tendency to choose coping over avoidance when faced with conflicts that involve fear and anxiety. It is, secondarily, a reflection of the way one is valued by others. Any change in either of these two factors can have a significant influence on one's self-esteem, but how one perceives oneself will always be more influential than how one is perceived by others.

For the remainder of our discussion, self-esteem refers to a psychological attribute that is responsive to consistent, credible feedback from either internal or external sources. We will discuss the potency and consequences of feedback from these different sources more fully in another section of this chapter. For now, we wish only to suggest that self-esteem can move along a continuum from high to virtually nonexistent. Dramatic movement along this continuum, however, is unlikely in the absence of equally dramatic changes in individual response patterns.

*2. Psychological threat is unavoidable!* In our discussion of the concept of coping, we have repeatedly emphasized that coping is the path of reality testing, insight, and the recognition of imperfections in the self. It should be clear that the very psychological attributes we have used to define the coping response will also guarantee the eventual recognition of personal limitations. In effect, we have a two-edged sword. First, personal limitations must be openly recognized and accepted before they can be faced and dealt with. This creates personal threat and discomfort. Second, learning to understand and face this threat is the basis for the most powerful forms of psychological learning.

In brief, psychological threat is a reality for us all. For some, the frequency and intensity of the threat can be consistently high. For others it can remain relatively low. But everyone is vulnerable to psychological threat in some areas, and overcoming this threat is one of the most basic processes involved in personal growth and development. Because of this, we suggest that the frequency and intensity of psychological threat can vary along a continuum from very high to relatively low.

*3. Self-esteem modifies psychological threat.* We suggest that there is an inverse relationship between levels of self-esteem and levels of psychological threat. As self-esteem increases, the frequency and intensity of psychological threat decrease. The converse is equally true. As self-esteem decreases, the frequency and intensity of psychological threat increases. There are two primary reasons for suggesting this relationship. Both are equally important, though one is based on a large body of empirical data and the other on a content analysis of avoidance and coping. We will start with our content analysis.

Coping and avoidance are based on attributes the intrinsic qualities of which lend themselves to either increasing or decreasing psychological threat. Let us explain. The act of avoidance virtually precludes the possibility of new learning. Its primary function is to avoid fear and anxiety. Avoidance does not provide a basis for learning new or more adaptive response patterns, or for reducing the number of areas in which a person's psychological function is impaired; nor does it provide any hope for personal growth and development. If avoidance does anything with surety, it provides people with personal experiences and perceptions of themselves as unable to deal with anxiety, fear, or conflict. Such experiences and self-perceptions can only be expected to further impair the person's ability to respond to threatening situations in the future. The result is an increase in the frequency and intensity of perceived psychological threats.

On the other hand, the act of coping with personal conflict requires risk taking, personal responsibility, and willingness to realistically face personal issues. When this is done successfully, people not only broaden their understanding of themselves and the world they live in, they also experience themselves as able to deal with threatening situations productively. This is a powerful consideration in any definition of self. It allows a person to approach threatening situations in the future with far less fear and anxiety than might normally be expected. High levels of self-esteem not only contribute to the ability to realistically face and learn from threatening situations, they also contribute to people's perceptions of themselves as able to resolve difficult issues. All of these considerations reduce the number of events a person finds threatening and increase the inclination to respond appropriately when one is threatened.

This content analysis is consistent with a substantial body of research literature. It has been repeatedly demonstrated that self-esteem and psychological health are related to favorable consequences in a variety of psychological situations. High ego strength, for example, is a good indicator of a favorable response to psychotherapy (Garfield, 1986). Not surprisingly, ego strength is related to high self-esteem as well as other measures of personal adjustment (Harmm, 1980). Similarly, individuals with a high internal locus of control as measured by the Rotter Internal/External Locus of Control Scale (I-E) generally have a more favorable response to psychotherapy than those with a more external orientation (Patrick, 1984). Again, we find that high self-esteem is related to an internal locus of control (Fish & Karabenick, 1971; Sathyavathi & Anthony, 1984) as well as other desirable psychological attributes, such as perceptual accuracy (Steger, Simmons, & Lavelle, 1973), better adjustment to old age (Carp & Carp, 1981), and less conformity (Singh, Prasad, & Bhagalpur, 1973). Finally, high self-esteem has been related to androgyny or sex-role flexibility (Flaherty & Dusek, 1980). Again, we find the same pattern as before. Androgynous people tend to be well adjusted and more flexible in responding to a wide variety of psychological situations (Bem & Lenney, 1976).

Collectively, then, there are both logical and empirical reasons to suggest an inverse relationship between self-esteem and the experience of psychological threat. The evidence from a wide variety of settings and researchers consistently describes the benefits derived from the psychological attributes typically related to high self-esteem. All of these observations suggest that high levels of self-esteem are associated with reduced levels of anxiety and fear, probably because the attributes associated with high self-esteem allow a person to respond to these situations more realistically and appropriately. Because of this, we suggest that the experience of psychological threat can vary on a continuum from high to low, depending on an individual's level of self-esteem.

*4. Self-esteem varies as a function of response styles to threat.* We have already discussed the role, function, and consequence of coping and avoidance in detail in an earlier section of this chapter. Our purpose now is only to highlight some of these considerations and describe the assumed relationships among self-esteem, psychological threat, and response styles. We have already suggested that individual response styles to threat can vary in degree from coping to avoidance. We defined coping as a process of realistically facing up to difficult issues that involve such desirable psychological attributes as self-examination, insight, reality testing, risk taking, and personal responsibility. On the other hand, avoidance and defense are based on a process of denial, distortion, and self-deception as a means of avoiding fear and anxiety. We have said that individual response styles contain varying degrees and mixtures of avoidance and coping. To the extent these response styles favor coping over avoidance, they tend to engender favorable self-evaluative thoughts and feelings. Conversely, patterns of avoidance can be expected to breed negative self-evaluative thoughts and feelings. These evaluations of the self and the feelings they engender can also be expected to vary from intense to mild. The more extreme the avoidance, the more intense the self-disapproval. The greater the risk and responsibility involved in the coping response, the greater the feelings of self-respect and approval. We will say more about these feedback loops shortly. For now we wish to emphasize our assumption that enduring response styles do exist, that they can usually be identified explicitly, and that these patterns of behavior are the basis for many self-evaluations.

## Summary

We have now described the continuum along which self-esteem, personal threat, and response styles can vary. The relationships among these three variables can be summarized as follows:

a. As self-esteem increases, there is a corresponding decrease in the frequency and intensity of psychological threat. This increases the probability of a coping response to conflict, which will usually generate favorable self-evaluations.

b. As self-esteem declines, there is a corresponding increase in the frequency and intensity of psychological threat. This increases the probability of an avoidance response to conflict, which will generate unfavorable self-evaluations.

With the relationship among these psychological variables now defined, we are ready to discuss the means and mechanisms by which feedback from the social environment, or the self, influences each variable. The remainder of the variables and propositions involved in our model of self-esteem are portrayed in Figure 1. Most of these variables define and describe the means and mechanisms by which self-evaluative processes and feedback from the social environment influence the development and maintenance of high or low levels of self-esteem. The following observations about Figure 1 are central:

1. Collectively, there are more sources of negative feedback than there are positive ones. Of the five feedback sources represented in the figure, two provide distinctly negative feedback (self-generated disapproval and credible negative feedback from the environment), and one provides positive feedback (self-generated approval). Of the two remaining sources, one provides feedback that is moderately positive (credible positive feedback from the environment), but the other is so untrustworthy that it need not be counted (noncredible positive feedback from the environment). Even though the last feedback source appears to provide positive feedback, it constitutes such a fundamental verification of one's impression management tendencies (avoidance) that its net effect is decidedly negative.

In brief, then, the most important source of enduring self-approval is internal positive self-evaluations. Disapproval, however, can be the result of credible negative feedback and noncredible positive feedback from the social environment, or from negative self-evaluations. It appears that there are more sources of negative information about the self than there are positive ones.

2. While external feedback and self-evaluations influence self-esteem, it is important to note that the two sources are not equal in their ability to do so. The relative potency of each source is suggested by the degree to which its lines of influence (the dotted and dashed lines in Figure 1) are extended to the extreme points on the self-esteem scale. Self-evaluations are clearly the most potent. Note that internal self-evaluations touch both extremes of the internal feedback scale, which in turn touches both extremes of the self-esteem scale, whereas feedback from the social environment does not. Credible negative social feedback is not quite as destructive as negative self-evaluations, and positive social feedback is not nearly as potent or uplifting as positive self-evaluations.

## Figure 1

*The Role of Internal Feedback, External/Social Feedback, and Personal Response Styles in the Development and Maintenance of High or Low Levels of Self-Esteem*

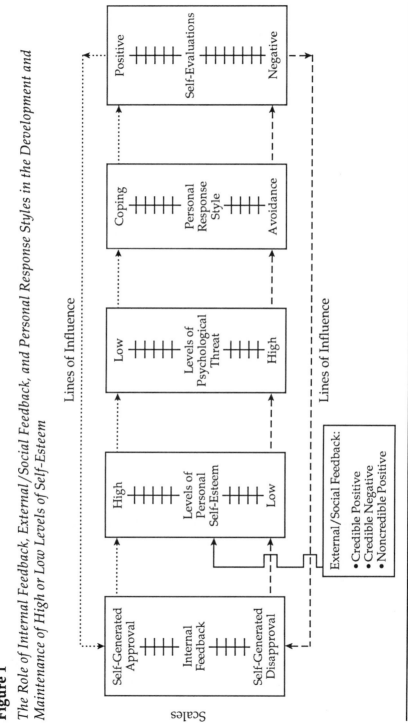

The differences in potency become particularly important when there are any inconsistencies between the feedback provided by internal and external sources. Favorable self-evaluations can more than negate the influence of negative social feedback. Similarly, negative self-evaluations can completely negate the influence of positive social feedback. In essence, we are suggesting that authentic high self-esteem *requires* reasonably high levels of self-approving thoughts. External social feedback can be influential, but usually on a supplementary basis, and only as long as the feedback is continuously available and consistent with other, more basic self-evaluations.

3. Based on our earlier discussion describing the relationships among self-esteem, psychological threat, and response styles portrayed in Figure 1, we would expect feedback to be processed as follows:

a. Positive feedback from either source tends to increase self-esteem, lowers the frequency and intensity of psychological threats, and increases the probability of a coping response when threat does occur. This sequence then provides the organism with feedback (1) to the self, (2) from the self, and (3) about the adequacy of the self. This is the internal self-evaluative process that we have suggested to be virtually continuous. This internal feedback influences the current level of self-esteem, sensitivity to threat, and tendency to avoid or cope with conflict as the cycle repeats itself over and over.

b. Negative feedback from either source is processed in essentially the same manner. Current levels of self-esteem are lowered, which increases the probability of an avoidance response when threat does occur. When this happens, the organism receives new internal feedback about the inadequacy of the self. Once again, this internal negative feedback and all of its consequences are entered into the cycle as it repeats itself over and over.

The units of time and behavior involved in any cycle can be highly variable, ranging from relatively brief episodes of appropriately assertive behavior to prolonged periods of self-control and restraint. Or they could be based on moral transgressions or prolonged periods of self-indulgence. These considerations are unique to each individual and need not be defined by any a priori theoretical considerations. We are proposing a mechanistic model that defines and describes some of more basic parameters affecting how evaluations by self and others are conducted. This process is assumed to be applicable to a wide range of behavioral considerations.

Finally, it is important to notice that we have deliberately avoided any attempt to provide profiles that would define coping, avoidance, or response styles. We consider our reasons for this compelling. The manifestations of each of these concepts are so varied that they cannot, and probably should not, be made more objective. It would simply be misleading. Remember that avoidance is not defined by any observable behavior patterns; it is defined by the function the behavior serves. We are referring to motivational constructs when we talk about avoidance and coping. One's intention to realistically face conflict and learn from it is the essence of a coping response. Similarly, one's tendency to escape from conflict is the essence of avoidance. Even though these personality dispositions shape behavior patterns, they cannot be identified by any specific behavior.

For example, simple politeness may be the first attempt by one person to become more sociable and overcome a fear of people, but for another person this same behavior may be the means of avoiding any interpersonal intimacy with others. The only reliable means of understanding human motives is on an individual basis. We consider the preservation of highly individualized and idiosyncratic considerations within a nonthematic framework of general principles to be one of the greatest strengths of this model. We can discuss the general principles involved in the model, but their application on an individual basis requires an understanding of each particular individual. In brief, we suggest that these general principles remain constant with different individuals, but understanding each individual's unique style of coping and defense is required before the general principles can be used. We will discuss this in more detail in Chapter 6.

## Theoretical Implications

Before discussing the important theoretical implications of this model, we want to provide a detailed case study to illustrate the clinical manifestation of the concepts we are discussing. We have two reasons for this. First, from past experience we have learned that it is easy to confuse the simplicity of the model with its subtlety. A clear conceptual understanding of basic principles does not imply a clear understanding of the behavioral manifestations of these principles. Admittedly, the model is not conceptually complex, but the manifestations of its most central concepts can be highly varied and are seldom obvious. Clinical illustrations contribute to a fuller understanding of the model for most readers. Second, clinical examples can also be used to illustrate the major theoretical implications more fully after these clinical examples are described.

## Clinical Illustration

Our first case study is of a pregnant, unmarried 20-year-old woman. We will discuss this case with regard to (a) a brief history, (b) presenting complaints, (c) treatment considerations, (d) critical incidents in psychotherapy, and (e) current status of the client.

**Brief history.** During high school this young woman, like so many teenagers from middle-class America, was preoccupied with personal appearance, peer acceptability, and personal self-consciousness. Her fondest memories of high school were attached to her senior year, when she was a cheerleader. Other than that, her life was more typical than remarkable. She was not particularly attractive, but she was certainly well-groomed and stylishly dressed. She had more friends than many of her peers but not nearly as many as she would have liked. She was, in essence, in the middle of the bell-shaped curve on most qualities, including feelings of inadequacy and inferiority.

She lived with two reasonably caring parents. Their marriage was probably better than most, though far from exemplary. She had a much better relationship with her mother than with her father, whom she described as detached. She had planned on continuing her college education before she became pregnant.

She had been dating her boyfriend for about 8 months before she stopped resisting his sexual advances. Actually, she agreed to sex more out of compassion for her boyfriend's frustration than her own sexual passion; it was just too difficult to say no. This was her first sexual experience. Even though her religious and moral values created a great deal of guilt about her sexual behavior, they were not sufficiently influential to curtail the sexual activity. She found out she was pregnant after 3 months of sex on an intermittent basis. Birth control measures had not been employed regularly.

**Presenting complaints.** In the initial interview she complained about depression, feeling deserted by her boyfriend, and confusion about what to do with the baby. She had already decided not to have an abortion, but the question of adoption still remained. Her voice was barely audible when she spoke, she avoided eye contact by looking at the floor, and she had a slight tendency to whine when she talked. With careful probing she admitted to some feelings of anger toward her boyfriend, but she quickly minimized their importance because they would only make him angry. She described herself as always having had very low self-esteem. Her major concerns focused on the confusion she felt about whether to keep the baby or place it for adoption, and the feelings of despair that accompanied her depression. From a clinical point of view, her symptoms varied from mild to moderate but fell far short of severe.

**Treatment considerations.** Major elements in the treatment of the client based on the principles we are discussing include:

1. The presence and pervasiveness of the client's impression management tendencies had to be ascertained, which was not difficult in this case. It was clear in the initial interview that this young woman was far more accustomed to gaining approval from others by impression management than by making herself known to those around her. Her proclivity toward impression management was repeatedly suggested by

a. her preoccupation with peer acceptance and approval;

b. denial of her feelings of anger toward her boyfriend because they would be unacceptable to him;

c. excessive and almost unquestioning conformity to conventional social standards (clothing styles, appearance, and value placed on being a cheerleader); and

d. a diminished sense of identity, as revealed by her willingness to engage in sexual intercourse in the absence of any intrinsic motivation to do so.

Future interviews provided additional evidence that she was a consummate impression manager and had been for many years. This was most evident in situations where anger and conflict could be avoided by denying her own thoughts and feelings or when acceptance could be enhanced by being what would be most pleasing to others.

2. Once her impression management tendencies had been clearly identified, it became important to understand the role and function of this behavior. Given that her impression management tendencies were far from isolated events, it was reasonable to assume the presence of some underlying motives that would account for the consistency of this behavior. Again, the answer was fairly obvious in the initial interview. It was part of a pattern she had developed to make herself more pleasing to others, and with the same stroke, avoid interpersonal conflict. She was, in essence, a person who had developed an interpersonal style of being a pleaser and placater. This is one of the most common conflict-avoidant strategies, and the only thing unique about it in this case was its embeddedness. She appeared to be so preoccupied with her personal acceptability to others because of low self-esteem that she had virtually no sense of self or personal self-direction. The following comments from the initial interview were consistent with this view:

a. She appeared to be just as concerned about how others would see her because she was pregnant as she was about such critical considerations as (1) adoption, (2) finances, (3) sin and guilt, and (4) the implications of all of the above for her future.

b. She was willing to provide sex to her boyfriend rather than argue about it.

c. She wanted to avoid conflict with her boyfriend's parents, even though it meant allowing them to mistakenly believe that she had seduced their innocent son.

3. Given the evidence that this young woman had developed chronic avoidance strategies, a major treatment consideration would be for the client to increase her awareness of her interpersonal style, the role and function it served, and the negative self-evaluations it generated. Generally speaking, as the role, function, and self-evaluations associated with avoidance patterns become

more explicit, the behavior patterns themselves become more un-acceptable to the client for reasons that are fairly obvious. They are, for the most part, behavior patterns that are seldom cherished or held in high personal esteem. Making patterns of avoidance explicit to the client only tends to make them more obviously un-acceptable.

4. Finally, and most importantly, a major treatment consideration for this client would be to actually engage in a series of coping behaviors during therapy sessions in response to the actual stress and conflict the therapy process will inevitably generate. This is probably the most reliable means of increasing a client's awareness of what a coping response is, what it feels like, and what self-evaluative thoughts and feelings are associated with facing rather than avoiding problems. Fortunately, this is not as difficult as it may at first appear. The very act of asking clients to realistically identify, describe, and label their avoidance strategies and the self-evaluations they generate is a *primary coping response.* It requires most of the psychological attributes we used to define coping, such as risk taking, reality testing, insight, and personal responsibility. Undoubtedly, this process can be extremely upsetting to the client. When properly understood, however, this distress is as inevitable to the therapy process as it is beneficial to the client. In the first place, the distress signifies that clients truly grasp the significance and consequences of their prior avoidance patterns. This is usually well worth being upset about. The presence of intense distress also verifies that clients are facing their own unpleasant psychological realities without resorting to their usual primitive methods of denial, distortion, and self-deception. Second, intense emotional distress becomes a powerful incentive for personal change provided clients clearly understand that it is the result of their own avoidant behavior, which they have already identified, described, and labeled.

Once these events have happened, *it is imperative* that the therapist assist clients in identifying any new behavioral elements present in their response to conflict. Identification of the self-evaluations that accompany any new behavior is equally central. We will say a great deal more about this process in the next chapter. For now, we will only illustrate this principle with examples of what a therapist might say to accomplish this purpose. Several alternatives are listed below.

a. "How do you feel about yourself for being able to talk openly about some problems you have always avoided in the past?"

b. "Even though you seem very upset about what we are talking about, how does it feel to be honest with yourself?"

c. "Have you noticed that you have been behaving differently for the last half hour or so? What differences have you noticed, and how do you feel about yourself when you act that way?"

**Critical incidents in therapy.** After about 30 minutes in the first therapy session, the client was asked to describe her way of presenting herself to the therapist. She passively resisted. After a short pause, she was asked to describe her voice, eye contact, and willingness to talk openly about her situation. She described each of these characteristics accurately. After another short pause, she was asked what impression she was conveying about herself. Again she resisted answering. She was now obviously uncomfortable. The therapist waited patiently, maintained eye contact, and eventually commented on her discomfort. The therapist said that she seemed to find his questions unsettling and it appeared that she wanted to avoid him. She nodded affirmatively. He asked if she typically tried to avoid unpleasantness. Again she nodded affirmatively. The therapist indicated that he would still like her to try to answer his question and wanted to know if she would try. She said yes. After a long pause she said that she probably appeared weak and helpless. She was complimented for her incisiveness and was asked to explain in more detail precisely what she thought would make her appear weak and helpless.

When she finished, she was much more relaxed. The therapist wanted to know if she was as weak and helpless as she was acting. She said NO, as if insulted by the question. (Actually, very few people would say yes to a question phrased this way.) The therapist thanked her for her honesty and indicated that he agreed with her. He asked her to think of an adjective that captured the essence of how she created the impression of being more weak and helpless than she actually was. A big smile came over her face as she said, "By acting like a dodo." The therapist smiled back and said, "Let's call this your dodo routine, then."

The task of identifying the self-evaluations generated by the dodo routine started at the beginning of the second session. She was asked to tell the therapist more about her routine, how she developed it, how well it worked, from whom she learned it, when she was most likely to use it, and how good she thought she was at it. Actually, all of these invitations for introspective speculation were preparation for a more fundamental question that could not be asked yet. Eventually the therapist was able to bring it up: "How do you feel about yourself for acting like a dodo so often?" The client paused, more out of thoughtfulness than resistance. Tears formed in her eyes before she said, "Ashamed." The therapist wanted to know more. Other adjectives were added, all of which were embarrassing and uncomplimentary. The client was allowed, and at times gently pushed, to experience the shame generated by her own self-evaluative thought. It was a difficult session for her, and she left with a severe headache.

In future sessions the therapist saw less and less of the dodo routine. The client also reported using it less frequently with others. Of course, there were occasional lapses in the session. When these occurred she was quickly asked if she meant to do her routine again. She almost always said no, but not always. The therapist faithfully asked how she felt about herself for allowing the dodo routine to reappear, either intentionally or unintentionally. "Ashamed" and "embarrassed" were the adjectives used most frequently to describe her feelings. There was also some resentment toward the therapist for catching it so quickly.

Two other basic avoidance patterns were also identified. These were described and labeled with equivalent care, as were the self-evaluations they generated. She called one "wimpy," which was nothing more than a simple extension of the dodo routine. The other was called "pleaser," which was her primary method of avoiding conflict.

About two-thirds of the way through the second hour of therapy, the therapist asked if she was using any of her dodo routine in this session. She paused thoughtfully and said she didn't think so. The therapist pointed out that she had maintained eye contact with him a good portion of the time, spoken up much more clearly, discussed her situation more openly, identified the concerns she was most worried about, and expressed many thoughts and feelings she usually kept private. He wanted to know if she had noticed the change. Because of the seriousness of her concerns and the stress they had created, she had not. This was not unusual. She was asked to reflect on her actual behavior for the past 30 minutes and identify everything that was new or not common for her. Most of her answers focused on being more honest with herself and feeling more upset about her situation than usual. She was asked if she approved of herself for being that way in spite of the distress it caused. She wasn't sure. However, when asked if she thought the session was good for her, she answered yes with no equivocation. Even though she was emotionally on edge, she reported feeling a bit more hopeful about her ability to solve some of the serious issues with which she was now confronted. When the therapist asked if she thought it would make much difference if she could learn to behave on a daily basis the way she acted in therapy, she talked at length about how hard it would be and the difference it could make.

The remaining ten sessions covered a variety of different topics. They included such basic and consequential matters as adoption, personal identity, anger, and plans for her future. In spite of the differences between these sessions, they all had two underlying similarities. The first was the therapist's continuing attention to the dominant style used by the client when considering these issues. The second was the client's experience of continually being asked to behave only in ways she could personally approve of.

**Current status of the client.** Therapy ended just prior to the birth of the client's daughter, who was put up for adoption. The client will always regret not having her daughter, but she believes any other choice would have been irresponsible. This way, her child will have a father. The client is actually proud of her ability to consider the well-being of her baby above her own wants and wishes. Giving up her baby may well prove to be one of the most difficult things she will ever have to do, but in spite of this she does not regret her decision.

Her depression is virtually gone. She is sad about many things from her life but not depressed. She is also quite determined not to make the same mistakes again. She clearly understands that her dodo routine and being a pleaser are the real reasons she was an unwed mother. In conflict situations she now forces herself to be more honest with others. This has made life more complicated and stressful than it used to be, at least on an immediate basis.

She is still waiting to see if the long-term benefits are worth it. For example, she terminated her relationship with her old boyfriend for the best of reasons, but now she is lonely. She has also talked with her boyfriend's parents and clarified their mistaken belief that their son was an innocent victim of her seductive talents. She is pleased with herself for all of these difficult accomplishments, but deep down she seems to wish there were an easier way to feel good about herself. She will continue to see her therapist on a once-a-month basis for about 6 months. The goal of treatment is to strengthen the linkage between her new behavior patterns and the feelings of personal approval that are clearly emerging. Ironically, now that she has earned the respect of her parents, her therapist, and the parents of her boyfriend, she seems surprised that it is less important than it used to be.

## Implications of the Model

Four primary theoretical implications that flow from this model should be identified:

1. Because high or low levels of self-esteem are the result of behavior patterns that have varying degrees and mixtures of coping and avoidance, one's enduring tendencies to cope or avoid will have a profound, long-term effect on the development of self-esteem. Remember that we have suggested that coping not only increases self-esteem, but increased self-esteem increases the probability of more frequent coping responses. Obviously, the converse is equally true. Avoidance not only decreases self-esteem, but lowered self-esteem increases the probability of more frequent avoidance response. It is as though the psychologically weak will become weaker with the passage of time, whereas the strong will become stronger. Because of this, any attempts to improve self-esteem require interventions aimed at the most fundamental and enduring dispositions of the personality.

2. The units of analysis for understanding the dynamics of self-esteem tend to be rather large. They focus on patterns, styles, dispositions, and traits. This is not meant to imply that discrete units of behavior are unimportant; clearly that is not the case. But one of the most important functions of small samples of behavior is to provide a miniature stage on which the enduring styles of the

personality can show themselves. Accordingly, understanding the dynamics of self-esteem as we have conceptualized them requires thinking in terms of processes and patterns that endure across time rather than in specific problems and solutions. Certainly both are important, but we are emphasizing molar levels of analysis.

3. The theoretical implications of this model for theories of psychological treatment are fascinating. It follows from this model that:

a. Psychological anguish induced in treatment is the first sign of personal change in the direction of coping. Thus, pain and discomfort are essential elements in the therapy process as long as they are understood by the client to be the result of increased psychological maturity. The model is based on the assumption that the immediate and long-term benefits of mature psychological responses will negate most of the undesirable consequences of facing up to disturbing problems. Clearly, one of the primary tasks of a therapist is to carefully attend to clients' understanding of the causes and consequences of their coping and avoidance behavior as they occur.

b. Intense personal distress can become a powerful incentive for personal growth and change if clients clearly understand that their distress is a result of their own avoidance patterns, which they have already discussed, defined, and labeled. For this reason, successful therapy requires clients not only to have a clear understanding of their own patterns of avoidance, but also to fully experience the negative self-evaluative thoughts and feelings that accompany these behavior patterns. This is usually the most distressing point in therapy. Ironically, the moment clients do this successfully, they have also engaged in a primary coping response that can be defined, described, and labeled, as can the self-evaluations that will accompany this change. This entire process is based on a high level of emotional arousal and intensity for clients, during which time their thoughts must remain relatively clear and lucid, as they attempt to shift from avoidance to a coping response in the therapy session.

c. Therapists must become more versed in the language and dynamics of psychological processes and patterns that endure across time. The actual treatment of clients requires careful observation and description of behavior and minimal inferences. Descriptive accuracy and labeling are central elements in effective therapy.

4. Finally, we have portrayed self-esteem as both a cause and a consequence of disordered and healthy human behavior. This position recognizes the reciprocal determinism between self-esteem and other crucial considerations in the development of the personality. For this reason, the implications of this model go beyond understanding the origins of high or low levels of self-esteem. They are extended into other areas, such as (a) understanding some of the underlying dynamics of normal and abnormal behavior, (b) major considerations in the treatment of disordered behavior, and (c) considerations for healthy development for the individual and family. We will discuss these considerations in the next chapter.

# 6

# Clinical Applications: Remedial Considerations in Psychotherapy

**W**e have now presented a preliminary model of self-esteem. Its most fundamental elements are the self-evaluative thoughts and feelings that accompany one's tendency to avoid or cope with anxiety-producing conflicts. Our thesis is that these self-evaluations not only accompany coping and avoidance, but also that they are the most fundamental source of intense and enduring feelings of personal approval or disapproval. We have suggested that the act of coping with conflict rather than avoiding it is based on a number of highly desirable psychological attributes, such as insight, reality testing, psychological risk taking, and personal responsibility. Each of these attributes also plays an essential role in the process of healthy psychological growth and development. Psychological avoidance, on the other hand, has emerged as one of the premier considerations in our attempts to understand disordered behavior and its treatment. The act of avoiding personal conflict because of psychological fear and anxiety is probably a staple ingredient in many forms of disordered behavior.

We have also provided a rationale to suggest that favorable self-evaluations are a consequence of a person's tendency to choose coping over avoidance. Our arguments are based on our observation that the very act of realistically facing personal or interpersonal conflict involves psychological responses that are intrinsically pleasing to most individuals and to our larger culture as well. Patterns of avoidance, on the other hand, breed negative self-evaluations. The very act of psychological avoidance, by denial, distortion, and self-deception, precludes the possibility of feeling personal adequacy because of the inadequacies inherent in these responses.

We now wish to turn our attention to the implications and applications of these general concepts in an applied context. This will undoubtedly clarify many facets of the model we have already introduced as well as illustrate some rather novel concepts and techniques involved in the remediation of psychopathology and the enhancement of self-esteem. We wish that we had 20 or 30 years of accumulated research evidence available to guide our thinking. Regrettably, that is not the case. What we do have is about 45 years of shared clinical experience to draw on, and that is precisely what we will be doing. There are three areas in which the implications of this model are the most obvious and probably the most useful: (1) remedial considerations in psychotherapy, (2) developmental considerations in psychotherapy, and (3) parenting and family relations. We will focus our attention on remedial considerations in psychotherapy in this chapter, and we will discuss each of the other topics in subsequent chapters.

## Psychotherapy: Procedures and Cautions

Our prior clinical experience with the methods we are discussing has demonstrated them to be influential methods of intervention. At times, they can arouse rather intense client affective reactions. High levels of emotional intensity and arousal can be good or bad, of course, depending on the therapist's skill and comfort in responding to the affect. It is fairly obvious that high levels of emotional arousal are often frightening or even harmful to some clients. The therapist clearly must use care in dealing with topics about which clients have strong feelings. However, it should be equally obvious that fear and anxiety (intense feelings) are staple ingredients in most types of psychopathology and most forms of psychological treatment. We can hardly expect to make reasonable advances in our understanding and treatment of disordered behavior by charting a course that cautiously steers clear of emotional intensity.

There are four indispensable steps involved in the remediation of psychopathology or in the development of self-esteem that have been derived from our model. Two of these steps are primarily remedial considerations, and the other two are more central in the enhancement of self-esteem. As most clinicians already understand, however, these are seldom mutually exclusive considerations. Because of this, we hope the reader will master the general principles we are discussing before making any attempt to apply them. It is our belief that once these general principles are mastered, they can be appropriately applied in varying degrees and mixtures to a variety of clinical cases with wisdom and discretion. *However, any attempt to apply the techniques illustrated in our examples without a clear understanding of the underlying principles upon which they are based could easily prove to be clinically inappropriate, and even harmful to clients.* More often than not, however, we have found that a client's ability to honestly explore the origin and meaning of his or her most intense feelings is an important and sometimes even necessary reaffirming psychological experience in the process of psychological treatment. The key to this, of course, is knowing how to handle intense emotions properly. The model we are proposing provides reasonably clear guidelines and explanations of the role and function of emotional intensity in disordered behavior and its treatment, which we hope the reader will attend to with considerable care. Of particular importance is the nature of the therapeutic relationship, which we will discuss more fully later in this chapter.

We will begin our discussion by identifying the four steps involved in the remediation of psychopathology or the development of self-esteem in general terms. This will be followed by several examples illustrating each of these steps. We will conclude with a more detailed analysis of each of these steps with additional clinical illustrations. The four basic steps are:

1. Identifying and clearly labeling the dominant avoidance patterns one uses in anxiety-arousing conflict situations. This generally requires that clients observe, describe, illustrate, and label their own style of conflict avoidance in specific and concrete terms.

2. Identifying and clearly labeling the self-evaluative thoughts and feelings associated with these dominant avoidance patterns. A cognitive understanding of the self-evaluative thoughts is essential but not sufficient. The emotions generated by these thoughts must not only be understood, they must also be fully experienced by the client. Simple recognition of these feelings is not sufficient, for reasons we will explain more fully later in this chapter.

3. Learning to realistically face negative self-evaluations and avoidance patterns. This is an important step in the model. It must be understood that the very act of clearly identifying and labeling one's own negative self-evaluative thoughts and feelings is a *coping response* to an anxiety-arousing conflict situation. It is essential that the therapeutic benefits of this response be fully realized. Note that clearly identifying the self-evaluative thoughts and feelings that accompany avoidance patterns creates the possibility for an in vivo corrective learning experience in what must be considered a uniquely penetrating anxiety-arousing conflict situation for the client.

4. Gradually learning how to cope with personal conflicts. Clients can then identify and label the ingredients of this new response as well as the self-evaluative thoughts and feelings that accompany it.

Each of these four phases is illustrated in the following clinical interview. Admittedly, it is unusual for all four steps to be covered in a single session. In this particular case, however, it was possible because the client was relatively nondefensive, with a fairly circumscribed problem. She came to the office complaining of excessive fatigue. The interview gradually revealed a woman whose primary means of avoiding rejection and gaining acceptance was by suppressing her own needs while making sure she satisfied the needs of all of those around her. The dynamics of this case, while interesting, are less important than this client's ability to quickly see her role in creating the very problem she was complaining about. This contributed to her ability to fully experience the emotions that accompanied her coping and avoidance responses as they occurred in the interview. While reading this interview, try to notice what factors seem to account for the client's rapid progress in spite of the fact that this is a first interview.

## Introduction and Rapport-Building

Therapist: Tell me, what led you to schedule a meeting for to-day?

Client: Well, I think that I'm just feeling so worn out and run down—you know, just physically and emotionally washed out.

Therapist: Please tell me more.

Client: Well, maybe if I talk a little about last week, I could describe what my life is like and why I'm feeling this way.

Therapist: Okay.

Client: Well, let's see, as I look back on last week I see myself wrapped up and so busy with the kids. It's just one thing after another. If it isn't sports, then it's plays and all these extracurricular things that they're in. And I feel like I need to be there to support them. It's just constant, just a steady kind of thing.

Therapist: So, as you see it, your fatigue is the result of the overwhelming amount of activity in your life?

Client: Yes, probably so.

Therapist: Why do you keep it up?

Client: Well, I think it's important for the kids to see that I support them in the things they do. I want to be a supportive person. If I love them, those are the kinds of things I should be willing to do for them. When I do, I think they feel better, and it makes them feel better about our relationship together.

Therapist: It sounds like you take your parental responsibilities very seriously.

Client: Maybe so, but I feel like sometimes I could just scream.

Therapist: A little angry there, huh?

Client: No! I'm not angry. It's just that I can't do any more, but I can't say that to them when I know they want me to be there. When it's important to them, I just feel like I really need to go ahead and do it anyway.

Therapist: Why?

Client: I'm sure they would be disappointed. They might think I wasn't interested in them or I didn't care what they did. It's easy to say you care, but I think it's important to do more than just say it—you have to show it by the way you act. You know, you have to have your behavior match your words.

The form and substance of this dialogue were essentially unchanged for another 15 minutes. The client repeatedly emphasized the "moral" and "socially desirable" reasons for her meticulous adherence to her parental role and responsibilities. She was not inclined to acknowledge that her behavior was motivated by a need for approval from her children or a fear of their rejection. Neither did she seem the least bit interested in exploring her style of developing and maintaining relationships within the family or acknowledging any anger or resentment to those who seemed to have so much control over her life.

As quickly as the therapist judged that the client felt understood enough to tolerate a moderate level of dissonance without becoming too defensive, the focus of the interview was changed so that it became more exploratory and incisive.

## Identifying Patterns of Avoidance and Self-Evaluative Thoughts and Feelings

Therapist:   Let me see if I can summarize what seems to be bothering you the most. You find yourself in a rather difficult situation. On the one hand, you feel a strong need to be supportive and involved in your children's lives as a way of building a strong relationship. On the other hand, you're tired, you want more time to yourself, and you may even resent others' controlling your life so much. The essential conflict is between what you think you should do for others and what you want to do for yourself. Does that sound like a fair summary of what's bothering you?

Client:   Yeah, I haven't thought of it that way before, but that sounds about right.

Therapist:   What precisely is it you usually do when other people want you to do something you're not really interested in doing?

Client:     What do you mean?

Therapist:  I mean what precisely is it that you usually do when
            other people want you to do something you're not
            really interested in doing?

Client:     [Long pause.] I usually do what other people want.
            I notice that other people do the same thing, though.
            [Note the defensiveness.]

Therapist:  It sounds like it's hard for you to say no to people.

Client:     It is! When people ask me to do things, I really feel like
            I should do it for them. But after I say yes, I'm so tight
            inside. How do you say no to those kinds of things?

Therapist:  What makes it so hard for you?

Client:     I think it's important to have pleasant relationships.
            You can't say no to people all the time and expect
            them to like you.

Therapist:  Let's see if we can get an accurate description of
            what you tend to do in situations where your desires
            are in conflict with the wishes of others.

Client:     I try to be cooperative and giving, to do my part in
            relationships even when it's inconvenient. That's
            my way of trying to be a good friend, or spouse, or
            mother.

Therapist:  You think of these as very desirable traits, is that
            right?

Client:     That's right.

The session is now at its first critical juncture. The therapist sees
the client's behavior as conflict-avoidant and approval-seeking.
The client is describing the same behavior as responsible and desirable. Attempts by the therapist to have the client identify anything negative or avoidant in her behavior patterns have been
unsuccessful. The therapist now changes the focus of the interview to the client's actual behavior in the therapy session because
it is less abstract, more immediate, and more revealing.

Therapist:  What you seem to be saying is that your style of deal-
            ing with conflict is to keep things pleasant by doing
            what others want and expect from you.

Client:     Well, yes. Maybe it is.

Therapist:  Maybe it is?

Client:     Otherwise, I guess I wouldn't have such a hard time
            saying no. People ask me to do things and I really

feel like I should do it for them, but after I say yes, I wish I'd said NO!

Therapist: Are you saying that you give in all the time so people will like and value you?

Client: I have to think about that. I imagine it could be. It's important, I think, to have a pleasantness in relationships.

Therapist: I would like you to determine if this is your way of avoiding unpleasantness and getting people to like you.

Client: I guess that could be true.

Therapist: Tell me about the ways it could be true.

Client: These are hard questions. No one likes to think that they are nice to people just so they will be liked.

Therapist: I agree, they really are hard questions.

Client: Yes, they are. Probably because they are hitting home with me.

Therapist: How does that feel?

Client: Not very good. I didn't realize I was doing that. But I hate people to be disappointed in me. I feel like they can't count on me, that I'm not willing to do things for them. I always thought it was worth the price that I guess I pay to do that. But now I'm not so sure.

Therapist: This way of thinking is kind of new to you?

Client: Yes.

Therapist: Let's try something. What you seem to be saying is that your style for avoiding conflict and gaining approval from others is by doing for others what pleases them the most. At least that's what we're considering so far. Does that sound about right?

Client: Well, yes. I guess I feel like I do that.

Therapist: Do you do that with me as well.

Client: Well, it's important to me, as a client, that you like me.

Therapist: Please try to describe as accurately as you can how you go about making sure that I will like you.

Client: I guess by cooperating with you and trying to do and say what you want me to.

Therapist: So that's what you're doing right now? I ask you these questions and you answer them even though

| | they're unsettling because that's what you think you have to do so I will like you? |
|---|---|
| Client: | Yes. It's really been hard for me to do, but I thought it was important to do that. |
| Therapist: | But it's for me you're doing it. |
| Client: | Yes, I think probably so because I know I trust you a lot, but I feel like maybe if I didn't you wouldn't like me, and maybe. . . . |
| Therapist: | So, in a sense, you're playing a role or pretending with me right now. |
| Client: | I guess so. |
| Therapist: | Do you have a word or a way of describing the way you treat me so I will like you? Do you know what I mean by that? |
| Client: | The way I behave so you'll like me? |
| Therapist: | Yes, can you think of a word to summarize the style or pattern of behavior you use to try and make sure I will like you? |
| Client: | Trying to be positive, pleasant, cooperative. . . . |

The client has now started to describe one of her styles for gaining approval from others with a reasonable degree of accuracy, but she continues to cast it in a favorable light by using terms such as "cooperative," "pleasant," and "positive." These terms accurately reflect her overt behavior, but they completely miss the underlying motives that sustain the behavior. These might include fear of rejection or loss of approval. The psychological consequences of her overly compliant interpersonal style are both obvious and consequential. And they are certainly not limited to the fatigue the client described in her initial complaint. They extend into such fundamental areas as (a) a limited sense of personal identity, (b) inability to regulate, balance, or resolve conflict, and (c) a life filled with frustration, guilt, and unhappiness. Because she is a relatively strong woman, the therapist decides to take a more active part in the labeling process to accelerate the movement of the therapy session and to increase the accuracy of the labels attached to the underlying motives of her behavior.

| Therapist: | How about "selling yourself out"? |
|---|---|
| Client: | That sounds horrible. [Long, long thoughtful pause.] I guess maybe so. I don't really say how I feel inside |

while I'm doing things for others, and I do feel real tight inside. And, you know, when I say yes to people, that's when the tightness starts.

Therapist: Are the terms "selling yourself out" or "buying approval" accurate descriptions? Is that what we want to call it?

Client: Those are harsh words.

Therapist: Yes, they are both harsh and unflattering, but are they accurate? It is important for you to try and describe your style accurately so we can understand what you do and why.

Client: I guess I see myself pretty much as a "yes" person. It's important that I do that for other people so that I won't disappoint them, so that we'll have a good relationship, so they won't know how I really feel inside. I hide that a lot.

Therapist: When I ask you to describe something, you describe it and then explain and justify it. You don't really need to justify it here. Let's just get a clear understanding of what it is you're doing.

Client: I guess when it gets down to the bottom line, maybe I'm just trying to be somebody I'm not.

Therapist: Okay, and you do that by saying yes when you don't mean it?

Client: Yeah, I do that a lot.

Therapist: Is there anything you want in return for being so nice to people?

Client: I want them to think I'm a good friend. I want my husband to think I'm a good wife. I want my children to think I'm a good mother.

Therapist: I understand. Basically, then, you are trying to gain the approval and acceptance of others by being what they want you to be.

Client: I guess so.

Therapist: Is that too harsh?

Client: I don't think I really realized that's what I was doing. It's kind of a hard thing to face.

Therapist: It really is hard, isn't it.

Client: I think so.

Therapist: So summarize all that we've said that describes how you are at relating to people. Let's see if we can get

|  |  |
|---|---|
|  | to a description that seems accurate to you even though it may be harsh. |
| Client: | I guess I basically hide myself and that I try to be something I'm not by doing what I think other people would like me to do. |
| Therapist: | And that description seems accurate to you? |
| Client: | I hear myself say it. I—yes, I think so. |

The client has a reasonably clear description of her behavior, which she seems at least partially willing to own. The next step is to start identifying the self-evaluative thoughts and feelings that accompany this behavior. This is frequently the point at which a great deal of the client's emotion comes to the surface, so the therapist proceeds with caution because it is late in the therapy hour.

|  |  |
|---|---|
| Therapist: | We need to go a step further with this, and this is going to be harder than what we just did. Should we wait for another session or should we start now? |
| Client: | Oh, let's give it a try. |
| Therapist: | Are you sure? It's going to be harder than what we just did. |
| Client: | I'll try. |
| Therapist: | Okay, you have a description of yourself, and at least tentatively it seems accurate to you. Now I want you to tell me how you feel about yourself because you're that way. |
| Client: | [Long pause, eyes begin to moisten.] I'm disappointed. I'm frustrated because I really would like to be able to say all these things I want to say and still have people not run away from me or push me away because I say how I feel. I'd like to know how to do that. |
| Therapist: | Know how to do what? |
| Client: | Be my own person! |
| Therapist: | You mean you want to stop pretending so much? |
| Client: | Yeah, that's a good way to put it. |
| Therapist: | How else do you feel about yourself for pretending so much? |
| Client: | I can't say that I think a whole lot of myself. Sounds kind of like a game. It's a game because I'm trying to |

fool people so they will like me. It's really disgusting.
How can they even like me if they don't know me?

Therapist:   And maybe you fooled yourself as well?

Client:   I guess I did.

This session is now to the point that it is *absolutely crucial* that
the therapist recognize that the very act of clearly identifying and
labeling one's own avoidance patterns and the self-evaluative
thoughts and feelings that accompany them is a primary coping
response. It is essential that the therapeutic benefits of this response be realized in the session in which it occurs. This is accomplished by having the client identify and describe this more
adaptive response and the feeling that accompanies it.

Therapist:   You don't seem to be fooling yourself right now.
How does that feel to you?

Client:   Feels kind of good.

Therapist:   Really?

Client:   [Tears are now streaming down her cheeks.] Yeah.

Therapist:   Even though it hurts that badly?

Client:   Yeah.

Therapist:   What do the tears mean?

Client:   Well, I'm kind of happy that I know this now. I'm
hurting, but I think I feel better now that I can say
these things to you. I feel better about myself, because you're still sitting here and I don't feel like you
hate me for what I've said or you're going to push
me away. That feels good.

Therapist:   What exactly have you done in this situation that has
allowed you to approve of yourself more than usual?

Client:   For the first time in a long time, I've been honest
with myself and another person about how I really
feel.

Therapist:   Are you saying that not being honest with yourself
and others is the real problem you came here about?

Client:   I think so. I didn't know it when I first came in, but I
think that has been a big problem for me.

Therapist:   An interesting thing has happened here today. You
have described yourself as a yes person, as someone
who hides herself from everybody. Then we had
what has to be considered a hard conversation,

where you presented yourself to me as you really are, and somehow we ended up with you feeling much better than when you walked in the door. Does that make any sense to you?

Client: Just knowing the truth, I guess. Besides, the problem seems more soluble now.

Therapist: Our time is up now, but before we end I would like you to summarize what you learned about yourself today.

Client: I need to learn how to say how I feel more. When I feel like saying no I need to be able to say that, and to tell my kids that I'm just being worn too thin and that even though I'd like to be there, I just can't do everything. And sometimes I will just tell them I still love and support them.

Therapist: So you're really talking about being more honest with yourself and others about your feelings?

Client: Yeah.

Therapist: And how do you feel about the prospect of going through a whole week without buying approval from others by being a servant to them?

Client: Well, if it makes me feel like I do now, I think that would be very important.

Therapist: Our time is just about up, but what we've done today would be worth thinking about and going over next week.

Client: Good, I'll try and see what I can do this week.

In a brief 50-minute session, this client was able to cut all the way through her socially conventional, pleasing interpersonal style and make explicit what she already knew about herself implicitly. She was able to accurately describe major portions of her conflict-avoidant interpersonal style and the negative self-evaluative thoughts and feelings it generated. She experienced moderate levels of her own self-disappointment, and during this very process started facing some of her personal conflicts with more realism and psychological maturity. As quickly as she did, the therapist started the process of describing and labeling these more adaptive responses and the more favorable self-evaluations they generated. This particular client had two more sessions, which further clarified the materials that were uncovered in the first session. She then terminated therapy but had another session about 4 months later. She was pleased with the changes her more self-approving interpersonal style generated.

Though this case is factual, it is unusual because of the obviousness of the client's avoidant style and her willingness and ability to face her personal issues quickly in a single session. Things are seldom this obvious or successful in most clinical cases. That is why we will now discuss, in more detail and with more complex cases, each of the four fundamental considerations involved in the remediation of psychopathology or the development of self-esteem in our model.

Our purpose is to illustrate each of these principles in considerable detail. Prior experience has taught us that the conceptual elements of these principles are easily mastered, whereas recognizing their varied and subtle behavioral manifestations during clinical interviews is far more difficult. Because of this, we will use a case study format for major portions of this chapter. We believe that actual case studies are not only more interesting to read, but also reveal the principles we are discussing with greater precision and clarity.

# Identifying and Labeling Avoidance Patterns

## Rationale

In our earlier discussion of avoidance and psychopathology, we suggested that one's tendency to try to escape from anxiety-arousing conflicts was the quintessential quality of disordered behavior. As you may recall, we reviewed the reasons to believe that the concept of avoidance serves essentially the same function in all of the major theories of disordered behavior: to protect and defend the individual from unpleasant or unwelcome psychological experiences. The specific means by which individuals try to defend themselves from psychological threat are far too ingenious, varied, and numerous to catalogue here. They range from the classical defense mechanisms first discussed by Anna Freud (Sandler, 1985) to the interpersonal styles discussed by Satir, Stachowiak, & Taschman (1975) and Millon (1981). Any, or all, of these patterns of avoidance can be used in different combinations by different individuals. It is the job of the astute clinician to assist individual clients with the task of clearly identifying and describing their own basic and enduring patterns of avoidance. The keys to successfully identifying and labeling these patterns include (a) careful and astute observation of patterns of behavior, and (b) skill in discriminating between clients' enduring patterns of avoidance and their situational reactions to conflict. Success in these two areas can pay handsome dividends in the therapeutic process. When both of these tasks are handled successfully, the therapist can reasonably expect the following:

1. Clients are highly motivated for personal growth and change after discovering that their patterns of avoidance are a major cause of their personal pain and unhappiness. This is an important consideration. The psychotherapeutic literature is filled with discussions of resistance, poorly motivated clients, and the powerful role of client motivation in successful psychotherapy (Garfield, 1986).

What we are suggesting is that the very process wherein clients clearly identify and label their own patterns of avoidance explicitly and deliberately accomplishes three important purposes. First, it increases clients' awareness of their own self-defeating behavior patterns. Second, it increases clients' level of subjective distress by making the link between their self-defeating behavior and their unhappiness both explicit and obvious. And third, as clients come to attribute the cause of their psychic unhappiness to their own patterns of avoidance, an increase in client motivation for personal change can be expected. In fact, we suggest that the clarity with which clients see their role in creating their own psychological difficulties will determine their level of personal motivation for psychological change.

2. Far more important, however, is the fact that asking clients to clearly and explicitly describe their own patterns of avoidance calls for a primary coping response from the clients. This task involves at least moderately high levels of risk taking, personal responsibility, and realistically facing an anxiety-arousing personal conflict; clients are immediately required to function at a higher level of psychological adequacy than they may be accustomed to. Though clients may experience distress and embarrassment, this is an absolutely crucial therapeutic maneuver because it creates

the possibility that the therapist can call clients' attention to their more adaptive psychological behavior and its consequences in the session in which it occurs. The self-approving thoughts and feelings that can accompany coping over avoidance can be very reassuring to clients even though the reality of many of their problems remains unchanged. Again, this is no small consideration. It can frequently provide clients with renewed hope and a will to persist, which, after all, are central considerations in almost any conception of normality, psychopathology, and cure.

## A Case of Sexual Addiction: Mary J.

**Introductory information.** This young woman, Mary J., was referred by a former client. She arrived for the first interview about 10 minutes early but waited until her appointment time before approaching my office. Mary was in her early thirties, modestly attractive, well-groomed, socially poised, and pleasant to talk with. She conveyed the impression that she was a highly qualified job applicant rather than someone distressed enough to seek the services of a psychotherapist. At my invitation, Mary proceeded to explain why she was seeking psychological help.

She indicated that she had a long-standing sexual problem that her husband now knew about. She had been sexually active outside her marriage since its inception, including male prostitutes, pickups at singles' bars, and chronic masturbation. Mary guessed that there were very few days, if any, in which she had not been sexually active with at least one person other than her spouse. Some days seemed to require more sexual activity than others. Mary also explained in graphic detail how some male images would sexually arouse her to a point of complete distraction. Once she saw someone who fit this description, she could not rest until she was sexually gratified. When this happened, the means of obtaining sexual gratification was of little concern to her. Mary considered it an obsession. She felt guilty about her behavior but said she couldn't seem to help herself no matter how hard she tried. On two prior occasions, she had entered therapy, but these efforts were quickly aborted.

Somehow, Mary had managed to keep her sexual escapades hidden from her husband and 4 children for over 7 years. Her guilt was sufficiently intense that she decided to confess her "sins" to her husband, beg for his forgiveness, and ask for his help in overcoming her problem. Mary indicated that she still loved him and their children dearly. They were now separated, with the understanding that they would try to restore their relationship if she could solve her sexual problems. After talking it over together, Mary and her husband mutually agreed that it would be in the best interest of her children for her to refrain from visiting them until she had reason to believe she could solve her personal sexual problems. She missed them a great deal and was deeply concerned about their not having a mother who would love them as much as she did.

Mary reported feelings of depression, despair, and hopelessness. Suicide had occurred to her on a fairly regular basis for over a year, but she did not meet the traditional criteria of being a high suicide risk at the time of our first meeting. There were no indications of psychosis, multiple personality, or serious dissociative states in which she might not be fully responsible for her behavior. Mary's thoughts and thinking patterns were clear and lucid. The possibility that her excessive sexual escapades were an expression of an underlying characterological disorder was diminished by the absence of other impulse control problems and by her persistence and success in other life pursuits (writing poetry and meaningful participation in civic activities).

**Background information.** Our second interview focused on Mary's early background. Two distinguishing features quickly emerged. The first was a psychologically ominous father whose behavior was consistent only in its unpredictability. Anger seemed to dominate situations where approval and acceptance would normally occur. Kindness and understanding were more common in situations where rejection would be more typical. Though it was not obvious how this affected Mary, it was clear that it had. It was a topic she could discuss at length and with intense emotions. It was obvious that Mary had few pleasant recollections of father, family, or childhood.

Second, Mary's masturbation habits had an early beginning. Her earliest recollections went back to 7 or 8 years of age. By the time she was 11 or 12 she was masturbating to orgasm with some regularity. By the time she was 15 she had mastered the art of distracting herself from stress with self-induced sexual pleasure, adding a touch of spice to an otherwise boring or stressful existence with an intense orgasm that was enhanced by specific and vivid sexual fantasies. The initial observation that suggested sexual arousal was a way of escaping from stress occurred in the therapy hour. Toward the end of each therapy hour, Mary seemed distracted and more tense. Upon inquiry, she reported that she was thinking more about "cruising" and wanting to stimulate herself than about receiving help with her problem. Although the hypothesis that Mary's sexual activity was primarily a means of distracting her from psychological unpleasantness was fairly obvious to the therapist, this possibility had clearly escaped Mary's awareness. Her problem might be better defined as anxiety management with sexual excess rather than as sexual addiction. It seemed that the activity took place outside of her marriage because she preferred sexual partners where intimacy was minimal and she could control the relationship.

**Identifying patterns of avoidance.** Because of Mary's openness and motivation to change, the third session turned into a crucial meeting. It was the first attempt by the therapist and client to explicitly identify her patterns of avoidance. Ironically, the task was made unusually difficult because the client had already provided the therapist with a plausible hypothesis regarding the meaning and function of her excessive sexual behavior. In spite of the fact that her overt behavior was the primary source of this hypothesis, Mary seemed oblivious of what appeared obvious. This made it difficult for the therapist to temporarily suspend his views and listen to the client with unbiased rigor as she attempted to identify and understand her own patterns of avoidance. Because of this, it was particularly important for the therapist to keep two important principles in mind while trying to assist the client.

The first was not selling or talking the client into the validity of any of the therapist's observations. To accomplish this, the primary task of the therapist was to ask the right questions of the client at the right time without being too suggestive. Clients can almost always become more aware of their avoidance patterns when they are asked to observe and describe their own behavior with care and precision. However, they must engage in this process in earnest. For clients to agree with the therapist's perceptions is simply not enough. They must formulate and "try on" their own perceptions. In this situation a therapist must not do anything for clients that they can do for themselves.

The therapist can ask valuable process questions without suggesting appropriate or even desirable answers to them. These questions are intended to suggest important topics that the client probably should consider while leaving it up to the client to provide all of the content regarding how they are considered. For example, clients can be asked how they feel about their anger without being given the slightest hint about how they should feel about it.

Second, the client's sense of freedom to answer questions spontaneously has to be scrupulously preserved. This is the only means by which the client can become a contributing member of a therapeutic alliance rather than a dedicated pupil to a skillful teacher. This is an important consideration. Maintaining the client's sense of freedom is the surest means of protecting the client's perceptions and information from being subordinated to the authority of the therapist, *whose perceptions and inferences are frequently wrong.*

More important, however, authentic self-discovery and self-exploration is an essential process in cultivating a disposition for personal risk taking and personal responsibility in the client. The importance of cultivating these two attributes simply cannot be overstated. They are essential ingredients in the coping response. What better way is there to develop risk taking and responsibility in clients than for the therapy process to encourage and reward them in an authentic problem-solving context! We contend that what clients actually experience in the therapy process is one of the best indicators of what they will actually learn.

In the early part of this session (her third), the discussion revolved around Mary's susceptibility and reaction to stress in very general terms. Gradually, the therapist moved the discussion closer to the stress that seemed obvious during the therapy hour. As this happened, the client became more resistant, defensive, and distracted. After about 15 minutes or so, the therapist asked Mary if she noticed what had happened to her during the last 15 minutes. She acted confused by the question. The therapist asked her to close her eyes and recreate vivid images of her behavior, thoughts, and feelings during the last 15 minutes of the session. She was asked to notice her posture, rate of speech, concentration, and personal comfort and discomfort. With no additional coaching, Mary started describing herself as becoming more tense. She was then asked to review the mental images of her behavior, thoughts, and feelings and to identify the best indicators of increasing tension. The important ones revolved around a feeling of subjective distress and anxiety. These were fairly common feelings, particularly in the face of uncertainty or evaluations by others. Mary left the session wondering if she were subject to more stress than she had previously recognized.

The next session was more of the same but with one crucial addition. She was now asked to identify and describe any changes she noticed in herself once she became overly anxious. The therapist thought it important that Mary become more aware not only of her anxiety and subjective distress but also of the patterns of behavior that accompanied it. Again, she acted confused by the question. Again, she was asked to close her eyes and try to create vivid images of her behavior, thoughts, and feelings once she became anxious. She was asked to pay particular attention to anything that seemed common to different situations. Increased sexual behavior was one of several possibilities mentioned. When Mary was asked which of these possibilities held the most promise for exploration, she indicated her sexual arousal. By the end of the therapy hour, the link between sexual arousal and increased tension was clearly established *in her mind.*

The remaining task was the most important but less difficult. It was for Mary to explore the reasons for increased sexual arousal in the face of psychological pressure. When asked to speculate about the connection between her sexual behavior and tension, she was able to suggest two possibilities with little assistance from the therapist. First, it was a means of temporarily minimizing psychological tension by distraction. Mary called it an obsession with pleasure-seeking. It was fairly obvious that the greater the tension, the greater the obsession. Second, it was a means of avoiding rejection by men by being involved in relationships where she felt indifferent, powerful, and in control. Both of these considerations seemed more than plausible to the therapist because they were crucial, life-long issues for Mary. The therapist summarized this session by saying, "You seem to be saying that you use sex in excess to distract you from your fears and anxiety, and to hide from your fear of men. Does that sound about right?"

The client concurred but in a most dejected mood. It was fairly clear that she felt overwhelmed by the hopelessness of her current situation as well as the growing realization that her most serious problems were the result of her attempts to avoid rather than face the stresses of everyday living. Because she was so upset, the therapist invited Mary to schedule another appointment during the week if she felt it was necessary.

This brings us to an interesting and probably controversial point in the management of this case, and the more general use of the model we are discussing. Some therapists might view their clients' distress as a signal to offer them reassurance or support during a difficult time. Our view is quite different. When clients are actually experiencing stress or engaged in avoidant behavior is the most opportune time to have them try to identify and describe their patterns of behavior and the self-evaluations that accompany them. We believe there are many important therapeutic benefits to be derived from this process even though clients don't usually find any pleasure in the process at the time it occurs; just the opposite is more likely to be true. This is usually a time of anguish, embarrassment, discouragement, dejection, and sometimes even despair.

Therefore, the therapist must comprehend the therapeutic reasons for exposing a client to such negative thoughts and emotions. More importantly, the therapist must have a clear understanding of how to manage these feelings so as to maximize their therapeutic benefits while minimizing the risks associated with exposing clients to intense negative feelings.

Earlier, we suggested the following four reasons for having clients clearly and explicitly identify and describe their patterns of avoidance: (1) it increases clients' awareness of their own style of psychological avoidance, (2) it increases clients' level of psychic distress by making the link between their personal unhappiness and their patterns of avoidance more explicit and obvious, (3) it increases clients' intrinsic motivation for psychological change by making it more likely that they will attribute both the cause and

consequences of their unhappiness to their own maladaptive behavior, and (4) the very act of clearly identifying and describing
one's avoidance patterns is a primary coping response that can be
used to generate more favorable self-evaluations.

These principles are illustrated during the next two therapy sessions. While reading them, remember that the therapist does not
create the intense emotions expressed by the client—merely helps
the client see the psychological reality she has created for herself.
The intense emotions Mary expresses are best understood as the
inevitable consequence of perceiving this distressing reality with
clarity and understanding. While her distress is obviously unpleasant, it is also a vital signal to the therapist that the client has
started realistically facing unpleasant psychological realities that
are usually avoided. In many cases, this will be new behavior for
a client, and it is vital that the new behavior be clearly labeled,
along with the more favorable self-evaluative thoughts that accompany it. As a result of going through this process, Mary
achieved a high level of intrinsic motivation for personal change
and a surprising amount of hope for the future given the poor
prognosis for this case, which was clearly understood by both the
client and the therapist.

The next therapy session was far from uneventful. The therapist continually asked the client for examples of how she used sex
to (a) distract herself from tension and anxiety or (b) add excite-
ment to an otherwise boring existence. After each example the
therapist would follow up with requests for clarification and de-
tails. Though expressed in different forms, the ultimate question
was always the same, however. What were you running from?
How aware were you that you were using sex to distract yourself?
What was it that initially frightened you? What are you learning
about your sexual cravings? Each example was followed by a request for another. With each example Mary's description of her
behavior became more exact, as did her understanding of the
function her sexuality played in trying to avoid stress or anxiety
or to avoid facing the fact that she was living a life she considered
hollow and meaningless.

The next session was more of the same. When Mary seemed too
distressed to go on much longer, the therapist would sympatheti-
cally comment on the difficulty of her task and the paramount

importance of her being able to clearly recognize and describe her own behavior patterns when she was under stress. With this modest level of support offered, he would then continue with the task of obtaining more descriptions of her behavior. Finally, after three therapy sessions, Mary was asked if she saw a pattern in her examples. She began to cry uncontrollably as she tried to explain that she now saw herself as a hopeless case. She considered herself a coward, someone who would not tolerate the slightest amount of stress, someone who played with her genitalia when she was upset just like a baby sucking a bottle, and someone who could probably never change because she had been that way so long. Mary was angry with herself for being so immature and angry with the therapist for making explicit what she had known implicitly for a long time. Regrettably, each of her comments was essentially true and insightful. She had now faced the truth about herself and understood the reasons for her self-hatred and low self-esteem, and the difficulty of the task that lay before her.

With this admission, the therapist asked her if her self-description seemed equally applicable to her behavior during the last three therapy sessions. Mary was stunned by the sudden change in direction by the therapist. She thought about it for a moment before saying no emphatically. Because it was so close to the end of the therapy hour, the therapist closed the session by asking Mary if she thought she would have such difficult problems to resolve now if she had a history of behaving the way she did during the past two sessions. Again, Mary considered the question thoughtfully before saying "probably not." She seemed more angry than pleased over this prospect. Her answer clearly implied that she might be more responsible for her personal problems than she would care to be. The therapist said that she might want to pursue that topic in some detail in a future session. Obviously, the client found the question both interesting and provocative. Mary was now remarkably composed, considering the intensity and difficulty of the session she had just completed.

**Summary.** One of the first steps in eliminating chronic patterns of psychological avoidance is for clients to be able to clearly recognize, identify, and describe their personal patterns of avoidance. We have described four therapeutic benefits that can be immediately derived from this process. Admittedly, the process can initially be difficult for clients because it requires them to start realistically facing many problems they usually avoid. However, this process can immediately set the stage for important therapeutic gains many clients desperately need. When clients clearly identify and describe their patterns of avoidance, not only do they become more aware of their self-defeating behavior patterns, they must also engage in a primary coping response during the therapy session. Though self-description is often difficult for clients because of the level of risk taking and personal responsibility involved, it is also essential for therapeutic progress. It is the surest means of exposing clients to the more favorable self-evaluative thoughts and feelings that can accompany coping and the easiest way to teach clients the cognitive, affective, and behavioral components of coping.

# Identifying Self-Evaluative Thoughts and Feelings

## Rationale

In an earlier discussion, we suggested that self-evaluative thoughts and feelings are based on a continuous process of noticing, monitoring, thinking about, and evaluating one's behavior. We also noted that these self-evaluations are a psychological reality for most people, and when necessary, such self-evaluative processes can be made reasonably clear and explicit by appropriate methods of observation and inquiry. Finally, we discussed the important differences between our conception of self-evaluative processes and traditional conceptions of self-talk growing out of the cognitive-behavioral models of psychotherapy.

Our analysis suggested that self-talk emphasizes the irrationality of many human emotions and acquired thoughts. Virtually all of these orientations share the assumption that the irrational beliefs contained in self-talk are without foundation. They are simply acquired irrational beliefs with few redeeming qualities and are best disregarded. Self-evaluative processes, on the other hand, are assumed to be based on an entirely different set of assumptions and psychological processes. In the first place, they are not considered to be irrelevant, irrational beliefs. Rather, self-evaluations are assumed to be at least partially valid self-perceptions. As a result, we have suggested that personal disapproval is the inevitable consequence of a personal response style that tends to favor avoidance over coping. The very act of avoidance, by denial, distortion, or self-deception by any means, virtually precludes the possibility of feeling personal adequacy because of the inadequacies inherent in these responses. Conversely, feelings of personal approval are just as inevitable when the personal response style tends to favor coping over avoidance.

The very act of coping involves highly desirable psychological attributes such as risk taking, personal responsibility, and perceptual accuracy. These not only lead to personal development but also reflect on the psychological well-being of the individual.

## Contradictory Emotions: A Paradox in Intensity

Increasing clients' awareness of their self-evaluative thoughts and feelings can be one of the most pleasing or distressing aspects of therapy within the confines of our model. We have seldom seen affect as intense, distressing, or long-lasting as that experienced by clients who come to unambiguously understand the role and function of their avoidance behavior and its consequences. Neither have we seen levels of personal approval more enduring than those earned by clients as they gradually learn to face personal issues they have chronically avoided. We hope that it is obvious that being able to gain access to a client's self-evaluative thoughts and feelings can be a potent therapeutic intervention. Doing so is not difficult. The most important consideration is consistently and carefully differentiating between a direct expression of clients' feelings based on past events and a conditional or contingent expression of their feelings based on current events. Let us explain this difference more fully.

The emotions aroused in clients as they identify and describe their patterns of avoidance are seldom pleasing to them. They are often embarrassed, ashamed, uncomfortable, tense, or agitated. In fact, a well-developed therapeutic relationship is generally considered a necessary prerequisite for such revealing self-assessment and self-disclosure. Not surprisingly, then, a generous

supply of tissues is usually required whenever a significant portion of a therapy hour is dedicated to an incisive exploration of a
client's avoidant behavior. Clients will almost always report extremely negative emotions (pain, remorse, anguish, shame, humiliation, embarrassment, and so forth) if they are asked how
they are feeling during this process. It could hardly be expected
to be otherwise. They are usually discussing the causes and consequences of what they consider their most obvious personal defects
and life failures.

An interesting thing happens if the nature of the question about
personal feelings is modified slightly. If clients are asked how they
feel for being able to face the truth, by being honest with themselves, or not playing games with themselves, their self-evaluative
thoughts and feelings will usually be positive. In effect, clients can
be feeling horrible about themselves as they recall their past but
pleased with themselves as they attempt to cope with these problems in the present. Though these two sets of emotions may seem
contradictory, there is no reason to suppose they cannot coexist at
the same time in the same person. Furthermore, they can be
equally potent, though that is seldom the case. What is important
to note is that the therapist can access either set of emotions. Nonspecific inquiries about how a person is feeling will generally elicit
the negative feelings from a person's past. More specific, conditional inquiries (e.g., "How do you feel about yourself for being
more honest in this session?") will tend to elicit the more favorable
self-evaluative thoughts and feelings generated by their adaptive
coping response.

Our contention is that either set of self-evaluations can be elicited from clients most of the time. Obviously, some approximation
to a coping response is a prerequisite for favorable self-evaluative
thoughts and feelings. However, this seldom presents a problem
to therapists working with our model because, as we have said,
the very process of having clients realistically identify and describe their patterns of avoidance is a primary coping response.
Nevertheless, the negative self-evaluative thoughts and feelings,
based on past events, are usually the most obvious and accessible
to both the client and the therapist. Because of this, these feelings
tend to get more therapeutic attention. This is regrettable in our

view for several reasons. First, it encourages clients to repeat stories of personal failure, sometimes endlessly. Aside from the temporary benefits of catharsis and having an attentive listening ear, we see little point in rehearsing and reliving past events in any detail. Besides, most clients have already engaged in a fair amount of personal rumination prior to coming to therapy. Second, and far more important, few therapists appreciate the therapeutic power of having their clients experience a sense of self-approval in the present for having the courage to face the agony of their past. Perhaps an example will help clarify the importance of this most fundamental distinction.

Several years ago a hardy, robust, middle-aged farmer was referred for psychological treatment by his local physician. His original medical complaint was that he periodically broke out with a severe case of hives. To say that the man found this problem annoying is an obvious injustice to his distress. His doctor found nothing wrong with him and referred him to an allergist. The allergist could not account for the man's symptoms on the basis of sensitivity to pollens. He referred him to a neurologist, who was equally unsuccessful in identifying the cause of the hives. The three physicians decided to refer the man to a therapist in case the hives were part of a stress reaction.

This man was an interesting client. Financially, he was a very successful farmer. He was also a prominent figure in the community and church. He was soft-spoken, slightly detached, but personable. Our first meeting consisted of nothing more than getting acquainted. The second was devoted to talking about his self-consciousness and feelings of inferiority. He seemed to enjoy learning about himself. In the third meeting, we probed his feelings of inferiority and fear of people in more depth and with greater care. As he came to see the personal distress caused by his fear of people, the man expressed considerable regret that he had not learned more about himself sooner. At one point he said, "I am 52 years old and I feel like I have given over half of my life away by being so private." Another time he said, "I feel as though I have cheated my wife and children out of a lot of the happiness we were entitled to." These are sober observations to make about one's life. His regrets were intense and well-founded. His insights were frightening to him.

Yet, when asked by the therapist how he felt now that he was facing the problems he had chronically been avoiding, the man replied, "It gives me a feeling of hope. I don't want to give the other half of my life away." With additional probing by the therapist, the client reluctantly acknowledged feeling proud of himself for being able to face his problems. It is important to notice that these favorable comments were made at precisely the time this man was most distressed about his past.

## Favorable and Unfavorable Emotions: A Paradox in Acceptability

Ironically, those clients with the greatest need for approval from self or others are usually the ones who become the most frightened when they receive it. Yet this seems to be the case more often than not. A clear understanding of the dynamics that sustain this paradox is crucial if one hopes to work effectively with both positive and negative self-evaluations.

There are three major elements involved in working with this paradox: (1) understanding the dynamics that seem to regulate this phenomenon, (2) developing the ability to accurately recognize this phenomenon when it is actually occurring, and (3) calling clients' attention to this paradox in their behavior as a means of increasing their awareness of the avoidance function it serves. We will discuss each of these elements briefly.

Most experienced clinicians have watched depressed clients start to feel better, and then, just when it becomes reasonable for both client and therapist to hope for significant client improvement, clients unexpectedly sabotage their therapeutic progress. The sabotage can take many forms, but the result is usually the same. It is seldom fatal to the therapeutic relationship and may not even seriously harm it. But it will almost always require that future therapy sessions be devoted to reviewing client material that was covered in earlier sessions. Clients seemingly make a strategic retreat to psychological areas they are more accustomed to, presumably where they feel more comfortable. This happens with enough consistency that one cannot help but wonder if the prospect of a client's starting to feel better, or having pleasant psychological experiences, or raising expectations for the future isn't in some paradoxical way a very threatening experience—so threatening that it almost automatically evokes a massive avoidance response that precludes further therapeutic progress until the avoidance response itself is clearly understood, described, and labeled by the client.

Our understanding of this phenomenon is based on two fundamental considerations. Both of these can be illustrated with our example of a depressed client. However, we have no reason to believe that the underlying principles illustrated in our example are confined to depression. In fact, we suggest that these principles probably have a very broad range of application when properly understood. The first principle involves what appears to be an almost automatic preference in many clinical populations for the known when compared to the unknown. The second has to do with the inherent fear of failing to meet the new expectations that can accompany improvements in psychological well-being. Let us explain each of these.

As miserable as depressed clients may be, they still experience a moderate level of consistency in their lives. Sometimes that consistency may be nothing more than lethargy, sleep, or sadness, but still, depressed persons know what to expect from each day, and far more important, hope for little more. On the other hand, there is substantial psychological risk involved in arousing these clients' belief and hope in themselves. There is even greater risk for them in believing in themselves and actually feeling better: it simply may not last. The depressive state, which was bearable in its consistency, can become unbearable when preceded by delicious moments of hope, happiness, and health. Enduring depression seems to deaden the senses and dilute despair. This somehow makes one's sadness and despair more tolerable. But when hope is reintroduced, the senses are rekindled and the taste of misery is no longer diluted. The same depression that was once tolerable in its constancy now becomes unbearable and in some cases even life-threatening. Clients simply do not want to believe too much in the happiness they desperately seek until it seems less risky and more obtainable.

The primary manifestation of the inherent risks in psychological progress is twofold. First, clients tend to feel safer endorsing negative emotions rather than positive ones. Second, because it is riskier for them to respond to favorable emotions, they approach these emotions with caution and resistance. Generally speaking, clients can be expected to oversubscribe to their negative self-evaluations and actively resist their more authentic and deeply felt favorable ones.

There are other risks associated with improved psychological well-being. As clients' expectations of themselves increase, the opportunities for failure and disappointment not only increase but also become more obvious. While heightened expectations for improvement are a favorable signal in many cases, it is important to remember that clients seldom have a history of success in satisfying their own expectations or those of others. Thus increased expectations for happiness or improvement, no matter how valid, can also resurrect intense fears of failure. It is little wonder, then, that many clients hesitate to believe in themselves or a brighter future, no matter how desperately they yearn for it.

Nevertheless, learning to be relatively comfortable in the presence of these risks is one of the primary reasons for being in therapy in the first place. We have repeatedly suggested that psychological risk taking and personal responsibility are the underlying qualities that mediate one's ability to cope with, rather than avoid, anxiety-arousing conflicts. The therapy hour is the place where these underlying attributes must first be understood and developed if they are to ever become an integral part of a person's more general psychological character. Generally speaking, the precise fear that the client wants to avoid is the grist the therapeutic mill must grind. Realistically facing what is usually avoided not only helps clients to identify patterns of avoidance and the self-evaluations that accompany them, it also cultivates their capacity for appropriate psychological risk taking at higher levels of personal responsibility. We hope the benefits of these two psychological attributes are now obvious. Without them, a deeply ingrained disposition to cope with personal conflict rather than avoid it is impossible. As we have said earlier, the first place to start developing these attributes is with the person's own patterns of avoidance in the therapeutic session in which they occur.

## Recognition of Emotions

Again, we find several paradoxes involved in accurately identifying self-evaluative thoughts and feelings. Our major concern is clearly differentiating between positive and negative emotions. The origin of a substantial amount of negative affect can be *healthy* psychological behavior, and, conversely, what appear to be pleasant emotions can be the result of *unhealthy* psychological behavior. Though this may seem contradictory at first glance, it really is not. It merely reflects two fundamental propositions about human affairs that are easily observed. Let us explain and illustrate.

According to our views, coping is a process in which a person is willing to realistically face personal conflict. The more clearly and realistically one faces these conflicts, the more abundant are the reasons for realistic anxiety, sadness, unhappiness, or distress. The natural result of realistically seeing and facing some of the inevitable psychological difficulties everyone must learn to deal with in the course of existence is intense emotion. The precise point at which clients are realistically distressed can be a meaningful signal that they have begun to cope with, rather than avoid, these difficulties. When this happens, the self-evaluative thoughts and feelings about current behavior are likely to be quite favorable even though the most obvious emotions will appear to be negative. An essential element of this treatment method is the therapist's continual and careful differentiation between the self-evaluative thoughts and feelings from past events based on avoidance and the thoughts and feelings about current events based on coping. This distinction is seldom clear to clients initially, and the therapist must assist clients to accurately identify and label their self-evaluative thoughts and feelings under both conditions.

The converse is equally true. What appears to be psychologically pleasing and pleasant is often nothing more than the relief clients experience temporarily as they skillfully avoid areas of personal or interpersonal conflict. The more intense the conflict, the greater the apparent pleasure derived from avoiding it. These moments of psychological relief and pleasure are as deeply felt and authentic as they are short-lived and self-defeating. But at the time they occur, the reality of these pleasant feelings cannot be denied. The sense of relief derived from temporarily avoiding difficult personal issues, no matter how intense or deeply felt, should not be confused with the more enduring feelings of personal well-being that reflect genuine self-approval. To illustrate this point, we would like to summarize a case of marital discord seen in our office several years ago.

As a result of an emotional as well as sexual affair by the husband, this marriage was strained well beyond the limits most marriages survive. It would be difficult to say if the wife was more distressed by the affair or the lack of remorse by the husband. In any event, the wife was devastated, and the husband felt entitled to a sexual fling after years of sexual deprivation and unsatisfying relations in the marriage. But he had not counted on actually falling in love with another woman. However, he did, and, furthermore, he had discovered parts of himself in this new relationship that had remained dormant and stifled in the marriage.

Even though both spouses indicated that they wanted to save their marriage, clearly the marriage would dissolve in the very near future unless some remarkable turnaround occurred. The wife was too hurt and humiliated to be able to respond to her husband's legitimate complaints, and the husband was far too liberated from the marriage to be very deeply concerned about the prospect of a divorce, and his wife knew it.

Fortunately, a short business trip provided the husband with time to carefully consider his past behavior and its implications for his future. He returned home realizing that the problems in the marriage were as much his fault as his wife's and that he was not entitled to an affair because of his frustrations. He was now more than willing to try to do his part in facing and resolving their marital problems. Simple honesty prevented him from saying that he was sorry about the affair, but he could say that it had been wrong of him to cheat on his wife both emotionally and sexually. He seemed sincere in wanting to try to correct the problems in the marriage that had made a less-than-desirable relationship. His renewed commitment to try to improve the marriage provided the wife with renewed hope for their future. Implicit in his comments was enough of an apology to allow her to face some of her own contributions to their marital difficulties. She tried hard to overlook her husband's past transgressions and work on improving the quality of the marriage relationship on a day-by-day basis.

Regrettably, however, her eagerness to improve the quality of their time spent together gradually pushed her across the line that divides behavior motivated by love, charity, and good will to behavior motivated by fear and anxiety. She started minimizing and avoiding her anger over the entire incident as a means of avoiding unpleasantness in the marriage. She also acted more seductive than she felt and systematically overattended to her husband's wants and wishes. Though subtle, her behavior was really a frantic attempt to buy reassurance for the marriage by self-sacrifice and denial. Outwardly, it appeared to be a gallant effort, but it was in fact both fundamentally dishonest and self-deceptive. True, her efforts did improve the general quality of the relationship almost immediately. The husband was so pleased with his wife's new behavior that he had little reason to doubt its authenticity. Furthermore, all these changes provided both partners with favorable experiences that renewed their hope in the future of their marriage. Their sex life improved—again, almost immediately. This was equally pleasing and reassuring. By most external appearances, the marriage had survived the storm and was well along the road to recovery.

In reality, however, this couple had quietly conspired to create an aura of tranquility, hope, and pleasantness as a means of reassuring themselves that the marriage could be saved. And while busying themselves with the task of creating pleasantness by avoiding unpleasantness, they failed to make progress on more serious marital issues such as trust, compatibility, consideration, and communication, which were the real cause of their marital difficulties.

The benefits of their sophisticated avoidance strategy were immediate and obvious: it provided reassurance and a sense of relief from imminent disaster. The classic illustration of immediate psychological relief and pleasantness that can result from unhealthy psychological behavior was occurring in their marriage. Its effects are usually short-lived, however. The cost of this avoidance will be equally obvious when the bill comes due. Not only will this couple have failed to prepare themselves for the next major stressor that hits their marriage, they will also be even less hopeful about their future because the results of their most recent problem-solving efforts have proven to be shallow and undurable.

## Interpreting Client Behavior

There are numerous and varied means by which a therapist can alert clients to the meaning and significance of their behavior.

Naturally, different styles are usually based on different assumptions and generally used for different therapeutic purposes. Most therapeutic styles have a loyal professional following that can argue or document the benefits of their approach, or both. Therefore, understanding the similarities and differences between approaches as well as their limitations and benefits is quite important, so we will review them again here.

The analytic approach, for example, is based on the assumption that awareness and insight are the most crucial elements in personality change (Ford & Urban, 1963; Greenson, 1967). Not surprisingly, we find their psychological interpretations and attempts to influence behavior to be heavily loaded with cognitive components designed to promote client insight and understanding into the workings of the personality. Although this is not explicitly stated, it is generally accepted that the positive influence of insight and understanding are not limited to improved understanding alone. Almost always the improved understanding of the personality is assumed to have a beneficial influence on other areas of psychological functioning, such as emotions and behavior.

The humanists-existentialists, on the other hand, are interested in increasing their clients' awareness and responsiveness to their own deeply felt human emotions (Rogers, 1961). To this end, we find their interpretations and therapeutic interventions to be aimed at increasing the frequency with which their clients experience their emotions more fully. An essential part of this process is helping the client get past the "blocks" or "resistance" they have to experiencing their own emotions. Once again, it should be noted that when this task has been successfully accomplished, most of these practitioners assume that the positive benefits of an improved state of emotional harmony are not limited to improved emotional well-being alone. They are more frequently thought of as a catalyst the influence of which naturally extends to the development of more appropriate cognitions and behavior patterns.

And, of course, we find the same pattern of thought in the cognitive-behavioral orientations. The primary emphasis of these approaches is regulating the reinforcement contingencies that most readily influence and shape observable behavior (Rimm & Masters, 1979). And while the ways and means of accomplishing this task are becoming increasingly more precise and sophisticated

## Table 1

*Units of Analysis and Affected Areas for the Major*
*Psychotherapeutic Orientations*

| Major orientation | Primary unit of analysis | Other areas affected |
|---|---|---|
| Analytical | Cognitive | Emotional-behavioral |
| Behavioral | Observable behavior | Thoughts and feelings |
| Humanistic-existential | Emotional | Cognitive-behavioral |
| Cognitive-behavioral | Cognitive-behavioral | Emotional |

in the psychological literature, the cognitive-behavioral approaches continue to assume that newly acquired behavior can shape the form and substance of the emotions and cognitions that accompany it.

## Sequential Determinism

In each case, we see that these major approaches to influencing behavior share two common assumptions. The first is the common belief of each that its particular unit of analysis (behavior, thoughts, or feelings) is the most potent entry point into the total system of psychological functioning. Second, each approach assumes that important changes in its primary area of intervention (thoughts, feelings, or behavior) will automatically stimulate changes in the other major areas of psychological functioning in a unidirectional manner. Table 1 summarizes these assumed relationships.

A moment's reflection on the assumptions of these major theoretical orientations reveals the following unsettling points.

1. Each orientation implicitly assumes that all three areas of psychological functioning are interrelated. This is fairly obvious from their common belief that improvement in one area of psychological functioning will affect all the other areas of psychological functioning. This is not an unreasonable assumption or an unlikely reality. However, the rationales that accompany this assumption are highly varied in quality, clarity, and completeness.

2. Any specific propositions or explanations about how these interrelationships are established or maintained are, for the most part, vague or nonexistent.

3. Each of the major orientations assumes that these areas of psychological functioning are sequentially and unidirectionally related. That is, the behavioral approaches suggest that once observable behavior has successfully been changed, different thoughts and feelings will follow. Similarly, if emotions are the primary target of therapeutic interventions (Gestalt), the improved emotional state is assumed to then influence thoughts and behavior. And, finally, a successful cognitive intervention will originally influence patterns of thought and self-talk, but these changed cognitions will then influence feelings and behavior.

In each case, changes in one area of psychological functioning are sequentially related to changes in the other areas of psychological functioning. It is regrettable that these assumptions are offered as declarations with little explanatory power or discussion of the psychological mechanisms that spread this influence. Two considerations have an important bearing on the vitality of this conceptual arrangement.

1. Little justification is provided for the suggestion that these variables are sequentially or unidirectionally related, or both. In fact, if they were sequentially related, one would expect the same sequence to apply in every case; thus there would be no possibility for different entry points.

2. Little justification exists for the belief that any of the three primary areas of psychological functioning represents the most potent entry point into the total system of psychological behavior. It seems more reasonable to simply consider all of them as important entry points. All of them can be useful, all of them have been useful, and all of them will probably continue to prove their usefulness in the future.

## Reciprocal Determinism

We are interested in trying to develop a system of intervention in which each of the major domains of psychological functioning is influenced simultaneously instead of sequentially. Our interest in this approach is based on a single assumption. We submit that every psychological event is the product of numerous and varied sources of psychological influence. The more of these sources of influence that are integrated into a conceptual whole, the more complete and useful the conceptual system and its clinical interventions are likely to be. Universally recognized sources of influence include (a) cognitions, (b) behavior, (c) affect, (d) peers and social systems, and (e) biochemical considerations. Bandura (1986) describes his conception of the interactions among behavior, cognitive and other personal factors, and environmental influences as "triadic reciprocality." Although the temporal relationship remains sequential, the nature of the relationship becomes bidirectional, with each variable affecting the other variables. While we have no hope of identifying or describing all, or even most, of the factors that go into shaping any specific psychological event, we do want to at least acknowledge and try to integrate some of the most obvious and interactive sources of influence into a unified conceptual system. In other words, we cannot explain the nature of the relationship among determining factors any better than previous theorists, but we believe that a description of this nature must evolve from a more accurate picture of the interaction of these factors, which are reciprocally affecting each other.

To accomplish this, one fundamental conceptual requirement must be satisfied. We must be willing to deal with units and levels of analysis that can accommodate multiple and bidirectional sources of psychological influence. The easiest way to do this is to deal with psychological events as they occur in the "here-and-now," which allows immediate access to the thoughts and feelings that accompany behavior as it occurs. In other words, by accepting as our unit of analysis behavioral products that represent an integrated sample of thoughts, feelings, and behavior, we can include all of these areas of psychological functioning for review and analysis in the context in which they occur and at the time they occur. Such an approach is based on the assumption that a person's behavior in the therapeutic setting will ultimately reveal the essence of maladaptive behavior, the function it serves for the individual, and the social conditions under which it tends to appear or disappear.

Experiential learning, then, is the crucial consideration in helping clients come to a fuller realization of their self-defeating patterns of avoidance. We are continually looking for opportunities during the therapy hour to "catch" the client fully engaged in a "Catch-22,"[1] or paradox. Our assumption is that when personal learning takes place simultaneously at a cognitive, behavioral, and affective level, it has more psychological impact than when these domains are insulated from each other.

**Summary.** Our discussion of self-evaluative thoughts and feelings is one of the most important sections of this book because of the paradoxes and contradictions it contains. Some key issues are summarized below.

1. Whereas most theorists consider self-evaluations to be expressions of irrational beliefs that are best discarded, we consider them to be at least partially valid self-perceptions. There are two major implications that flow from this formulation. First, a personal response style that favors avoidance over coping cannot completely escape the awareness of most individuals. Because of this, the very act of avoidance—by denial, distortion, or self-deception—virtually precludes the possibility of feeling personal adequacy because of the inadequacies inherent in these responses. Personal disapproval is the inevitable result of a personal response style that tends to favor avoidance over coping. Similarly, feelings of personal approval are just as inevitable when the personal response style tends to favor coping over avoidance.

2. Nonspecific inquiries about how a client is feeling while discussing a specific problem will generally elicit the negative feelings associated with that problem. However, specific conditional inquiries (e.g., "How do you feel about yourself for being more

---

[1] This expression comes from Joseph Heller's 1961 novel *Catch-22*, in which the leading character's attempts to be discharged from the army are frustrated by contradictory regulations. The phrase has been widely adopted to mean any situation with contradictory or conflicting demands.

honest with yourself about this problem?'') tend to elicit more favorable self-evaluative thoughts and feelings when the client is attempting to cope with the problem rather than avoid it. We see no contradiction in having a client experience an overwhelming sense of personal self-approval in the present for having the courage to face and experience the agony of the past. Neither do we see the value in trying to protect clients from the unfavorable psychological realities they create for themselves when these negative self-evaluative thoughts and feelings can provide the basis for increased motivation for personal change. We submit that these feelings can coexist, and that it is the responsibility of the therapist to judge which set of feelings will best serve the development of the client at any particular point in the therapy process.

3. Generally speaking, clients will find it more threatening to openly acknowledge and experience their basic feelings of self-approval than their enduring feelings of disapproval. This paradox was discussed in terms of underlying dynamic considerations as well as the means by which the therapist can help the client recognize and escape from it.

4. Finally, we suggest the value of having all three major domains of psychological functioning (thoughts, feelings, and behavior) involved in any attempt to work with self-evaluative thoughts and feelings. We suggest this can most easily be accomplished by working with client behavior as it occurs in the therapy hour. By accepting, as our unit of analysis, behavioral products that represent an integrated sample of thoughts, feelings, and behavior, all of these domains can be subjected to review and analysis by the client and therapist in the context in which they occur, and at the time they occur.

We will now proceed with our case study of Mary J. as a means of more fully illustrating the principles we have discussed.

## The Self-Evaluations of Mary J.

As you may recall from our earlier discussion, Mary has now completed about ten therapy sessions, several of which were rather intense. The focus of each of these sessions was on increasing her awareness of her personal style of avoidance. This process has gradually contributed to the clarity and precision with which she now understands the meaning and function of her excessive sexual behavior. It is her means of providing some pleasure in an otherwise boring and uneventful life; equally important, it is a means of distracting herself from almost any form of psychological tension, boredom, or pressure. It is now fairly obvious to Mary that her level of sexual activity is clearly related to each of these factors. She has arrived at the point where she is willing and able to clearly identify and describe the role of her sexual conduct in her style of avoidance. Mary also understands she has gone to substantial lengths to avoid clearly facing the possibility that she likes and enjoys her sexual behavior and that she has no particular interest in abandoning it, given the important role it plays in her life. She has not found these insights pleasing to face. Naturally, Mary prefers not to talk this way, but this reality is no longer as obscure as it once was. Furthermore, she finds it most unsettling to even consider the possibility that she actually enjoys and uses her sexual behavior to avoid pressure and create pleasure. For obvious reasons, she prefers thinking of herself as a victim of her parents' abuse and an overdeveloped sex drive she gallantly fought to control.

While none of this has been easy or pleasant for Mary, it should be noted that she already takes some pride in her accomplishments and is considering increasing her sessions to twice a week. Ironically, her sense of progress is not based on any improvement in her sexual behavior. Her sexual cravings are as intense as ever, as is her willingness to satisfy them at almost any cost.

Up to this point in the therapy process, the client has come to understand two major dimensions about her style of avoidance. As we discuss these patterns of avoidance, the reader should keep two points in mind. First, these patterns cannot possibly be portrayed in the diverse and complete forms in which they present themselves in the therapy room. Our characterizations are, of necessity, oversimplifications. And second, these are deeply ingrained patterns of conflict avoidance that have been refined by over 38 years of functional use—highly polished skills of self-deception that have survived the misery they have created because they have worked so well. There simply is no substitute for clinical experience in truly grasping the subtle sophistication and psychological influence these strategies have for self-deception and conflict avoidance. The two components in Mary's style of avoidance are described below.

1. She has developed an effective, highly sophisticated, and subtle "poor-me" story that she regularly employs to legitimize the sexual behavior she really disapproves of. In essence, the function of Mary's poor-me story is to convince herself that she is entitled to any pleasure she can derive from her sexual conduct because her life is one of misery and deprivation related to the hardship, cruelty, and emotional abuse her parents imposed on her. In its simplest form, her poor-me story is an attempt to distance herself from the responsibility for her volitional acts of sexual excess. She now clearly recognizes this pattern of conflict avoidance in her personal life and in the therapy sessions as well.

2. Mary has also developed another highly effective strategy: the type of avoidant behavior we call "the dodo routine," a phrase coined during our work with the unwed mother discussed in Chapter 5.

In Mary's initial sessions, this style of avoidance became apparent as she would ask her therapist to clarify questions or appear slightly confused about a relevant topic they were discussing. Finally, her therapist caught on to the fact that she really understood more about the topic they were discussing than her questions indicated.

The benefits of this all-too-common style of avoidance are both numerous and obvious. In Mary's case, pretending to know or understand less than was really possible for her allowed her to avoid (a) discussing emotionally laden topics in the therapy hour by keeping the therapist busy explaining terms and their importance to her problem, (b) showing any meaningful initiatives in solving her personal problems because she couldn't quite understand the meaning of important events without the expert assistance of someone smarter than herself, (c) the possibility that others might come to want or expect more from her than could be expected from a struggling dodo, and (d) feeling any significant sense of personal responsibility for her life problems.

Mary is also very aware of the role and function of this avoidance style in her personal life as well as in her therapy sessions. In fact, she now catches herself almost immediately when she starts this routine in the therapy hour, and she now chides her therapist when she catches herself in the act before her therapist does. In good humor, she has asked if the threat of a fee reduction would help keep the therapist more alert! In any event, Mary is able to clearly identify and describe at least two of her main styles of avoiding unpleasant psychological realities.

It is now time to discuss the means by which the self-evaluative processes that accompany avoidance behavior can be integrated into the therapeutic dialogue. Naturally, this takes place at a pace and in a context that is far more gradual than we can present in brief segments from therapy sessions. Our primary interest, however, is to clearly illustrate some of the governing principles of our model, and these segments seem suitable for this purpose.

Two guidelines are useful when the therapist is trying to decide when to start clarifying self-evaluative thoughts and feelings. First, *never* call attention to them before important patterns of avoidance have been clearly identified, described, and owned by the client. Second, *always* call attention to them (1) as quickly as the clients see the role and function these behavior patterns serve in their current life problems, or (2) in any therapy session in which they present themselves in unmistakable form. Both of these conditions were satisfied after Mary's third session. The client was starting to catch a glimpse of the meaning and significance of her avoidant behavior; additionally, she was actually engaged in the avoidant behavior in the therapy session. It was in the third session that the therapist first started making oblique inquiries about Mary's self-evaluative thoughts and feelings.

The first 30 minutes of the session had been devoted to Mary's exploration and clarification of the role of her poor-me story in her excessive sexual behavior. She was willingly explaining the stupidity of ruining the rest of her life simply because of her parents' personal problems. Mary stated that she had to find some way of getting control of herself before she ended up with AIDS, dead in an alley, or so depressed she would kill herself out of personal self-disgust. Doubtless Mary meant everything she said, but only her head was participating in her comments. Emotionally, she was already running away from the implications of the cognitive understanding she was acquiring.

Finally, the therapist stopped her, summarized the essential content she had been discussing, and asked how she felt about herself for always running to sex when confronted with the every-day hassles of life. Obviously, the therapist already knew the answer to this question, as did the client. But so far, the client had only presented these feelings in words. The therapist believed she needed to experience these emotions in their full intensity if she were ever to effectively combat her sexual problems. It was always assumed by the therapist that emotions as powerful as those that appeared to lie just below the surface of her verbal reports could induce a state of psychological dissonance so powerful that it might actually interfere with her long-standing patterns of avoidance.

Mary briskly responded by saying she didn't understand what her therapist wanted from her. She felt she had answered the therapist's question before he even asked it. She appeared agitated and angry. The therapist asked if she recognized what she was doing. After a short pause she said yes, but not with the cordial tone that usually accompanied her insights. It was obvious she didn't want to feel these feelings.

The therapist asked if she was thinking about stroking herself *now*, or if she was thinking about having sex as soon as she could get out of his office, or perhaps remembering one of her more satisfying encounters. Mary's agitated state visibly melted into the despair of melancholy as she quietly said yes. The confrontation was about over and the client was almost through trying to defend the indefensible. And the therapist supportively but nevertheless insistently asked, "And how do you feel *about yourself* for wanting to run away from me right now?" There were no words now, only tears. Mary seemed to physically hurt as she cried. It was the kind of emotion that can be frightening, particularly to inexperienced therapists. When the first wave of tears started to subside, the therapist quietly asked her to help him understand the meaning behind all the tears. There were no big surprises. There was self-hatred, despair, dejection, discouragement, disgust for being weak, anger for having thrown in the towel, and hurt because of the loss of love and esteem from her family. Mary's most enduring self-evaluation was self-hatred, at levels of intensity that are usually life-threatening. The truth was now out; she had heard herself say it all. She left the session with all the benefits of a full catharsis and all the burdens of seeing what she was really up against. The session ended with no further discussion of her sexual cravings and an invitation to schedule another appointment if she needed one. She called for another appointment two days later.

After the usual greetings, the eighth session got off to a quick start. She indicated that her anguish was becoming intolerable. She didn't know what to do. The therapist listened attentively as she talked for about 15 minutes before he responded. He needed to see if she was starting to realistically face up to these most unpleasant psychological realities or if avoidance was still the dominating force. If denial, avoidance, or self-deception were still reasonably prominent considerations, then a continued emphasis on identifying and describing avoidance patterns and the self-evaluations that accompany them would have been the most reasonable therapeutic course to follow. Though this may seem strange or even cruel, it is important to remember the two primary objectives of this phase of therapy. The first is to induce an affective level of psychological dissonance so strong that it can be satisfied only by personal change. The second is to create the opportunity for clients to start realistically facing the very problems they usually avoid as a means of teaching them about coping responses and the self-evaluative thoughts and feelings that accompany them. Premature termination of this therapeutic process, once it is started, is seldom in the best interest of the client.

Fortunately, Mary was deeply moved by her last session. She didn't know how she could ever stop such deeply ingrained patterns of avoidance, but her disapproval of herself would no longer allow her to continue as she had in the past. Ironically, the client failed to notice that she had been less preoccupied with her sexual "addiction" since the last session than she had been for the past 5 years. Mary was not particularly confident that she could ever break her long-standing patterns. Though the client offered this as a message of despair, the therapist was pleased to hear it. Clients realistically facing problems of this magnitude should not be sure of themselves: only a fool is certain of things that aren't certain.

Mary was already becoming more reality-bound in areas that mattered to her a great deal. Because of this, the therapist asked her if she had noticed anything new in the way she was now handling her problems. Of course, he would eventually want to know how she felt about herself for her new behavior, but we will say more about that in Chapter 7.

An abbreviated case study presentation such as this one can create misunderstandings about the model we are trying to clarify. Two points strike us as particularly important. First, in actual clinical practice, the event we have just described would probably be repeated many different times and at many different levels of clarity and precision. We are not advocating one-trial learning in the process of psychotherapy. Like most of our colleagues, we see effective therapy as a relatively slow, stable process in which progress is cumulative across time. We are simply illustrating some basic principles that play a crucial role at critical times in the therapy process.

Second, we are using rather difficult and dramatic cases to illustrate these principles for reasons we have already discussed earlier in the book. Therefore, we want to provide a brief, less dramatic illustration of how to introduce and integrate self-evaluative thoughts and feelings into the therapy dialogue. This time, however, we will use an example that illustrates the development of positive self-evaluations in a marriage relationship. Remember that the underlying therapeutic principles we are discussing do not change because of the type or intensity of self-evaluations involved. Basic styles of coping or defense must first be carefully identified, described, and owned by the client. Then the self-evaluative thoughts and feelings associated with these behavior patterns can be exposed, explored, and experienced.

This particular marriage had been dying a tedious death for several years. There was nothing dramatic about the decline—just a gradual, insidious loss of interest and good will. Initially, it wasn't clear why the couple had contacted a therapist instead of proceeding with a divorce; this appeared to be a hopeless case. In fact it was not. This couple's apparent detachment was far too calculated to be taken at face value, and what appeared to be supreme indifference was betrayed by sweaty palms and tapping toes.

Once therapy got started, it didn't take long for each partner to unveil a long list of documented complaints against the other. Each complaint brought out a counter-complaint, and each counter-complaint was more heated than the one preceding it. The underlying style of interaction was not unusual for a troubled marriage: "I would take out the garbage if you would iron my shirts like you're supposed to." "Well, if you would just pick up after yourself once in a while, I might have time to iron your shirts." The variations on this theme were endless, but the style remained constant. Both partners blamed the other for their inconsiderate and retaliatory behavior. This type of blaming could have gone on indefinitely, but the therapist quickly made a concerted effort to have the couple try to describe their style of interacting, and they accurately labeled their pattern of reciprocal blaming. With a little additional exploration, both spouses quickly became aware that the other was neither responsible for, nor the cause of, their undesirable behavior. It became embarrassingly clear that both partners were simply using the behavior of the other as a convenient excuse to express their anger and to camouflage their more authentic and tender feelings of personal hurt and disappointment.

The self-evaluations accompanying this behavior pattern became apparent to the husband and wife about as quickly as the pattern of blaming behavior. Simple yet accurate descriptions of the meaning and function of their reciprocal blaming allowed this to occur. They were deeply embarrassed and ashamed. Certainly neither spouse approved of this behavior once it was described with clarity, and each of them started searching for more responsible ways of behaving. Nevertheless, there were frequent slips of the tongue. These were seldom consequential, however. What their individual embarrassment didn't stop, the therapist did by simply asking if they were aware of what they were doing at the time.

Under these conditions, it didn't take long before one of the partners started expressing feelings of personal hurt and disappointment. Naturally, the therapist immediately inquired if this type of communication was typical in their marriage. Clearly it was not. "How is it different?" the therapist inquired. They described it as more honest, direct, revealing, and candid. The therapist then asked several questions: "Is this something you approve of? Would it help your marriage if you learned to be more honest about your feelings? How do you feel about yourself when you communicate this way?" The list of potential questions is endless, but they all ask the same thing: *How do you feel about yourself when you act this way?* When self-approval had been clearly established, the therapist focused on clearly identifying and labeling the new behavior, which provided the basis for more favorable self-evaluative thoughts and feelings.

*A word of caution:* Confusion frequently arises in this process when a client merges the meaning of "self-approving" with that of "self-pleasing." We are not sure why this happens so much, but our experience shows that it does. When this takes place, clients come to think self-approving means self-pleasing, and in some cases even doing only what they find pleasing. Our conception of self-approving behavior has little tolerance for such hedonism. Far more often than not, as we have said before, self-approving behavior involves realistically facing difficult personal issues that are typically avoided because of the fear and anxiety associated with them. Certainly this is not always the case; there are undoubtedly many psychological events that generate authentic and enduring levels of personal approval that do not involve facing issues that are more easily avoided. But when problems of chronic low self-esteem are involved, we suggest that overcoming one's disposition to avoid is generally a crucial consideration. Obviously, then, this process will seldom be pleasing in the sense that fun is. The self-approval we are talking about results from our clients' coming to understand that they can direct their personal affairs in a manner congruent with their most deeply held personal views and values regardless of the difficulty in doing so. Self-approval is a clear sense of personal identity and adequacy, not personal pleasure or indulgence. It is knowing oneself and having a comfortable and realistic belief in the adequacy of the self derived from prior life experiences.

# 7

# Developmental Considerations in Psychotherapy: Enhancing Coping Responses

We hope it is clear from our earlier discussion that we consider the remediation of deeply ingrained patterns of avoidance to be a vital precondition for personality development. We hope that it is also obvious that the very act of controlling patterns of avoidance constitutes a major therapeutic achievement and is a basic remedial improvement in the structure of the personality. Therefore, we have devoted a full chapter to explaining how to therapeutically respond to long-standing patterns of avoidance. Our intent has been to illustrate how the intense negative self-evaluative thoughts and feelings that are generated by patterns of avoidance can be used to eliminate the behavior that first created them. Obviously, we consider it nearly futile to make any serious attempt at facilitating personality development until pervasive patterns of avoidance are exposed and their debilitating influence at least partially immobilized.

But not everyone is a victim of enduring patterns of avoidance—at least not all the time. Some clients have more patterns of avoidance than do others. Still others are inclined to use their patterns of avoidance more extensively and consistently than the rest do. And some clients gradually improve as a result of psychotherapy and abandon their patterns of avoidance. Gradual improvement during psychotherapy usually implies a need for gradual changes in treatment plans, which generally flow from remedial to developmental. In light of these considerations, we suggest that successful psychotherapy calls for continuous and sometimes subtle transitions between remedial and developmental considerations. Knowing when to do which is important.

Though the distinction between remedial and developmental considerations can be less obvious than we might hope for at times, there are profound differences in how they are treated. The essence of a remedial approach involves having the client (1) clearly identify and describe patterns of avoidance, and (2) directly experience the self-evaluative thoughts and feelings this response generates. On the other hand, strengthening a coping response involves having the client (1) clearly identify and describe styles of coping, and (2) directly experience the self-evaluative thoughts and feelings this response generates.

Though the two different types of interventions share many structural similarities, the psychological experience they provide for the client and, for that matter, the therapist, have little in common. Strengthening a coping response is a rather reaffirming psychological experience that involves progressively higher levels of risk taking and personal responsibility on the client's part. It requires higher and higher levels of client self-direction (autonomy) and the ability to face personal issues squarely. Psychological adequacy is based on personal integrity, authenticity, and accurate self-knowledge more than on practical outcomes or the responses of others. Inhibiting an avoidance response, however, is similar to stopping a runaway train going downhill. For the client, it is usually scary, involving intense fear and anxiety, but it is an essential step if one hopes to regain control of the train.

Because focusing on developmental or remedial therapeutic processes is such a pivotal choice in the therapy process, we will discuss the primary means for assessing a client's disposition to cope or avoid. The adequacy of this assessment provides the essential information that can guide the therapist's judgment regarding the relative balance between remedial and developmental treatment approaches.

## Direct Assessment

Let us begin this discussion by being clear and specific about our assessment question. Our question is to determine the degree to which a person is inclined to realistically face or avoid personal conflict when fear and anxiety are involved. Obviously, this is not a problem in which dichotomous answers are likely. The disposition to cope or avoid exists in varying degrees and mixtures in different people in different circumstances and situations; the assessment problem is highly idiosyncratic. In a literal sense, what we want to know is if the probability is high, medium, or low that our client will realistically face or avoid personal conflict in general. The key considerations in this problem are threefold: (1) the general disposition of the personality to cope or avoid, (2) the level of fear and anxiety that must be present for the process of avoiding or coping to be present or absent, and (3) the general form, style, and substance of the coping and avoidance response.

When viewed in this light, our assessment problem is substantially simplified. We are now looking for an opportunity to directly observe our client's response to personal problems involving different levels of fear and anxiety. What better time, place, and circumstance for this to occur than in the first meeting between a therapist and a client? This is seldom a moment of glorious euphoria for most clients. They don't usually know what to expect from the meeting, they are almost always uneasy during most of the meeting, and, most important, they usually have a limited understanding of the purpose of the meeting. With so much inherent ambiguity, it is hard for the client to impression manage; equally important, it is hard for the client to know what impressions to try to manage. The first session is thus an opportune time for the therapist to observe how a client reacts to stress, fear, and anxiety. Furthermore, the adequacy of this assessment situation can be enhanced by the therapist's level of skill in describing client problems at different levels of clarity and precision, and with word variations that imply different levels of client responsibility for their problems. And, of course, the level of fear and anxiety associated with this conversation can be increased or decreased by the therapist, along with the type and frequency of questions that are asked.

From our point of view, then, the assessment starts as soon as the client enters the room and the therapist asks why the person is there. While the content of this introductory story is usually fascinating, it should not necessarily command most of the therapist's attention. There is also a client process to be observed quite carefully. It is the style the person uses to respond to the stress and fear associated with this intake interview. Are clients embarrassed, awkward, or withdrawn? Can they define their problems with reasonable clarity? Are they able to forthrightly provide relevant information? Can they say what they want and need? Are their explanations of the causes and consequences of their difficulties realistic or defensive? Are their expectations for help realistic? Do they seem more interested in blaming or improving? Are they already doing what they can to help themselves? In essence, at what level of psychological responsibility (see our discussion in Chapter 4) does the client function in this interview?

But these preliminary observations are not all there is to the assessment. The next steps are more revealing. They occur when the therapist starts to openly discuss with the client the validity of these preliminary observations about the client. Of course, a skilled therapist will proceed with this task with extreme sensitivity to the client's tolerance for stress and discomfort. Nevertheless, this is a situational stress assessment. The task of the therapist is to determine two things during the interview. The first is to evaluate client process reactions during the interview; the second is to focus on client content and substance.

## Process Evaluation

Our first task is to determine the client's capacity for a candid and realistic conversation about the meaning and significance of personal problems with a nonpunitive, reasonably astute professional person. The therapist accomplishes this by patiently but consistently pressing clients for more than they would normally provide voluntarily. Clients who describe their problems with anger in general terms can be asked what it is about them that makes anger a problem in the first place. If they answer evasively, the therapist should ask them if they are aware of how evasive their answer was. If they answer reluctantly, they can be asked if they are aware of that. If clients eventually take offense at being pressed in this manner, the therapist should ask if it is customary for them to act indignant (or however it is they act) when they feel offended or misunderstood.

It is equally likely that clients will be questioned about alternative responses they could have offered. For example, clients can be asked if they were aware at what point they found themselves annoyed with the questions. Did it occur to them to say they found the questioning offensive? If they were aware, what stopped them? Do they now wish they had expressed their feelings more directly? Is it likely they might now be more inclined to speak up under similar circumstances sometime in the future? Are these response tendencies typical outside of this interview?

And so it goes. Each question in the interview leads to another. And the style as well as the content, revealed in the answer, is carefully observed by the therapist and becomes the basis for the next question. There is a high focus on the here-and-now because it is assumed that behavior within a social microcosm is a reliable guide to the enduring dispositions of the personality. We are much more interested in observing these events directly in our assessment process than we are in having the client tell us about them. At each point in the interview the therapist is looking for the same thing—what makes this client defensive and avoidant, and when? How deeply ingrained are the patterns of avoidance? And, most important, do the patterns of avoidance quickly crumble or evaporate as they are exposed in the process of seeking clarification, or do they tend to become more rigid and entrenched?

When this process is finished, it is our assumption that the client will have been provided with an opportunity to engage in a cordial, nonpunitive, realistic conversation with an unbiased professional who is willing and able to have such a conversation for the purpose of understanding the client's problems. But, more important, the therapist has seen at least part of the client's capacity for coping and the pervasiveness of avoidance. If the intake interview has been done properly, these preliminary observations have been made under relatively optimal conditions. This, we suggest, is the essence of the assessment process, which begins with the intake interview and continues throughout the course of the therapy. The information from this continuous assessment process is what should guide the therapist's judgment about the client's need for remedial work, intended to help control or eliminate long-standing patterns of avoidance, or for developmental work, intended to strengthen one's understanding and ability to offer coping responses in the face of personal conflict.

## Evaluation of Content and Substance

Our second concern in this assessment process is more substantive. It is to ascertain the specific psychological elements that seem to dominate the client's response patterns, whether they be coping or avoidance. Differences between people are fairly obvious regarding the level of development apparent in their behavioral skills, cognitive capacities, and level of emotional comfort. Not surprisingly, we also find that these same elements usually play a central role in sustaining patterns of avoidance or coping. For some, patterns of avoidance are clearly a function of intense emotional fears that immobilize them; for others the ability to cope is the result of high levels of emotional well-being that allow them to face with comfort that which is intolerable to others. Similarly, some individuals manifest patterns of avoidance sustained by confusing and unrealistic expectations of personal harm; others, however, are able to cope with extraordinarily difficult situations because they can literally "see" (think about) alternatives and options that virtually guarantee a solution to the most difficult problems. Knowing the psychological domains (thoughts, feelings, behavior) in which individuals are the most adequate and inadequate is an essential prerequisite for understanding their patterns of avoidance and styles of coping. Valid information about how clients use their emotions, thoughts, or feelings in either the process of coping or avoidance can provide a valuable guide for clinical thinking and interventions.

**Clinical illustration.** The case of Mary J. provides a good illustration of this point. As you may recall, Mary had a history of chronic and almost compulsive sexual activity outside of marriage for a number of years. She finally became so disgusted with her inappropriate sexual conduct that she voluntarily confessed to her husband and asked for his assistance in overcoming her sexual problems. Mary was fully cognizant that her husband might leave her as a result of her confession and, furthermore, that she might lose custody of her children in a divorce. She found these prospects terrifying because of her professed love for her husband and children. In spite of these realities, she was willing and able to voluntarily "tell all" and accept these risks as a necessary step in her rehabilitation.

These few facts provide us with three important pieces of information about Mary's psychological composition. First, she has an extraordinary capacity to endure emotional trauma, at least under some circumstances. Relatively few people have the courage to face consequences as severe as those waiting in the wings for Mary after her voluntary confession. Additionally, her feelings during the intake interview covered a broad spectrum, ranging from despair and disgust to cordial pleasantness. Clearly, this is a woman with relatively easy access to a wide range of emotions, none of which frightens her to the point of avoidance.

Second, we know that Mary has a broad range of behavioral assets at her disposal. She can talk about intense personal problems, she can love and care for her children, she can function effectively in her civic responsibilities, she can manage her personal problems with discretion, and she can function effectively in most of her interpersonal relationships. More could be said, but we think the point is clear. She is not a person plagued with behavioral deficits.

Third, we know that Mary is perfectly able to understand the meaning and consequences of her behavior and be appropriately self-regulating most of the time. This is evident by the clarity of her understanding that her confession could easily lead to a loss of affection by her husband and children. In spite of this, she was able to proceed with her confession because she considered it an essential step in the process of no longer living a life of lies. This observation becomes invalid only when she becomes sexually aroused. Under these conditions, her ability to be self-regulating is seriously impaired. We must wonder why. More importantly, we must wonder why is one who is so psychologically capable in most situations so inept in others. Our ability to answer these questions will also expose the style and substance of Mary's dominant patterns of avoidance.

Because we know that Mary can respond appropriately to most events in her life, we also know that assessing her when she is sexually aroused is the best way to clearly identify the major components in her avoidance responses. As you may recall from our earlier discussion of Mary's case, she eventually described two dominant patterns of avoidance. The first was a well-developed poor-me story. This was the means by which she would try to convince herself that it was all right for her to break the rules of good conduct—because of her oppressive and impoverished past. It was also her way of trying to justify doing what she really found unjustifiable. Because her sexual behavior was incompatible with her standards of morality, she desperately needed an excuse to blunt the harsh discrepancy between her values and her behavior. Her poor-me story helped provide that excuse and thereby allowed her to escape the full force of her own wrath.

Her second pattern of avoidance was her dodo routine, a close relative to her poor-me story. The essence of this response was a philosophical questioning of right and wrong, and on select occasions, wondering if there was really anything wrong with her own behavior. Its most frequent manifestation, however, was appearing to understand far less about herself and the meaning and function of her behavior than she actually understood. The type of questions she asked would suggest her to be an enlightened thinker trying to grapple with issues of personal morality in an objective and detached manner. The fact that these questions were raised by a beleaguered woman in therapy during a major life crisis involving transgressions of her private code of moral conduct reveals them to be impoverished attempts to hide from her own moral condemnation.

Both of these styles of avoidance rely on cognitive distortions. The poor-me story is essentially a system of organized rationalizations intended to distort and excuse the self from what one considers inexcusable. The dodo routine is an attempt to obscure personal accountability by creating ambiguity and confusion in those areas where personal conduct is inconsistent with deeply held personal beliefs.

The style and function of these avoidance patterns now becomes obvious. It is to allow Mary to escape, or at least minimize, the personal distress and self-recrimination that would inevitably accompany her sexual misconduct if she acknowledged that this was her way of distracting herself from stress and adding an element of pleasure to a tedious existence. The psychological implications of this harsh reality were simply too demeaning and embarrassing to face. The psychological functioning of her behavior is to hide the truth about herself from herself; the style is cognitive distortion, and the pattern is long-standing and effective.

The necessity of having clients clearly identify and describe their patterns of avoidance should now be more obvious than ever. Identification is the means by which clients make explicit the function and style of their avoidance. Description removes the camouflage that hides the processes clients use to strategically deny, distort, evade, and escape. But, more importantly, self-identification and description of client patterns instructs the therapist on how to deal with each client. Understanding how a client's system of avoidance works tells us a great deal about how to respond to it when it does occur.

In Mary's case, for example, the function of her cognitive distortions was to minimize the unacceptableness of her behavior in her own eyes, as illustrated by the following example. After one period of prolonged sexual abstinence (3 months), Mary became discouraged and appeared to have lost her will to abstain any longer. In one respect, this was surprising because she had made a herculean effort to get through the first month of abstinence. Additionally, Mary was becoming progressively more aware of the intense self-approval and hope she was feeling because of her abstinence. Nevertheless, a major argument with her husband that further delayed their reconciliation date, along with two financial setbacks, reinstated her poor-me story in its most spectacular form. The following conversation took place in a crucial session. Note how just a modest understanding of this client's style of cognitive vagueness and distortions guides the clinical intervention.

> Mary: I'm not sure what will happen between now and our next session.
> Therapist: I'm not sure I understand what you are trying to tell me. [The therapist wants the client to be clear and specific.]
> Mary: I just don't know how much longer I can keep this up. It's tough doing this alone. Just at the point I am

starting to make real progress, my husband jerks the rug out from under me. His timing couldn't be worse. And the bank isn't going to extend my loan. I'm not sure I see the point of trying as hard as I have. No one is going to give you a break when you really need one.

Therapist: So you are angry and discouraged—and about to do what? [The therapist still wants the client to be clear and specific.]

Mary: Just give up, you know, bag the whole damn thing.

Therapist: It sounds like you are on the verge of doing something, but you don't want to come out and say what it is.

Mary: You know what I mean! What do you want me to do, draw you a picture?

Therapist: Now you sound angry at me.

Mary: Give Wonder Boy a star. He has figured out the obvious. You're no better than the rest of them when I get in a pinch. I was hoping I could get more from you when I needed it the most. The bank has let me down, my husband has let me down, and it looks like you will, too. [Note cognitive distortions.]

Therapist: Do you recognize what you're doing now?

Mary: I know what you want me to say, that this is my poor-me story. But you forgot it's also very true.

Therapist: You're not going to say it, are you?

Mary: [Long pause.] All right, I don't care any more, I want sex, and I'm going to have it tonight.

Therapist: I thought that's what you meant all along, but I wanted you to speak clearly so neither of us would misunderstand what you meant.

Mary: I guess that does make it clear, but that doesn't really change anything, does it?

Therapist: Not unless you want it to.

Mary: It always seems to come to this, and I just can't seem to help myself. I have never been successful before. Why should it be any different now?

The poor-me story is just now starting to go into remission, and the client is becoming slightly less belligerent. The client is still vulnerable and not really able to resist her sexual impulses. This is a crucial point in this therapy session inasmuch as the progress of the last 3 months now hangs in the balance. The therapeutic task is to intervene in a way so that the full impact of the client's imminent sexual acting out is not diminished by her system of cognitive distortions. This must be done in a way that makes these consequences immediate, concrete, and undeniable. The principle that guides the intervention is to make clear and explicit that which the system of cognitive distortions wants to make vague and obscure.

Therapist:    It sounds like you have given up, that there is no point in fighting a losing battle, and the best thing for you do is to leave now, go get your sex, and schedule another appointment for next week so we can start over again.

Mary:    That sounds great, except for the starting over again.

Therapist:    Starting over feels like a real setback?

Mary:    More than you can imagine, but I don't think I will be able to help myself.

Therapist:    How will this affect your reconciliation date with your husband?

Mary:    Not very much. I will have a sexual fling, then start abstaining again. We can be reconciled by September 1 instead of June 1.

Therapist:    You mean you're not going to tell him about it?

Mary:    Absolutely not, he would divorce me immediately.

Therapist:    I think it is important that you be honest with your husband. This is important information for him to have while he is deciding if he wants to reconcile or not. Besides, he will probably find out sooner or later, and it is hard to reestablish a trusting relationship when deception is involved. I would like to encourage you to pick up the telephone right now, call your husband, and explain your feelings, what you are about to do, and suggest a postponement of the reconciliation date.

Though this may sound like a form of "reality therapy," it is really much more than that. It is a very specific and limited intervention designed specifically for this client's style of avoidance. The intention of this intervention, as we said before, is to bring the full impact of the meaning and consequences of Mary's sexual behavior into the present discussion. Again, this is being accomplished by making clear and explicit that which Mary's system of cognitive distortions is trying to make vague and obscure.

|          |                                             |
|---------:|---------------------------------------------|
| Mary:    | I won't do that.                            |
| Therapist: | Why?                                      |
| Mary:    | He would divorce me today.                  |
| Therapist: | What would you expect?                    |
| Mary:    | I guess I want to have my cake and eat it, too. |
| Therapist: | It sounds like you're in a real bind.     |

This crisis was over, and the client did abstain from sexually acting out, but there was no reason to suppose this same crisis, or variations of it, would not reappear in future sessions. The next session was devoted to having Mary describe her behavior during this session and the negative self-evaluative thoughts and feelings that accompanied her avoidance behavior. The next several sessions focused more on Mary's coping response when it was present. This stage of her therapy involved numerous transitions between remedial and developmental work. It was becoming progressively more difficult for Mary's system of cognitive distortions to work or go undetected when they were the object of such intense interventions.

Please remember that this example and all of the client/therapist dialogue it contains is not an illustration of how to do outpatient psychotherapy in general terms. Rather, it is an illustration of how to make clinical interventions that are consistent with one's assessment of the style and function of the client's avoidant behavior. If this case were one in which the function of the client's avoidant behavior was to avoid intimacy with her husband because of deep-seated fears of rejection, and the style of avoidance involved emotional fears and anxiety, it could not be treated in the same way.

The model we are proposing is a mechanistic, process-oriented model of human behavior. It describes the processes involved in coping and avoidance, but requires the clinician to make careful observations of these processes in each client. These observations provide the information to design and direct clinical interventions. In this sense, the model is both particular and universal. General principles are described, but they cannot be applied to the individual without an accurate understanding of the style and function of the client's avoidance and coping responses. That is why the direct assessment of client adequacy and style of coping and avoidance is central to our model.

# Coping and Self-Evaluative Processes

## Avoidance: The Origins of a Creative Coping Response

From a practical point of view, the ability to quickly differentiate patterns of avoidance from styles of coping is as important to successful psychotherapy as any other single consideration. We would hasten to add that failure to regularly make this distinction can not only neutralize therapeutic progress, it can also be hazardous to client well-being. Remember that the first phase of psychotherapy can be a rather tense and tortuous time for clients. This is the time they are asked to do what they usually avoid—to realistically start facing intense personal conflict by clearly identifying and describing their own patterns of avoidance. This can be difficult for clients. It requires them to function at higher levels of personal risk and responsibility than they are generally accustomed to. This involves candid self-disclosure, realistic self-examination, and a willingness to try to face unpleasant psychological realities that are usually at the very heart of their avoidance tendencies. Fortunately, successfully accomplishing this task can be spread over as much time as the client requires, and the therapist can provide a supportive therapeutic relationship as well as professional assistance in managing the discomfort and anxiety that will inevitably accompany this difficult task. Gradually, clients will complete the assigned task and honestly, candidly, and explicitly identify and describe their own patterns of avoidance. There are many important client benefits to be derived from this process that have been discussed in an earlier chapter. But the most important is that the client cannot possibly accomplish this task without successfully engaging in a series of high-level coping responses, usually in a content area saturated with intense affect, fear, and anxiety. And while the immediate goal of this task is to sensitize clients to some of their undesirable psychological attributes by having them repeatedly ponder the power of their chronic patterns of avoidance, the long-term objective is to create a primary coping response for tutorial purposes within the therapeutic relationship.

However, the intense negative emotions that almost always accompany a client's explicit labeling of patterns of avoidance are so dominant that clients seldom if ever even notice the more mature psychological behavior this process involves unless the therapist calls attention to it. Of course, the therapist must see through the intensity of the moment and respond to the higher levels of personal risk and responsibility inherent in this level of psychological inquiry and activity. That is why it is essential that the therapist be able to clearly recognize and differentiate coping from avoidance at their most fundamental levels, and at the time these responses actually occur.

Inability to make this distinction regularly and accurately can compromise the entire therapeutic program. Every time this happens, clients will be left submerged in a quagmire of intense, negative self-evaluations at the precise moment their behavior is the most adaptive and likely to lead to successful conflict resolution. We cannot think of a therapeutic failure more consequential than this one. Each time it happens, clients are not only left to needlessly relive intense negative feelings from the past, they are also denied the opportunity to explore the meaning, significance, and immediate psychological benefits that accompany realistic coping responses in the face of intense personal conflict.

Because of the importance of identifying the coping response inherent in realistically facing one's patterns of avoidance and their consequences, it seems appropriate to review the reasons for having clients identify their patterns of avoidance in the first place. There are three primary reasons. First, clients must make explicit the style and function of their avoidant behavior. Second, clients are introduced to the scope and intensity of the negative self-evaluations that accompany their avoidant behavior. And third, clients are engaged in a therapeutic task that can be accomplished only with a series of high-level coping responses.

Creating the opportunity for the client to engage in high-level coping responses is crucial for three additional reasons. First, it provides an experiential basis for clients to (1) identify and describe the most influential elements involved in their own coping responses, (2) understand the consequences that generally accompany coping as opposed to avoiding, and (3) understand the scope and significance of the favorable self-evaluative thoughts and feelings that can accompany a primary coping response.

Obviously, none of this can be accomplished if the therapist is unclear about the most fundamental differences between psychological coping and avoidance. Of course, this can be difficult to do at times. We have not defined either coping or avoidance in behavioral terms that are easily recognized. Rather, we have defined them with regard to the underlying psychological attributes that are assumed to drive them. Coping is based on psychological risk-taking and personal responsibility. In our view, these are the psychological attributes that seem essential to the process of realistically facing personal conflict and productively learning from it. This is the path of personal insight, reality testing, self-exploration, and personal growth through conflict resolution. Each of these responses involves relatively high levels of psychological risk taking as well as personal responsibility.

One of the first and most obvious manifestations of coping, as we have defined it, is a willingness to accept the self as one of the primary causal agents in creating its own psychological difficulties. It is a willingness to see and accept imperfections in the self, and as a result of these perceptions, to try to improve by self-examination and the acquisition of a more accurate understanding of the self and the world that surrounds it.

We wish to make it clear, however, that we are not suggesting that identifying the negative self-evaluations that accompany patterns of avoidance are the only relevant coping responses we can work with. Actually, any will do. This particular response just happens to be one that will appear regularly because of the way we have structured the therapy process. However, any significant coping response can serve the same tutorial purposes for the client as long as the self-evaluations that accompany it are still fresh. What is most central to this entire process is the skill and ability of the therapist to quickly and accurately respond to authentic coping responses when they occur. The fact that the transition from avoidance to coping can be both gradual and subtle only suggests the need for the therapist to review this judgment regularly, and with considerable care.

Remember, in both coping and avoidance, it is the underlying function the behavior serves for the personality that defines coping or avoidance. Avoidance is based on denial and distortions of various kinds, but the result is always the same. It is to flee from the fear and anxiety associated with the conflict. The inadequacies inherent in these responses virtually preclude the possibility of psychological growth and development. Coping, on the other hand, is a process in which the short-term discomfort of facing imperfections in the self is tolerated as a means of cultivating psychological enrichment for the future. The ultimate reward is developing a life-style in which the quality and integrity of one's psychological experiences are every bit as important, and perhaps even more important, than other, practical considerations such as acceptance by others, appearance, and achievements. In the long run, we suggest that a firmly rooted sense of personal well-being is the source of a great deal of human happiness and personal success.

Perhaps the best way to illustrate how a primary coping response can have its origin in one's attempt to describe patterns of avoidance is with a clinical illustration. Note how the therapist capitalizes on the appearance of this coping response once it is clearly established and how oblivious the client was of its existence right up to the time the therapist called her attention to it.

**Clinical illustration.** Mary J. has now completed over 6 months of intensive therapy. During this time, she has made more progress than had originally been anticipated. Nevertheless, she is still far from reaching an enduring resolution to her most pressing sexual problems and personal concerns. Some may wonder why we consider her progress so satisfactory while she is still plagued with so many of her original complaints. We have several reasons for suggesting this.

First, Mary is now able to clearly and consistently identify and describe her patterns of avoidance any time she really wants to. They are simply no longer a mystery to her. She is equally aware of the contempt she feels for herself when she engages in her poor-me story or dodo routine. More than anything else, Mary seems to despise the personal weakness that the use of these avoidance strategies implies about her. Nevertheless, she still uses these routines occasionally, more often outside her therapy sessions than during them. But she seldom fools herself about the meaning and purpose of her avoidant behavior, and she now clearly understands the origins of much of her self-contempt. Her avoidance patterns are gradually becoming psychologically useless, and because of this, Mary is continually confronted with the unpleasant reality that she is the author and architect of most of the personal problems she complained about that brought her to therapy. Additionally, Mary is starting to develop an idea of what it might be like to be truly different. This conception is far from clear or explicit, but she does understand that it would involve substantial increases in personal honesty with herself and others. Translating this abstract idea into the practice of living on a daily basis is consistently problematic because of the immediate consequences it always seems to involve, but the idea is starting to take shape. Finally, her relationship with her therapist is almost fully developed. She talks openly and honestly about her concerns. She feels a full range of emotions in many therapy hours. Relationship issues between Mary and her therapist are discussed openly, frequently at Mary's insistence. The therapist's exaggerated power base has become more realistic in Mary's eyes, and he is now accepted in the relationship as both a person and professional therapist eager to help her change and grow. Most importantly, however, Mary likes and approves of the way she acts while she is with her therapist. She describes herself as open, spontaneous, and more alive than usual. Feeling her personal distress is part of what she calls being alive. Paradoxically, she is finding most of her therapy hours to be intensely enjoyable even though they usually involve tears, uncertainty, and facing the very life issues she has usually avoided.

At this time, Mary had successfully abstained from sexual intercourse with anyone for more than 23 weeks. Remember that she and her husband had temporarily separated until her sexual problems were resolved. She masturbated on several occasions but that was the full extent of her sexual activity. Several factors played a role in her abstinence. Certainly her therapy helped by immobilizing her ability to deny and distort the real meaning and consequences of her inappropriate sexual behavior. But her wish to save her marriage was even more influential. She was simply afraid that any inappropriate sexual activity on her part would not be accepted by her husband; he would divorce her immediately. Her abstinence proved to be a daily struggle, and finally the inevitable happened. She spent some time alone with a friend one evening and they ended up in bed. Even though she was racked with guilt the next morning, her sexual activity persisted through the next several days. Finally, in a state of near desperation and panic, she called her therapist and they met immediately.

The therapeutic issues involved in this meeting were both consequential and emotional but not terribly complex. The first concern of the therapist was to determine the effects of this most recent incident on Mary's well-being. Even though such a relapse was almost entirely predictable, it could be perceived by Mary as a major blow to her therapeutic progress. These effects had to be carefully assessed. The therapist's second concern was to ascertain the degree to which she was going to attempt to avoid or cope with the issues raised by her most recent sexual behavior. Divorce was now a clear possibility, as was a loss of hope for future improvement. For the first 45 minutes of the session, the therapist patiently and attentively listened to Mary explain all of her views and feelings about her sexual episode. She was clear in her expression and offered few excuses. Her sexual cravings and the tension associated with them simply became more than she could tolerate. Her decision to have sex was quite deliberate.

Mary was facing this problem with far more honesty than usual. She became avoidant only when she started considering the potential consequences if her spouse knew what had happened. The prospect of a divorce was now more imminent and terrifying than ever before. This made it very difficult for Mary to not avoid the obvious issues she was now faced with. Even though her massive system of avoidance was not operative, she was not inclined to tell her husband what had happened. Mary was ready to be honest with herself about the meaning and significance of her behavior in the privacy of her therapist's office, but she was not at all sure she wanted to extend that candor to her husband. The session ended at this point and another meeting was scheduled for the next day.

Early in the next meeting, Mary's major concern was the prospect of divorce if she let her husband know about her most recent sexual incident. She knew she should tell him about it, that he was entitled to know about it, and, actually, she wanted to tell him about it. But she was sure he would divorce her if she did. The therapist focused on letting Mary talk about her ambivalent feelings and occasionally paraphrased her dilemma. Finally, she decided that she could not and would not tell her husband. The therapist had been waiting for her decision, and now he simply asked for her description of the means by which she was trying to save her marriage.

"I'm a liar!" she snapped back. "You know it, I know it, but my husband isn't sure about it, and this marriage has to be saved. I can't stand the thought of losing my children. And I love my husband. He's the kind of person I've always wanted, and I'm not going to give him up. I can tell him about this later, maybe in 6 months or so. This won't happen again, and by then it will be easier for him to understand and accept what I've done." The therapist indicated that there were many good reasons for her not to tell her husband and that he was particularly pleased about her ability to accurately call herself a liar at appropriate and limited times. For obvious reasons, she did not like his comment. She was now caught in the classic struggle of feeling compelled to do something she disapproves of because it seems to be the only means available of accomplishing what she does approve of.

The heart of this conflict was quickly exposed in its completeness in the following session. Mary could no longer lie to herself or her spouse without feeling a great deal of self-recrimination, nor could she willingly submit herself to the prospect of a divorce by being honest. In the past, Mary easily avoided such a dilemma by hiding the truth about the meaning and consequences of her behavior from herself and others. This allowed her to postpone negative consequences almost indefinitely. But now there was an immediate price to be paid for avoidance or coping. Avoidance was now explicitly associated with feelings of personal weakness and a relatively clear understanding of its self-defeating nature. Coping required realistically facing the possibility of losing the family she loved. Her past had now caught up with her on all counts.

The therapeutic issue was now becoming clear. Mary had to decide what kind of a person she wanted to be in these intensely difficult conflict situations. And that is what the therapist focused on for the next two sessions. The client was repeatedly confronted with the same difficult question in a variety of forms and formats: What do you need to do in this situation so you can approve of yourself whether your husband files for a divorce or not? Mary sought reassurance from the therapist that honesty was the best policy, but the therapist kept asking what she needed to do to have her own approval! This was hard for Mary. She was accustomed to thinking in strategic terms—of how to get what she wanted from other people. But she had virtually no experience in thinking about what she needed to do to earn her own approval.

Mary struggled with this problem without even noticing her self-candor and courage in facing what was probably the most difficult and conflicted choice in her life. At this point the therapist started asking her if she had noticed how she was handling this problem. Though this type of questioning can be developed in many different ways, it always involves the same underlying issues: What do you notice about the way you are trying to deal with this problem? What are you doing differently? Is it typical of you to try to face problems as realistically as you are now? If you had tried to deal with other problems in the past in the same way you are dealing with this one, would your life be different? What specifically are you doing differently now? What do you think of yourself when you act this way? How does it feel to be the person you have been for the last 30 minutes? If you could be like this more often would you be happier with yourself?

These questions are all reducible to the same two essential points. The first is a simple description of how clients actually behave while they are in the middle of the conflict and how this is different from the past. The second is how clients feel about themselves for their honesty, courage, lack of deception, or willingness to face problems rather than avoid them, or whatever they do when they actually start facing problems instead of avoiding them.

Mary was so caught up in her dilemma that she had difficulty even understanding the therapist's new set of questions. She was deeply concerned about how much she would tell her husband, and the prospect of looking at the underlying processes involved in her own problem solving did not arouse much interest or enthusiasm in her. Nevertheless, Mary's therapist explained that it could be valuable to clearly understand what she was doing that was different from her past behavior. With this encouragement, she discussed what she considered to be the new ingredients in her current problem solving. She started by describing herself as comfortable in her relationship with her therapist. This was the first time she had really been known by another person. It seemed to Mary that anything was all right with the therapist as long as she stayed "straight" with herself about what she was doing and why. This made it easier for her to face things she usually avoided and not play games with herself. This resulted in her being more honest and open about her real thoughts and feelings. She also indicated that she liked herself when she acted this way and hoped she could learn to be like this without the assistance of her therapist.

The therapist then paraphrased this message back to Mary and asked if his understanding was accurate. She indicated it was. He then asked what turned out to be a poignant question: What would she do in her current dilemma if she were to act just like the kind of person she wanted to be? Mary's answer was disarming in its simplicity. She would tell her husband simply because he was entitled to know. She would also face up to whatever consequences followed because it was more important to be honest with her husband than to live a lie with him. Mary quickly added that she did not believe she had the courage to actually do what she had just described, however. The therapist asked how it felt to be clear in her own mind about what she wanted to do even if she wasn't sure she could actually do it. She was glad she understood but was afraid of the whole situation.

When she returned for her next session, Mary reported that she had gone ahead and told her husband everything. A divorce now seemed unavoidable. She indicated that she had been crying all week, felt seriously depressed about what she had done to her life, and didn't know if she could go on. Interestingly, Mary did not regret being honest with her husband. She still felt she had done the right thing but deeply regretted the consequences that were sure to follow. She wished this were all a bad dream that would end. It seemed to her that her whole life was about to fall apart.

## Commentary

In spite of the intensity of these meetings and the serious consequences they involve, we hope two points are clearly illustrated in this example. The first is how the process of clearly describing patterns of avoidance can be turned into a primary coping response. The second is the high level of personal risk and responsibility that can be involved in coping as opposed to avoidance. Both of these points could have been illustrated with examples that would be far less controversial than this one. Additionally, other examples could have been selected that would not involve such negative real consequences as a result of coping at high levels of personal risk and responsibility. We thought it best, however, to use an illustration that contained complex issues involving serious life consequences at the outset and to save the less drastic and more typical examples for later. This is our way of trying to flush out the conceptual and practical issues involved in clinical interventions that can be as potent as those we are describing. Once these basic issues have been given the thoughtful consideration they deserve, the reader can judge the merits of these interventions on principle and merit rather than on carefully selected clinical examples that would have almost universal appeal.

There are several points about the way this case was managed that should be discussed. A severe critic could point out that the management of this case was seriously flawed for the following reasons:

1. The therapist played a major role in causing a divorce needlessly by showing too much allegiance to preconceived theoretical assumptions on how to manage a case without enough regard for client welfare.

2. The therapist was guilty of overinfluencing the client in the direction of personal values and patterns of behaving that were not of the client's choosing.

3. The therapist had too much control over the client's behavior without the client's fully understanding the nature and extent of that control.

As a result, the critic could say, the client's autonomy and ability to be self-directing were fundamentally compromised because of the therapist's influence.

Each of these criticisms should command the attention of any serious professional. We are, in fact, trying to describe incisive methods of intervention that are intended to influence client behavior. Additionally, we view the task of the therapist, at least partially, as being able to intervene in client behavior in such a way that it will make a difference. The issue we face is not one of therapist influence but the appropriateness of that influence. From our point of view, therapeutic influence should improve a client's willingness and ability to cope with personal conflict rather than avoid it. This involves realistically facing problems and oneself, improved perceptions of reality, high levels of personal risk and responsibility, and an increased capacity for self-direction. Note that we do not suggest that the job of the therapist is to protect the client from any of the unpleasant realities or consequences that accompany their self-defeating behavior patterns. Neither have we suggested that coping will automatically lead immediately to outcomes that the client will find pleasant or enjoyable. What we have suggested is that clients can gain their own approval by coping instead of avoiding, and that this self-approval can be an enduring and helpful element in personal growth and self-direction. We suggest this is true whether the immediate external consequences of coping are favorable or unfavorable. Our view is that the long-term consequences of coping will *always* be more favorable than those of avoiding, and a major responsibility in case management is to assist clients in overcoming their disposition to accept the short-term benefits of avoidance at the cost of the long-term benefits of coping. And, as difficult as this task may appear, we suggest that one of the therapist's greatest tools in this process is the immediate feelings of client self-approval that can be generated by coping with difficult real life situations. In this light, we ask the reader to consider the following observations about the interaction between client and therapist in our previous example:

1. The therapist did not create the client's avoidance tendencies or the intense negative self-evaluations that accompanied them. His role was to help the client remove the camouflage she had carefully put in place to protect herself from having to face her conflict avoidance tendency and the problems it created.

2. The client's own clear identification and description of herself as a liar in the crisis situation was a psychological reality, and once this was clearly perceived by the client it served as a catalyst for much of her subsequent behavior.

3. The negative self-evaluative thoughts and feelings the client associated with being a liar were also a psychological reality, and once these feelings were clearly perceived and understood by the client, they became a primary source of her motivation for change during the crisis situation. The client came to believe that lying was not an appropriate means of saving an important relationship, and the act of accepting the consequences of telling the truth constitutes a primary coping response of the highest order. The spouse's response (seeking a divorce) to Mary's truthfulness does not diminish the psychological maturity inherent in her response, nor is it likely to diminish the client's sense of self-approval for behavior she considers appropriate.

4. Mary clearly understood the possible consequences of being honest with her husband, and she took this step voluntarily and deliberately. She did not report any regrets about the act of being more honest; in fact she felt proud of this achievement. She did, however, have solemn regrets about the sexual activities she had engaged in which led her husband to initiate a divorce.

Taking these observations into consideration, we suggest that this client was functioning at an extraordinarily high level of personal self-direction under the most difficult circumstances imaginable. We also suggest that if she continues to function at this same level, her prognosis for the future is outstanding even though she is now confronted with several major adjustment problems because of the imminence of a divorce. Finally, and perhaps paradoxically, we suggest that the behavior that precipitated this crisis in Mary's life (candor with her husband) is also the basis for her rapidly improving prognosis for the future. Mary's disposition to avoid is gradually being replaced by her ability to cope with conflict. This ability will gradually become more obvious as she cultivates the two underlying psychological attributes essential to coping. These are psychological risk taking and personal responsibility, both of which are now becoming apparent in Mary's style of coping.

## Strengthening the Disposition to Cope

For a variety of reasons, it is not always necessary to create a coping response during the therapy hour for the benefit of the client. As we said earlier, not all clients are complete victims of chronic and pervasive patterns of avoidance. Still others can move more freely between patterns of coping and avoidance, depending on the situations they find themselves in. And some clients gradually improve in psychotherapy and start to volitionally abandon their patterns of avoidance. For any of these reasons, the major therapeutic task can shift from creating new coping responses to strengthening already-existing ones. Of course, the disposition to cope must be strengthened in those areas in which the client is most inclined to be defensive and avoidant. Even though this process can be similar to that which we have already described (identifying patterns of behavior and the self-evaluations they generate), several important differences should be noted.

In the first place, strengthening a coping response does not generally involve the high levels of emotional intensity portrayed in our last example. This is not meant to imply that this type of intervention is less important or that it should be undertaken casually. In fact, strengthening the disposition to cope is the "harvest" of the entire therapeutic process, and the point with which client gains will be the most obvious and profound. The therapist cannot catch a quick nap just because the client is not immersed in the chaos of filing emotional bankruptcy during emotionally depressed times.

Strengthening the disposition to cope is different from and more pleasant for the client than describing avoidance patterns because it does not involve attempts to alter the personality in such fundamental ways. It does not call for the acquisition of brand-new behavior patterns or profound increases in the client's level of personal risk and responsibility. These interventions are more comfortable for clients simply because so much less is asked of them. Equally important, however, is the obvious fact that this stage of therapy asks clients to focus their attention on the patterns of behavior they most approve of. It is a time to learn how to think well of one's self, to identify and describe one's favorable patterns of behavior and the self-evaluations they generate, to learn how to graciously and appreciatively accept self-compliments, and to explore the significance and risks involved in being a self-approving, self-directing human being who cares deeply about the self and others.

Certainly, some psychological tensions will be associated with these tasks. It is not easy for clients to accept the burdens of personal self-direction and personal approval. Also, in our culture there are many negative associations with these terms, which may require therapeutic discussion. Nevertheless, it should be obvious this can be a pleasant and rewarding experience for clients. It is certainly an essential one, and one that does not feel remotely similar to the grueling experience of describing one's patterns of avoidance.

Second, strengthening the tendency to cope is perceived by most clients as being more relevant to their reasons for being in therapy. It has an immediate and obvious problem-solving orientation that seems to be welcomed by many clients. More than client perceptions are involved in this difference, however. The therapist's primary role in this phase of therapy is to help clients identify and describe the main elements involved in their best coping responses and the self-evaluative thoughts and feelings that accompany them. When clients complain of mild depression or a series of unsatisfying interpersonal relationships, for example, they can be asked quite early how they feel about themselves for the way they conduct their lives within the problem area they have identified. The source of disapproval can be quickly identified, and, more important, clients' attention can then be focused on what they need to do so they can approve of themselves in the problem area.

When a therapist is attempting to strengthen coping responses, a major portion of each therapy hour should be devoted to (1) understanding the conditions that tend to increase the tendency to avoid, (2) careful exploration of the sources of anxiety in that situation that seem to be the source of the avoidance, (3) careful exploration of what clients need to do in the conflict situation to approve of their behavior in that situation, and (4) careful exploration of the self-evaluative thoughts and feelings that accompany clients' coping responses in general and in this specific problem situation.

A good example of the entire process is contained in our earlier example of a housewife who tried to avoid the possibility of being rejected by those she valued and respected. She did this by continually placing herself in the service of those whose approval she valued the most as a means of obtaining their appreciation and approval. This case study is presented in Chapter 6.

As you may recall, this housewife started her first therapy hour by complaining of fatigue and depression and ended it with a relatively clear understanding that (1) she attempted to buy approval from others by being conflict avoidant and denying her own wants and wishes, (2) she was basically dishonest with herself and others about her true feelings regarding many important topics and events in her personal life, (3) she considered herself weak and inadequate because of her attempts to buy approval rather than present herself as the person she really was, (4) it felt very pleasing to her to be honest with herself and the therapist during her first meeting (coping response), (5) a major portion of her future happiness depended on her being as honest with herself and others as she was during this first therapy hour, and (6) it was well within her psychological capabilities to be more honest with herself and others immediately. Those who are interested may wish to reread this case study in its entirety (see Chapter 6) because it contains much of the original therapist/client dialogue, which basically focuses on strengthening an already-existing coping response.

Returning to the case study of Mary J., one of the best examples we have seen of strengthening a coping response occurred two weeks after Mary told her husband about her most recent sexual encounters. Mary had accepted the prospect of a divorce and was now struggling with her own emotions of anger, loneliness, and fear for her future. By sheer coincidence, Mary received a letter that week from a sibling. It was an open letter to the family in which he confessed to all that his life was falling apart, that he had had serious sexual problems, that a divorce was imminent because of these sexual problems, and that he desperately needed support from the family. Mary called all of the siblings and found out that many of the children had serious sexual problems, that all of them were in therapy at the present time, and that the origins of these problems went back to sexual abuse they had suffered as children. Even though everybody knew something about the abuse, none of them had spoken to each other or their parents about them.

Mary arranged a family meeting for a weekend in which the children flew home from all over the country to confront their parents. It was a meeting intended to be helpful by bringing all their problems out into the open where they could be dealt with, including confronting the parents with their inappropriate sexual behavior. When Mary returned from this meeting, she spent an entire hour talking about her behavior while at home. She had confronted a highly manipulative mother and refused to accept the burden of her emotional problems any longer. She had confronted her father with things that should have been dealt with years ago. And she expressed love and appreciation to her parents and siblings for all the good things that had been done for her. Mary declared herself fully and openly to her entire family and no longer had anything to hide from any of them. She also indicated that she wanted close relationships with all of them, but that she would no longer act in ways she disapproved of for their benefit. She won the respect and admiration of her family for bringing them together.

When Mary finished telling her story, the therapist simply asked how she felt about herself for all she had done. "Proud," she replied. "What is it that you are most proud of?" the therapist asked. She described the elements in her behavior she was pleased with. "Brave" and "courageous" were among the first words she used. When she had exhausted her description, the therapist then focused on how she felt about herself for being able to do all she had done. She consistently reported feelings of personal pleasure and integrity she had never felt before. At one point, the therapist asked if she considered herself to be "healthy" while she was at home over the weekend.

At first she said yes but then reconsidered her answer. She talked about all of the problems she had left to solve. The implication seemed to be that until all of these problems were resolved, it would be unwise to consider herself healthy, even on a temporary basis. It appeared to the therapist she was starting to experience the risk of considering herself an adequate person who could trust herself to run her life in ways she approved of. This is always a critical point in the therapy process, and she seemed afraid to believe in herself in spite of the overwhelming evidence it was starting to be true. Having noticed this slight digression, the therapist asked if she was being as honest with herself right this minute as she was while she was at home. She said no, adding that she considered herself to have been extremely healthy while she was at home and that she had actually fulfilled all of her fondest expectations of herself. Her greatest concern was her ability to keep it up. The therapist considered that a valid concern but not one that negated the maturity of some of her emerging behavior patterns.

It is doubtful that Mary will now encounter many conflict situations in which she can engage in her avoidance routines oblivious of their meaning or not have some rather clear ideas about how she can be different in conflict situations so she will approve of herself both at the time and when the conflict has been resolved. Whether she will consistently be different in these situations is still an open question, but it should be obvious that Mary has experientially learned a great deal about coping in the last month, and this learning has taken place at many different levels of psychological functioning (cognitive, behavioral, and affective).

## Some Important Questions

Because this model and the treatment methods it generates have been demonstrated and discussed in a number of professional forums prior to this publication, we are aware of some of the most common questions and concerns it raises. The three questions that appear most frequently are:

*1. Aren't these treatment techniques unnecessarily confrontational and hard on clients?*

*2. Why is it necessary to be so confrontational with clients?*

*3. A client's presenting complaints seem to play a minimal role in the actual therapy process. Instead, you*

*seem to assume that decreasing the tendency to be con-
flict avoidant and increasing the disposition to cope
will benefit most clients. How do you actually judge
therapeutic progress?*

We find the first two questions on confrontation puzzling, and,
frankly, we have spent a considerable amount of time trying to
understand them. We have concluded that each of these two
questions is probably best understood at two different levels of
meaning. The first is substantive and is a literal request for additional explanation and information. The second is more emotional
and is an expression of the personal discomfort frequently associated with emotional intensity and the unpleasant experiences it is
assumed to generate in the self and others. We would like to try
and answer both of these questions at both levels of meaning.
This will be followed by a discussion of how to judge therapeutic
progress.

**Substantive commentary.** The first two questions focus on
confrontation. Obviously, how these questions are answered depends on how one defines confrontation. We think the term has
two general meanings. The first and most common conception is
that of one person confronting another, usually with unpleasant
feedback, though this is not always the case. The other is when
people confront themselves or face something about themselves
they had previously been unaware of. Again, it is most generally
assumed that what one faces is unpleasant or undesirable. We
would amend these popular conceptions by altering their preoccupation with negative attributes. Confrontation can and usually
does involve both positive and negative considerations. And,
frankly, we have come to consider the immediate and direct expression of meaningful regard or affection to be more frightening
to most clients than facing a list of well-documented personal
faults. In our view, then, confrontation can be both interpersonal
and intrapsychic, and it involves both positive and negative attributes or feelings.

With this definition in mind, we suggest that our model is not
unnecessarily confrontational or hard on clients! Certainly clients
are asked to face themselves (self-confrontation) by identifying
and describing their patterns of avoidance and coping. And the

therapist is clearly an adjunct to this process when necessary (interpersonal feedback), but all forms of psychotherapy ask clients to face themselves in one form or another. Increased self-awareness is a staple item in almost all treatment forms. What distinguishes this treatment format from others is not that it is more confrontational or unnecessarily confrontational, but the relevance of what clients are confronted with. Asking clients to identify and describe their patterns of avoidance and the self-evaluative thoughts and feelings associated with them is serious psychological business because it is so revealing and relevant. The same is true of the coping response. We consider the relevance of the psychological material this model has selected to focus on to be one of the major strengths of the model.

This brings us to the question of how hard this relevance (as opposed to confrontation) is on clients and why it is necessary. Two points seem obvious to us.

First, we can't imagine any theory proposing to focus on psychological material that is considered irrelevant! The real issue, then, is not relevance, but the intensity of client reactions to such relevant material. This we consider a vital and valid concern. We have no wish to see clients overwhelmed by emotional reactions they find frightening, unhelpful, or distressing. This makes therapeutic timing as crucial a consideration in this model as in all other treatment forms. Clients must be ready to deal with material that would be rated high on psychological immediacy and intensity. That is also why we always ask clients to identify and describe their own patterns of avoidance and the self-evaluations that accompany them. Though it may not appear to be so at first glance, we are proposing a treatment model in which the client controls the pace of therapeutic movement far more than the therapist. One of the primary responsibilities of the therapist is to keep the therapeutic process and content focused on highly relevant materials. Certainly a nudge here and there can be helpful to the client, but having clients identify and describe their patterns of avoidance during the therapy session is far more important than pushing them through these experiences. This is our way of helping clients recognize and respond to the anxiety associated with problem areas before these problems are the focus of therapy. We are basically describing a therapeutic process in which the therapist keeps clients focused on relevant material, and the rate at which clients move forward is determined by their own progress with each therapeutic task. We suggest, then, that the therapist interventions we are proposing are no more intrusive than those of most other treatment techniques. They are more relevant and incisive, and that is why it is important to allow clients a great deal of latitude in the rate at which they move through the developmental tasks in this model.

**Emotional considerations.** We cannot help wondering if some of the concern expressed about client discomfort is not partially an expression of therapist discomfort as well. Certainly in the treatment format we are describing, emotions can be intense at times, and much of the conversation is both relevant and consequential. These are not conditions commonly associated with fun and relaxation; neither should they be. Certainly, some of the emotionally intense, and cognitively poignant, therapy sessions we have already described are not the place for a therapist who has many unresolved emotional issues that need to be kept under control. In our view, a good therapist is one who has a reasonably high tolerance for the emotional distress of others without becoming overly protective or nurturing.

In our view, one of the most important underlying principles in effective psychotherapy is never to do something for clients that they can do for themselves. Equally important is remembering that the therapist's emotional comfort and stability when a client reports emotional confusion can be a source of immense reassurance to the client. Probably one of the most unfortunate events that can take place in therapy is for a client to try to protect the therapist from emotional discomfort by not talking about the emotionally laden issues that are most in need of therapeutic discussion. Regrettably, our experience as clinical supervisors suggests this happens more than most of us would guess.

In brief, we are asking therapists to be sure they can tolerate the emotional discomfort of their clients reasonably well before they make any attempt to protect them from the distress that is frequently a consequence of a radically improved awareness of their own self-defeating behavior patterns. Though most therapists abhor client suffering just as we do, the intensely negative feelings that are a result of more accurate client perceptions are an important source of motivation for the client to change. Furthermore, realistically facing these negative feelings can become an immediate and primary coping response that generates high levels of client self-approval, which can more than offset the distress of facing problems that are usually avoided.

**Therapeutic progress.** If low self-esteem is a major consideration in the development of dysfunctional behavior, as we believe it is, and if human development is based on the development of progressively higher levels of personal self-esteem, then client improvement is a multidimensional phenomenon based on the following assumptions:

1. Disrupting chronic or pervasive patterns of avoidance must generally precede any serious attempt to enhance the development of the personality. The very act of successfully controlling patterns of avoidance is a major therapeutic achievement and constitutes a basic remedial improvement in the structure of the personality.

2. Developmental progress is most readily assessed by observing the relationship among (a) internally directed behavior patterns, (b) levels of appropriate risk taking, (c) improved human functioning, and (d) improved feelings of self-worth and personal approval.

The interrelationships among these variables are sequentially summarized as:

a. Internally directed behavior is necessary for responsible risk taking. The appearance of appropriate psychological risk taking is one of the first developmental signs of client improvement.

b. Responsible risk taking is a necessary condition to correct patterns of self-defeating behavior.

c. The sense of self-efficacy that generally accompanies correcting self-defeating behavior is intrinsically rewarding and enhances self-esteem. This is the second developmental sign of client improvement.

d. A secure sense of self-esteem is the underlying basis for self-directing behavior.

e. Responsible risk taking can be initially promoted in the therapeutic relationship even when it has been totally absent in the client's prior psychological experiences.

The circular relationships among these variables are portrayed in Figure 2.

## Figure 2

*The Development and Maintenance of High or Low Levels of Self-Esteem*

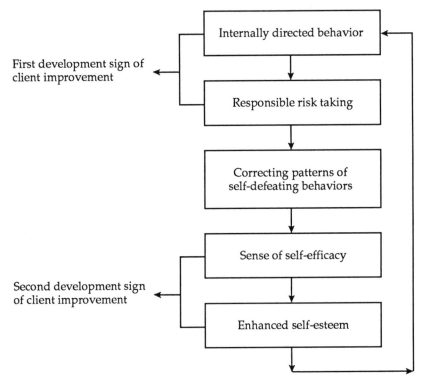

*Note.* The level of personal self-esteem influences the degree to which life events can be stressful. This in turn affects the personal response that is most likely to appear. If coping prevails, the individual faces problems honestly, realistically, and nondefensively. This produces favorable self-evaluative thoughts, which provide the self-generated approval that raises self-esteem, and so forth. The converse is true if low self-esteem, high personal stress, and a defensive response style prevail. Unfavorable self-evaluations trigger denial, deception, and avoidance in an attempt to disavow that which has already been glimpsed to be true. This process provides self-generated disapproval as a form of feedback to the self about personal inadequacy.

Inspection of the figure reveals that each of these variables can sequentially enrich the other variables in a continuous cycle that gradually leads to progressively higher levels of appropriate client risk taking, personal responsibility, internally directed behavior, and improved levels of self-esteem. The psychologically healthy individual is one who has a sufficient amount of self-esteem to support internally directed behavior. These people are aware of, but not entirely controlled by, the demands, pressures, and constraints of their social environments. As a result, they can take appropriate psychological risks (both interpersonal and intrapsychic), which provides them with a continuous source of learning about themselves and their social relationships. The willingness to engage in responsible risk taking enables them to correct self-defeating behavior when it does occur, which in turn demonstrates self-efficacy and improves self-esteem.

One of the major goals of psychological treatment is for the therapist to help the client initiate this process of personal growth if it is not operative or to enhance its effectiveness if it is only partially operative. We ask the reader to note that we are not attempting to discuss client improvement in more generic terms. We are restricting our comments to the evaluation of self-esteem and its antecedents, which are the focal considerations of the model we are discussing.

## Summary

We started this chapter by differentiating remedial and developmental considerations in the therapeutic process. The major therapeutic task in a developmental framework is increasing the client's understanding and ability to realistically and forthrightly face personal conflict. We suggested that the more adequate the adjustment of the client, the less time and attention remedial considerations should require. We also indicated that it makes little sense to seriously attempt facilitating personality development until deeply ingrained patterns of avoidance are at least exposed and their debilitating influence at least partially immobilized.

Even though the distinction between remedial and developmental considerations may be less obvious than we might hope for, we suggest that successful psychotherapy is likely to consist of a series of balanced transitions between remedial and developmental considerations. That is why we devoted a substantial amount of space to discussing how a therapist can assess a client's disposition to cope or avoid during the therapy session. Judgments about a client's disposition to cope or avoid at any given moment are the basis for a therapist's choosing between remedial and developmental therapeutic work. Our view is that a therapist's choice to focus on remedial or developmental considerations is one of the most important choice points in the entire therapy process.

We discussed the therapeutic means of actually creating a coping response by the client during the therapy hour. This was proposed as one of the most reliable means of experientially teaching clients about the elements and consequences of this more mature psychological behavior. This was followed by a discussion of how to strengthen the disposition to cope in clients who are not the victims of chronic and pervasive long-standing patterns of avoidance. Creating new coping responses or strengthening existing dispositions to cope was considered essential to a developmental approach to psychotherapy. This is the means by which clients can experientially identify and describe the elements most central to their own coping responses, and the self-evaluative thoughts and feelings that accompany them.

# 8

# Unique Qualities
# of the Therapeutic Relationship

## Types of Therapeutic Relationships

There can be little doubt that the quality of the client–therapist relationship is a primary component of the therapeutic process. Its importance seems to be universally understood and accepted among all therapeutic orientations (Orlinsky & Howard, 1986). Although some radical behavior therapists argue that the therapeutic relationship is an irrelevant consideration in client improvement, most orientations consider it to be at least a prerequisite to positive change and possibly a primary curative factor in and of itself (Frank, 1973; Prochaska, 1984).

There are serious differences of opinion about the most essential ingredients of a healthy therapeutic relationship. Discussions about helping relationships regularly include such diverse qualities as the carefully calculated neutrality of the analyst (Greenson, 1967) to the transparent involvement and authenticity of the humanistic and existential approaches (Rogers, 1957). In spite of this diversity, any discussion of the therapeutic relationship cannot lose sight of the complexity of this phenomenon or its centrality in the therapeutic process. In our discussion, we will emphasize what we consider to be the two cardinal considerations in any therapeutic relationship. The first is the relationship characteristics that are essential to the treatment model we have proposed. The second is the role these attributes are assumed to play in the therapy process.

Before discussing these two considerations in detail, however, we will outline some of the most important dimensions along which therapeutic relationships regularly differ. It will quickly become obvious that what one considers a good therapeutic relationship is usually an extension of other, more basic views such as (1) the underlying causes of disordered behavior, (2) the nature of human beings and their potential for perfectibility, (3) the optimal conditions for human growth and development, (4) the degree to which humans are considered to be unique creatures or simply another of nature's creations bound by natural laws, and (5) the practitioner's guiding theory of psychotherapy and the treatment techniques it emphasizes.

We have selected five bipolar dimensions[1] that seem to represent the major views and values out of which different types of therapeutic relationships grow in the mental health professions. As you might expect, there are serious and substantive disagreements about the relative merits of each of these dimensions as well as what the optimal mixture of ingredients might be for an ideal therapeutic relationship. These disagreements make it both interesting and useful to note the similarities and differences among the types of therapeutic relationships that can be created.

Of course, we understand that the descriptive dimensions we are proposing are not exhaustive; neither are they mutually exclusive of each other. In some cases, they may not even be applicable to all systems of psychotherapy. We consider them to be useful descriptive tools that can help clarify some of the important ways in which therapeutic relationships can differ. The five dimensions include (a) therapist involvement—high to low, (b) therapist time orientation—past or present, (c) therapist role—teacher or facilitator, (d) emphasis on client content or personality style, and (e) individual autonomy—high to low.

## Therapist Involvement

One of the most obvious ways in which therapeutic relationships differ is the degree to which therapists retain a detached neutrality

---

[1] Much of the material included in this section was developed by Dr. Richard L. Bednar and Dr. Theodore J. Kaul in an unpublished manuscript entitled "Group Psychotherapy: A Comparative Review and Analysis."

in their dealings with clients or become personally involved and allow their own primary thoughts and feelings to become part of the therapeutic process. The end points of this continuum can be represented by the later views of Carl Rogers (1980), when he was emphasizing the importance of experiencing and encountering clients, and the early writings of Freud (1912/1957), in which the therapist's carefully calculated neutrality was essential if client projections and transference were to be complete and uninterpreted.

Therapists who remain technically neutral avoid direct personal involvement with their clients for a variety of reasons. It can be the means of avoiding countertransference problems, retaining the objectivity necessary for dispassionate diagnosis, or a recognition of the power and status ascribed to a therapist in any therapeutic relationship. These therapists may appear ambiguous, unapproachable, or even invulnerable to their clients. However, they assume this orientation as a consequence of some important beliefs about the origins of abnormality and its cure.

In contrast is the therapist who defines an ideal relationship as one in which both the client and the therapist are open, congruent, and authentic in their respective expressions of thoughts and feelings. These therapists are likely to deal directly with their clients and expect to be dealt with as individuals of equal worth and power in the therapy relationship. It would not be uncommon for these therapists to offer direct feedback, interpret the here-and-now, and be as open in their expression of negative reactions as positive ones. Some would even go so far as to suggest that the very process of encountering another individual in the here-and-now is the essence of the therapeutic process, though many would disagree with this view. These therapists tend to be anything but passive, and they do not view themselves as a mirror for improving client self-perceptions.

## Time Orientation: Past or Present

Therapists who assume that the past is the dominant determinant of psychological distress create a different type of therapeutic relationship from those who view the present as a microcosm representing all of the important psychological elements from the past.

These differences are apparent in most therapy sessions. They are reflected by the degree to which clients are systematically encouraged to experience and express psychological events as they occur, or recall and reconstruct them from the past. The level of cognitive or affective arousal closely parallels this continuum, with experiential learning in the here-and-now being associated with the highest levels of affective arousal.

The dominant tool of a therapeutic approach that emphasizes historical considerations is the interpretation of the meaning of present behavior in terms of historical conflicts. This mode of psychological activity is generally quite cognitive and takes place at relatively low levels of immediacy, intensity, and affective arousal. Of course, this is not always the case. High levels of emotional expression are common in moments of intense catharsis or accompanying particularly poignant insights. But these events are less common than continuous attempts to understand the present by acquiring more penetrating insight into the past. The ideal relationship for this type of psychological activity would appear to be one that is *calm, patient, stable, reassuring, analytical,* and *accepting.*

In contrast, therapists who emphasize the importance of the here-and-now tend to ignore historical interpretations of behavior. They recognize the existence of the past, of course, but they try to deal with it as it manifests itself in the present. When they interpret, they stress the immediacy and intensity of the experience in the moment. Because these therapists assume that historical conflicts can find full expression in the here-and-now, these conflicts need not be intellectually reconstructed to be understood; they can be reexperienced in their fullness and resolved in the present. Accordingly, these therapists work in an intense and volatile relationship because of the intensity that can accompany their evocative and, at times, provocative interventions, designed to bring the psychological traumas of the past right into the consulting room. Terms that could be used to describe this therapeutic relationship include *confrontational, probing,* and *experiential.*

## Therapist Role: Teacher or Facilitator

This is an interesting dimension because the two end points of this continuum represent two distinct philosophical orientations toward psychological treatment. Other terms have been used to describe this continuum. Two common ones are (1) structured versus unstructured, and (2) directive versus nondirective. No matter what terms are used to describe this continuum, however, the underlying dimension and its most fundamental attributes remain essentially unchanged. So do the relationship characteristics they breed.

One end of this continuum is represented by proponents who argue that treatment technologies exist. Because they exist, and because we have good evidence that they work, they should be used. Naturally, it is therapists who understand how to apply these technologies to the problems of their clients. According to this view, it is both efficient and responsible for therapists to plan the activities of their clients, much as teachers plan the learning activities of their pupils. They go into the therapy hour with the intention of creating situations designed to provide clients with the type of learning experiences that will maximize their growth. This point of view is most clearly represented by the behavioral and cognitive-behavioral approaches, in which clients are taught new patterns of thinking or behaving (Beck, Rush, Shaw, & Emery, 1979; Ellis, 1973). And while the relationship between the client and therapist during this process can be both warm and nurturing, few clients will fail to recognize or respond to therapists as the informed expert. Therapeutic relationships of this type tend to be *task centered, cordial, focused, hierarchical,* and *problem centered.*

Other approaches champion a more idiographic and democratic attitude toward their clients. Denouncing the role of the therapist as a teacher as too proscriptive and prescriptive, they argue that what is important is the uniqueness of the individual and each therapy hour. In this context, the therapist is a facilitator of experiential learning. What is valued is that clients increase their awareness of themselves and others and learn to present themselves more congruently. According to this view, this uniqueness cannot be elicited or commanded; it must be allowed to evolve and appear naturally. The most effective means of eliciting that uniqueness is to leave the therapy hour unstructured by having the therapist abandon the role of expert teacher and assist clients to express their most deeply felt needs and problems. With few exceptions, therapists of this persuasion see attempts to structure the therapy process as controlling and intrusive. This type of therapeutic relationship is usually described as *client centered, supportive, expressive, democratic, exploratory,* and *genuine.*

## Client Content or Personality Style

At first glance, this dimension may appear to represent a therapeutic focus factor rather than a relationship characteristic. In a sense, that is entirely true. But, as we have already noted, the way in which therapy is conducted virtually defines the therapeutic relationship. A therapist closely aligned with the content end of this continuum assumes that it is the literal content of the client's complaints that warrants the therapist's interventions. These therapists orient their treatment activities toward clarifying the meaning and consequences of the clients' concerns and then developing problem-solving strategies to alleviate them. These relationships are generally seen as *collaborative, cooperative, problem centered,* generally *more cognitive than affective,* and *reality bound.*

Those therapists who emphasize client styles, or patterns of behavior, assume that content is important only in its revelation of the client's enduring styles of functioning. Styles are presumed to be based on trait-like dispositions about which people may have limited awareness. These styles are generally considered to be deeply ingrained patterns that produce consistent and wide-ranging effects. Examples of some frequently discussed psychological styles include (a) approval seekers, (b) conflict avoiders, (c) noncompliers, (d) nurturers, and (e) pleasers and placaters. The therapist's primary task is to increase clients' understanding of the underlying psychological dispositions central to their recurring problems. Insight alone, however, is not enough. Therapists' efforts are also directed toward influencing clients' general style of behavior, though not necessarily any specific problem situation revealed by the client. These relationships usually have high levels of trust and warmth to support the depth of self-exploration involved. They also have relatively high levels of psychological immediacy and intensity because many of the clients' trait dispositions find expression during the therapeutic hour and become the grist for the therapeutic mill.

## Individual Autonomy: High to Low

The final relationship dimension we have elected to discuss is the role of individual autonomy in the therapeutic relationship. This continuum closely resembles that of the therapist as an expert teacher or facilitator of experiential learning, but it differs in several important respects and deserves additional comment in its own right.

Therapeutic relationships that are high on individual autonomy (for both the therapist and client) place a heavy emphasis on personal responsibility, individual accountability, personal freedom, and an absence of client caretaking. Client problems, no matter how serious, tend to be viewed by the therapist as opportunities for the clients to learn more about themselves. These therapists are not very inclined to do for the client what clients could do for themselves. Though therapists who create this kind of relationship can be warm, supportive, nurturing, and caring, they are more likely to require that clients explore the meaning and significance of their dependency, for example, than they are to provide the approval and reassurance these clients seem to need.

These relationships appear to have some of the same attributes associated with the concept of "tough love" (York, York, & Wachtel, 1982), which has emerged in recent years. Individuals are cared for, but in a context in which they are expected to exercise their individual freedom and assume the responsibilities that go with it. Of course, these therapists also expect the same thing of themselves and tend to avoid symbiotic involvements or dialogues with their clients.

Other therapeutic approaches minimize the client's sense of individual autonomy, at least in early sessions, as when the therapist assumes the responsibility for teaching the client new ways of thinking or behaving. Understanding that the client must learn techniques of behavior change, the therapist takes complete responsibility for directing the therapy process. Clients are literally dependent on the counsel and expertise of the therapist and must learn to be good students. It is important to notice that we are not suggesting that this type of dependence is bad or undesirable. In the restricted way we are using this term, all of us are dependent on the expertise of others as we learn throughout our life span.

This, of course, does not alter the fact that these relationships would still be rated low on individual autonomy.

**Summary.** In this section we have described some of the dimensions along which therapeutic relationships can differ. Even though these dimensions are not all-encompassing or mutually exclusive, each one provides different descriptive information about the ways in which therapeutic relationships can differ. These nine dimensions and their most important relationship characteristics are summarized below:

*1. Therapist involvement*—The degree to which the therapist's personal presence, thoughts, and feelings are part of the therapeutic process is measured on this dimension.

*2. Therapist neutrality*—The therapist is primarily reactive to client verbalizations and is a consistent, careful, and objective observer of the client and the therapeutic process.

*3. Historical orientation*—The meaning of present behavior tends to be interpreted in terms of historical, unresolved conflicts. Therapy sessions tend to be more cognitive than affective, with interpretation being a primary treatment technique.

*4. Here-and-now orientation*—Clients are encouraged to experience and express their feelings about psychological events as they occur. Therapy sessions tend to be more affective than cognitive, with experiential learning being a central consideration.

*5. Therapist as an expert teacher*—The therapist teaches clients new ways of thinking and behaving based on expert knowledge. The teaching process is relatively explicit rather than implicit in the orienting theory.

*6. Therapist as a facilitator*—These relationships tend to be client-centered, supportive, and democratic as a means of increasing client sensitivity to self and others and more congruent expressions of the authentic self.

*7. Client content*—The literal content of client complaints becomes a central consideration in the therapy process. The therapist tries to help clarify and interpret the meaning and significance of the client's concerns, and then explores the means for solving these problems in a collaborative, cooperative, problem-solving relationship.

*8. Client personality style*—High levels of trust and support are required to sustain the depth of self-exploration required for

## Table 2

*Descriptive Characteristics of Four Therapy Orientations*

| Dimension | Psycho-dynamic | Humanistic-existential | Strict behaviorist | Cognitive-behavioral |
|---|---|---|---|---|
| Personal involvement | L | H | L | L |
| Therapist neutrality | H | L | H | H |
| Historical orientation | H | L | L | L |
| Here-and-now orientation | L | H | L | M |
| Expert teacher | M | L | H | H |
| Experiential learning | M | H | L | M |
| Content-centered | L | L | H | H |
| Personality styles | M | M | L | L |
| Individual autonomy | L | H | L | L |

*Note.* H = high, M = moderate, L = low.

clients to obtain a greater understanding of their underlying trait-like disposition, which seems to be the cause of a variety of their recurring psychological problems.

*9. Individual autonomy*—High levels of individual autonomy are most apparent in relationships in which individuals can be cared for, but are still expected to exercise their individual will and accept the responsibility of making their needs known and finding acceptable ways to satisfy these needs.

Inspection of Table 2 reveals that a variety of different therapeutic relationships can be described with reasonable accuracy using these dimensions.

Even though there may be some disagreement about the way we have applied these descriptors to the treatment systems in Table 2, there can be little doubt that therapeutic relationships do differ based on the philosophical underpinnings of the orienting theory. Also, notice that these relationship dimensions tend to cluster in patterns or profiles. For example, high ratings on the therapist-as-expert-teacher category appear to be systematically related to other categories such as therapist neutrality, involvement, and autonomy. Similarly, high ratings on therapist involvement seem to vary with other categories such as facilitator, experiential learning, and time orientation. This interdependence should not be surprising, however. Most new therapy orientations are created as a reaction to the deficiencies in existing treatment approaches, and new theories tend to emphasize new and opposite elements. The development of behaviorism, for example, was a reaction at least in part to the psychoanalytic influence of the time. And, over the years, each changing philosophy has added new dimensions to what can be considered a therapeutic relationship.

## Relationship Characteristics

In this section, we will describe what we consider the optimal combination of relationship characteristics to be for the therapeutic relationship we are proposing. To illustrate the type and level of these relationship attributes, we will use the clinical example we first used to illustrate the major elements in our model. This was the example in which a young housewife chronically tried to avoid rejection and gain acceptance by suppressing her own needs and meticulously attending to the wishes of others. She originally came to therapy complaining of fatigue, but the definition of her problem was altered dramatically in her first session as her therapist had her focus on her style of gaining approval.

We will reproduce this session in its entirety to illustrate each of the relationship dimensions we will be discussing. Brief explanatory notes have also been inserted in the text to help clarify important relationship considerations in this session. All of this material is intended to help illustrate and clarify the role and function of the relationship characteristics we will be discussing right after this clinical case illustration.

## Introduction and Rapport-Building

Therapist:   Tell me, what led you to schedule a meeting for today?

Client:   Well, I think that I'm just feeling so worn out and run down and—you know, just physically and emotionally washed out.

Therapist:   Please tell me more.

Client:   Well, maybe if I talk a little about last week, I could describe what my life is like and why I'm feeling this way.

Therapist:   Okay.

Client:   Well, let's see, as I look back on last week I see myself wrapped up and so busy with the kids. It's just one thing after another. If it isn't sports, then it's plays and all these extracurricular things that they're in. And I feel like I need to be there to support them. It's just constant, just a steady kind of thing.

Therapist:   So, as you see it, your fatigue is the result of the overwhelming amount of activity in your life?

Client:   Yes, probably so.

Therapist:   Why do you keep it up?

Client:   Well, I think it's important for the kids to see that I support them in the things they do. I want to be a supportive person. If I love them, those are the kinds of things I should be willing to do for them. When I do, I think they feel better, and it makes them feel better about our relationship together.

Therapist:   It sounds like you take your parental responsibilities very seriously.

Client:   Maybe so, but I feel like sometimes I could just scream.

Therapist:   A little angry there, huh?

Client:   No! I'm not angry. It's just that I can't do any more, but I can't say that to them when I know they want me to be there. When it's important to them, I just feel like I really need to go ahead and do it anyway.

Therapist:   Why?

Client:   I'm sure they would be disappointed. They might think I wasn't interested in them or I didn't care what they did. It's easy to say you care, but I think it's important to do more than just say it—you have

>to show it by the way you act. You know, you have
>to have your behavior match your words.

The form and substance of this dialogue was essentially un-changed for another 15 minutes. The client repeatedly empha-sized the "moral" and "socially desirable" reasons for her meticu-lous adherence to her parental role and responsibilities. She was not inclined to acknowledge that her behavior was motivated by a need for approval from her children or a fear of their rejection. Neither did she seem the least bit interested in exploring her "style" of developing and maintaining relationships within the family or acknowledging any anger or resentment toward those who seemed to have so much control over her life.

As quickly as the therapist judged that the client felt understood enough to tolerate a moderate level of dissonance without becom-ing too defensive, the focus of the interview was changed so that it became more exploratory and incisive.

## Identifying Patterns of Avoidance and Self-Evaluative Thoughts and Feelings

Therapist:   Let me see if I can summarize what seems to be both-ering you the most. You find yourself in a rather difficult situation. On the one hand, you feel a strong need to be supportive and involved in your chil-dren's lives as a way of building a strong relation-ship. On the other hand, you're tired, you want more time to yourself, and you may even resent oth-ers' controlling your life so much. The essential con-flict is between what you think you should do for others and what you want to do for yourself. Does that sound like a fair summary of what's bothering you?

The therapist has now taken the role of expert teacher and will begin to shape the session in such a way that the client can be-come aware of her self-defeating style. Notice how the succession of questions leads the client to more and more specific descrip-tions of her behavior and the purpose it serves. Despite client con-tent concerning her physical symptoms, the discussion is centered around her personality style.

Client:      Yeah, I haven't thought of it that way before, but that sounds about right.

Therapist:   What precisely is it you usually do when other people want you to do something you're not really interested in doing?

Client:      What do you mean?

Therapist:   I mean what precisely is it that you usually do when other people want you to do something you're not really interested in doing?

Client:      [Long pause.] I usually do what other people want. I notice that other people do the same thing, though. [Note the defensiveness.]

Therapist:   It sounds like it's hard for you to say no to people.

Client:      It is! When people ask me to do things, I really feel like I should do it for them. But after I say yes, I'm so tight inside. How do you say no to those kinds of things?

Therapist:   What makes it so hard for you?

Client:      I think it's important to have pleasant relationships. You can't say no to people all the time and expect them to like you.

Therapist:   Let's see if we can get an accurate description of what you tend to do in situations where your desires are in conflict with the wishes of others.

Client:      I try to be cooperative and giving, to do my part in relationships even when it's inconvenient. That's my way of trying to be a good friend, or spouse, or mother.

Therapist:   You think of these as very desirable traits, is that right?

Client:      That's right.


The session is now at its first critical juncture. The therapist sees the client's behavior as conflict-avoidant and approval-seeking. The client is describing the same behavior as responsible and desirable. Attempts by the therapist to have the client identify anything negative or avoidant in her behavior patterns have been unsuccessful. The therapist now changes the focus of the interview to the client's actual behavior in the therapy session because it is less abstract, more immediate, and more revealing.

| | |
|---|---|
| Therapist: | What you seem to be saying is that your style of dealing with conflict is to keep things pleasant by doing what others want and expect from you. |
| Client: | Well, yes. Maybe it is. |
| Therapist: | Maybe it is? |
| Client: | Otherwise, I guess I wouldn't have such a hard time saying no. People ask me to do things and I really feel like I should do it for them, but after I say yes, I wish I'd said NO! |
| Therapist: | Are you saying that you give in all the time so people will like and value you? |
| Client: | I have to think about that. I imagine it could be. It's important, I think, to have a pleasantness in relationships. |
| Therapist: | I would like you to determine if this is your way of avoiding unpleasantness and getting people to like you. |
| Client: | I guess that could be true. |
| Therapist: | Tell me about the ways it could be true. |
| Client: | These are hard questions. No one likes to think that they are nice to people just so they will be liked. |
| Therapist: | I agree, they really are hard questions. [Therapist involvement through support.] |
| Client: | Yes, they are. Probably because they are hitting home with me. |
| Therapist: | How does that feel? |
| Client: | Not very good. I didn't realize I was doing that. But I hate people to be disappointed in me. I feel like they can't count on me, that I'm not willing to do things for them. I always thought it was worth the price that I guess I pay to do that. But now I'm not so sure. |
| Therapist: | This way of thinking is kind of new to you? |
| Client: | Yes. |
| Therapist: | Let's try something. What you seem to be saying is that your style for avoiding conflict and gaining approval from others is by doing for others what pleases them the most. At least that's what we're considering so far. Does that sound about right? |
| Client: | Well, yes. I guess I feel like I do that. |
| Therapist: | Do you do that with me as well? |
| Client: | Well, it's important to me, as a client, that you like me. |

With this intervention, the therapist has become intensely involved in the therapeutic process in the here-and-now. The following interventions highlight the here-and-now experiential learning nature of the treatment.

| | |
|---|---|
| Therapist: | Please try to describe as accurately as you can how you go about making sure that I will like you. |
| Client: | I guess by cooperating with you and trying to do and say what you want me to. |
| Therapist: | So that's what you're doing right now? I ask you these questions and you answer them even though they're unsettling because that's what you think you have to do so I will like you? |
| Client: | Yes. It's really been hard for me to do, but I thought it was important to do that. |
| Therapist: | But it's for me you're doing it? |
| Client: | Yes, I think probably so because I know I trust you a lot, but I feel like maybe if I didn't you wouldn't like me, and maybe. . . . |
| Therapist: | So, in a sense, you're playing a role or pretending with me right now? |
| Client: | I guess so. |
| Therapist: | Do you have a word or a way of describing the way you treat me so I will like you? Do you know what I mean by that? |
| Client: | The way I behave so you'll like me? |
| Therapist: | Yes, can you think of a word to summarize the style or pattern of behavior you use to try and make sure I will like you? |
| Client: | Trying to be positive, pleasant, cooperative. . . . |

The client has now started to describe one of her styles for gaining approval from others with a reasonable degree of accuracy, but she continues to cast it in a favorable light by using terms such as cooperative, pleasant, and positive. These terms accurately reflect her overt behavior, but they completely miss the underlying motives that sustain the behavior. These might include fear of rejection or loss of approval. The psychological consequences of her overly compliant interpersonal style are both obvious and consequential. And they are certainly not limited to the fatigue the client described in her initial complaint. They extend into such fundamental areas as (a) a limited sense of personal identity, (b) inability to regulate, balance, or resolve conflict, and (c) a life filled with frustration, guilt, and unhappiness. Because she is a relatively strong woman, the therapist decides to take a more active part in the labeling process to accelerate the movement of the therapy session and to increase the accuracy of the labels attached to the underlying motives of her behavior.

Therapist:    How about "selling yourself out"? [Therapist involvement through nonneutrality.]

Client:    That sounds horrible. [Long, thoughtful pause.] I guess maybe so. I don't really say how I feel inside while I'm doing things for others, and I do feel real tight inside. And, you know, when I say yes to people, that's when the tightness starts.

Therapist:    Are the terms "selling yourself out" or "buying approval" accurate descriptions? Is that what we want to call it?

Notice how the therapist explicitly maintains client autonomy throughout this next section by always asking the client to improve or validate the descriptors used to describe her style.

Client:    Those are harsh words.

Therapist:    Yes, they are both harsh and unflattering, but are they accurate? It is important for you to try and describe your style accurately so we can understand what you do and why. [Therapist involvement through support.]

Client:    I guess I see myself pretty much as a "yes" person. It's important that I do that for other people so that I won't disappoint them, so that we'll have a good relationship, so they won't know how I really feel inside. I hide that a lot.

Therapist:    When I ask you to describe something, you describe it, then explain and justify it. You don't really need

THE THERAPEUTIC RELATIONSHIP    237

|            |                                                                                                                    |
|------------|--------------------------------------------------------------------------------------------------------------------|
|            | to justify it here. Let's just get a clear understanding of what it is you're doing.                                |
| Client:    | I guess when it gets down to the bottom line, maybe I'm just trying to be somebody I'm not.                         |
| Therapist: | Okay, and you do that by saying yes when you don't mean it?                                                         |
| Client:    | Yeah, I do that a lot.                                                                                              |
| Therapist: | Is there anything you want in return for being so nice to people?                                                   |
| Client:    | I want them to think I'm a good friend. I want my husband to think I'm a good wife. I want my children to think I'm a good mother. |
| Therapist: | I understand. Basically, then, you are trying to gain the approval and acceptance of others by being what they want you to be. |
| Client:    | I guess so.                                                                                                         |
| Therapist: | Is that too harsh? [Therapist maintains client autonomy.]                                                           |
| Client:    | I don't think I really realized that's what I was doing. It's kind of a hard thing to face.                         |
| Therapist: | It really is hard, isn't it? [Support and involvement.]                                                             |
| Client:    | I think so.                                                                                                         |
| Therapist: | So summarize all that we've said that describes how you are at relating to people. Let's see if we can get to a description that seems accurate to you even though it may be harsh. |
| Client:    | I guess I basically hide myself and that I try to be something I'm not by doing what I think other people would like me to do. |
| Therapist: | And that description seems accurate to you? [Note again the emphasis on client autonomy.]                           |
| Client:    | I hear myself say it. I—yes, I think so.                                                                           |

The client has a reasonably clear description of her behavior, which she seems at least partially willing to own. The next step is to start identifying the self-evaluative thoughts and feelings that accompany this behavior. This is frequently the point at which a great deal of the client's emotion comes to the surface, so the therapist proceeds with caution because it is late in the therapy hour.

|            |                                                                                 |
|------------|---------------------------------------------------------------------------------|
| Therapist: | We need to go a step further with this, and this is going to be harder than what we just did. Should |

|              | we wait for another session or should we start now? [Again, the explicit expectation of client autonomy and decision making.] |
| Client:      | Oh, let's give it a try. |
| Therapist:   | Are you sure? It's going to be harder than what we just did. |
| Client:      | I'll try. |
| Therapist:   | Okay, you have a description of yourself, and at least tentatively it seems accurate to you. Now I want you to tell me how you feel about yourself because you're that way. |
| Client:      | [Long pause, eyes begin to moisten.] I'm disappointed. I'm frustrated because I really would like to be able to say all these things I want to say and still have people not run away from me or push me away because I say how I feel. I'd like to know how to do that. |
| Therapist:   | Know how to do what? |
| Client:      | Be my own person! |
| Therapist:   | You mean you want to stop pretending so much? |
| Client:      | Yeah, that's a good way to put it. |
| Therapist:   | How else do you feel about yourself for pretending so much? |
| Client:      | I can't say that I think a whole lot of myself. Sounds kind of like a game. It's a game because I'm trying to fool people so they will like me. It's really disgusting. How can they even like me if they don't know me? |
| Therapist:   | And maybe you fooled yourself as well? |
| Client:      | I guess I did. |

## Strengthening the Coping Response

This session is now to the point that it is *absolutely crucial* that the therapist recognize that the very act of clearly identifying and labeling one's own avoidance patterns and the self-evaluative thoughts and feelings that accompany them is a primary coping response. It is essential that the therapeutic benefits of this response be realized in the session in which it occurs. This is accomplished by having the client identify and describe this adaptive response and the feeling that accompanies it.

| Therapist:   | You don't seem to be fooling yourself right now. How does that feel to you? |

The therapist has now shifted from describing the client's avoidance to describing the client's coping in the session. Notice how the method of learning still emphasizes here-and-now experiential learning, with the expert teacher helping the client to see the immediate change in her typical style of behaving.

Client:    Feels kind of good.

Therapist:    Really?

Client:    [Tears are now streaming down her cheeks.] Yeah!

Therapist:    Even though it hurts that badly?

Client:    Yeah.

Therapist:    What do the tears mean?

Client:    Well, I'm kind of happy that I know this now. I'm hurting, but I think I feel better now that I can say these things to you. I feel better about myself, because you're still sitting here and I don't feel like you hate me for what I've said or you're going to push me away. That feels good.

Therapist:    What exactly have you done in this situation that has allowed you to approve of yourself more than usual?

Client:    For the first time in a long time, I've been honest with myself and another person about how I really feel.

Therapist:    Are you saying that not being honest with yourself and others is the real problem you came here about?

Client:    I think so. I didn't know it when I first came in, but I think that has been a big problem for me.

Therapist:    An interesting thing has happened here today. You have described yourself as a "yes" person, as someone who hides herself from everybody. Then we had what has to be considered a hard conversation, where you presented yourself to me as you really are, and somehow we ended up with you feeling much better than when you walked in the door. Does that make any sense to you?

Client:    Yes, just knowing the truth, I guess. Besides, the problem seems more soluble now.

Therapist:    Our time is up now, but before we end I would like you to summarize what you learned about yourself today.

Client:    I need to learn how to say how I feel more. When I feel like saying no, I need to be able to say that, and to tell my kids that I'm just being worn too thin and that even though I'd like to be there, I just can't do everything. And sometimes I will just tell them I still love and support them.

Therapist: So you're really talking about being more honest with yourself and others about your feelings?

Client: Yeah.

Therapist: And how do you feel about the prospect of going through a whole week without buying approval from others by being a servant to them?

Client: Well, if it makes me feel like I do now, I think that would be very important.

Therapist: Our time is just about up, but what we've done today would be worth thinking about and going over next week.

Client: Good, I'll try and see what I can do this week.

## Therapist Involvement

Therapist involvement can take many different forms. It can vary from session to session, or minute by minute, within a session. Its manifestations can be subtle or obvious, as can be its effects. But high involvement generally involves unambiguous personal expression by the therapist, and at least minimal levels of congruence between important therapist feelings and behavior. This is not to say that this is all therapists do, or that they even do it a lot. Rather, on selected occasions therapists are willing to make some of their feelings and values known to the client. Expressions of personal support and encouragement for the client are probably the most common form but not necessarily the most important. Openly challenging and confronting clients with their incongruities is an expression of involvement in which therapist observations directly influence the course of therapy. No matter what specific form the therapist's involvement takes, its cardinal feature is always the same—the introduction of the therapist's views in such a way that the client can react to them. And in this process, the therapist generally becomes a less ambiguous person to the client.

There are two noteworthy observations about therapist involvement in our case illustration. First, the therapist's observations and thoughts about the client's behavior plays an obvious and influential role in the therapy process. There is very little about the therapist's comments that is neutral or reactive. The therapist is far more proactive and provocative than neutral. The most obvious example takes place as the client describes her behavior. The client's description was socially appropriate and emphasized terms such as cooperative, pleasant, and positive. The therapist suggested another label (selling yourself out), which was psychologically more relevant and designed to capture the avoidant nature of her behavior. This new label represented a dramatic shift in the explicit and implied meaning of her behavior that could hardly be ignored. It was a form of confrontation, dissonance induction, and reality testing in one sentence. And the increased level of client distress that followed this comment suggests the value and validity of the new label. The client's tears, depth of self-exploration, and self-disclosure all increased after this comment. So did the value of the therapy session.

But it is important to notice the timing and style of this confrontation. The confrontation itself was delivered as a question, not a statement. It was a nonhostile, matter-of-fact invitation to consider an alternative. Implicitly, such statements demean the value of the client's socially appropriate and conventional behavior. Explicitly, they suggest the value of candor and realism, even when it is painful. But once the confrontation was delivered, the client was asked if the label was too harsh, which, of course, creates the opportunity to modify or disown it. The value of these confrontations resides in their ultimate validity and usefulness to the client, not the persuasive power of the therapist. They are occasions in which therapists openly share their perceptions and then create opportunities for clients to examine them to determine their value and accuracy.

But our second point is equally important. What about the client's level of comfort or distress during this process? Lieberman, Yalom, and Miles (1973) made it quite clear that the charismatic therapist can be quite dangerous, at least in group work. Their data indicated that therapists who were overly provocative, confronting, or demanding were associated with the highest frequency of client casualties. We believe that the essential dynamics of this process (overwhelming the client) are equally applicable and destructive in individual therapy. That is why it is absolutely essential that therapist involvement also convey a high level of support, encouragement, patience, humanness, and commitment to the client. The therapist's most benevolent motives are critical here, and they must be clearly perceived and understood by the client. They must also be authentic. Our assumption is that even the most revealing information, interpretations, or confrontations can be helpful as long as the therapist is perceived as offering them for the benefit of the client. In this particular example we have a limited but relevant number of examples of therapist support. Notice the frequency of statements such as (a) "Are you ready to go further now, or should we wait until the next session?" (b) "Yes, these are really hard questions," (c) "Is that too harsh?" and (d) "Does that description sound accurate to you?"

We want the humanness of the therapist to show for other reasons as well. In our view, it is easier for a client to have a meaningful relationship with a therapist who is comfortable showing his or her human qualities some of the time. We see nothing wrong with it if the client and therapist exchange an occasional joke or the therapist self-discloses a bit about a bad day. These brief retreats from the core business of therapy are enlightening to the client. They personalize the therapist and make it easier for the client to feel comfortable in the relationship. Sometimes it makes the relationship more comfortable for the therapist as well.

**Summary.** A high level of therapist involvement has two major components and purposes in our view. First, it is a personal tool for relationship development. It allows the therapist to be seen, at least partially, for the type of person he or she is. It brings an element of informality, casualness, and humanness to the relationship. This can improve the basic nature of the relationship, which can be developed by increasing candor, trust, psychological risk taking, and interpersonal comfort.

And second, it is the quality of the therapeutic relationship that allows the therapist to productively introduce the client to levels of psychological dissonance that would normally be intolerable and unproductive. Highly dissonant materials cannot profitably be introduced into the therapy process by a therapist whose personal qualities are essentially unknown and whose response to intense client distress is uncertain. High levels of therapist involvement are essential for those times the therapist's interpretations, confrontations, or opinions are offered as a means of inducing high levels of client dissonance or "unfreezing."

## Time Orientation: Past or Present

It is probably obvious to the reader by now that we consider the most potent treatment interventions to be those that take place in the psychological present, or the here-and-now. Naturally, we have no rule against discussing historical events with clients; these are excellent opportunities for rapport-building. They also provide the therapist with valuable information that can help clarify the origins of the client's current patterns of thinking and behaving. But when it is time for the serious business of therapy to begin, we offer the following guidelines for the therapeutic use of the here-and-now for your consideration:

1. The units of analysis involved in our model are rather complex. As you recall, they are deeply ingrained patterns of behavior that are assumed to transcend time, place, and circumstances. They also involve cognition, emotion, and behavior. Because of this, we have suggested that when a client is continually encouraged to experience and express thoughts and feelings as they occur, sooner or later these enduring patterns of behavior are certain to make their appearance in the therapy.

2. Once these patterns of behavior emerge in the therapy session, the astute therapist can have the client (a) describe them in their completeness as they occur, (b) identify the psychological function the behavior patterns were serving when they first appeared in the therapy session, (c) attach summary labels to the patterns of behavior, and (d) inquire about the self-evaluative thoughts and feelings that accompany these behavior patterns. Our belief is that this entire process takes place at high levels of precision, clarity, and intensity when the behavior in question is taking place in the therapy room rather than simply being recalled from past events.

3. We have also suggested that human thoughts, feelings, and behavior are best considered as integrated rather than separate systems. Each of these components (thoughts, feelings, and behavior) affects, and is affected by, every other component in a

continuous cycle of reciprocal influence. While we have no guiding theory to lead us through this complex maze of interacting human elements, we still consider it important to try to deal with them (cognitions, feelings, and behavior) as though they were interrelated systems. This is a difficult task, but one that is simplified when the client's behavior in the consulting room is the topic of the therapy session. Asking clients to clearly observe and describe their behavior patterns as they occur (behavioral focus), label the meaning and function of the behavior (cognitive activity), and then identify and experience the self-evaluative thoughts and feelings that accompany that behavior (affective experiential activity) is an important step in responding to client behavior as a unified system. The alternative, of course, is to continue developing treatment approaches that emphasize primarily one of the three: behavior, thoughts, or feelings.

If we return to the example of the young housewife, we find another useful illustration of bringing client issues into the here-and-now. A critical phase of this interview occured as the therapist helped the client describe her style of avoiding rejection (being a pleaser and placater of others), and the self-evaluative thoughts and feelings accompanying that pattern of behavior (self-recrimination and embarrassment). To help the client deal with this problem once it had been made explicit, the therapist asked the client if she were also trying to please him in the same way during the therapy session. In this segment, the therapist asked her how she tried to gain his approval, and more importantly, how she felt about herself for pretending during her therapy hour. This intervention was pivotal in the process of diminishing this client's inclination to be a pleaser and placater in the therapy sessions. It also created the opportunity, and an implicit demand, for the client to be more honest in her self-presentation and to experience the benefits of a more authentic self-presentation. All of this took place at high levels of cognitive, emotional, and behavioral immediacy and intensity because the topic of discussion during the therapy hour was the psychological events taking place in the consulting room.

**Summary.** We suggest three important points from this example. First, clients do have a tendency to bring their enduring patterns of behavior into the therapy room with them. This is hardly a startling revelation to most of us. Second, these patterns of behavior can become the primary grist for the therapeutic mill. They can be identified, labeled, and experienced in the fullness in the consulting room. And at the precise moment the client becomes the most disheartened, the therapist can ask how the client needs to act in the relationship *right now* to be the type of person he or she has always wanted to be. These new behaviors can also be identified, labeled, and experienced by the client to enhance learning. And third, cognitions, affect, and behavior are all the focus of therapy during this process. It is our assumption that the more psychological domains are involved in the change process, the more durable the changes will be. And, finally, the relationship between the client and therapist provides a format for all of these events in the here-and-now that can facilitate learning at three levels simultaneously (cognitive, affective, and behavioral). We suggest this will result in therapeutic outcomes in which people understand more, feel better, and act differently.

## Therapist Role: Teacher or Facilitator

We have a bit of a problem here. On each of the relationship dimensions we have already discussed, we have consistently suggested the merits of one side of each relationship characteristic over its opposite. We have opted for high involvement and low neutrality, and more emphasis on the here-and-now compared to the there-and-then. However, on this relationship dimension we are going to straddle a fine line. We will suggest that the therapist is both an expert teacher and a facilitator of experiential learning. Our discussion will strive to clarify the fundamental differences between these two roles and the conditions under which each is called for. This is a therapeutic relationship that attempts to preserve the role of the therapist as an expert teacher, but what the client understands is more experiential than cognitive, and what the client learns is more personal than universal.

**Therapeutic process.** When we talk about the therapist as an expert teacher, we are referring to someone who understands the general principles of self-approving behavior and teaches them to the client. In our mechanistic model, the treatment format is an expression of general conceptual principles that are applied in such a way that the client ultimately acquires a clear understanding of them. This is accomplished by having clients clearly identify and describe their patters of coping and avoidance and the self-evaluative thoughts and feelings that accompany them. As a result of this process, clients can be expected to learn such generalizable statements as (1) "My personal approval depends a great deal on how I react to situations I have a tendency to fear," (2) "Realistically coping with situations I have had a tendency to avoid adds to my perception of myself as capable, strong, and brave," (3) "Avoiding difficult situations adds to my perception of myself as weak, inadequate, and spineless," (4) "Realistically and candidly determining what I can and should expect of myself in conflict situations is my responsibility," (5) "Responding to conflict situations in ways that I thoughtfully approve of is in my long-term best interests."

Other examples could be listed, but these will suffice for now. That clients learn these general principles is central to the treatment. It is the means by which clients can convert their therapy experiences into more abstract and generalizable principles. When these principles are clearly and properly understood, they can also be applied to new conflict situations. One of the primary roles of the therapist is to arrange events in therapy so the client will actually experience the value of each principle being taught. This is the sense in which we consider the therapist to be an expert teacher. In other words, expert therapists should have such a clear understanding of the theoretical issues that they can plan for and make happen experiential learning moments for the client.

**Therapeutic content.** Even though the overall therapeutic process is shaped by the expert therapist, as we have already discussed, the content of every case is peculiar to that client. Admittedly, clients will eventually be asked to discuss their unique style of avoidance or the feelings they have about themselves because of their avoidance. Similarly, clients will ultimately be asked what they can do in conflict situations so they will be more approving of their own behavior. But this is where the similarity ends. Theory does not provide answers to these questions; only the client can. And this is where general therapeutic skills are important. Before clients can provide meaningful descriptions of their own behavior patterns, the therapist will usually have to help clarify, probe, observe, interpret, and provoke. And when this is done well, clients will describe themselves and their unique feelings and reaction patterns in considerable depth. Many insights occur along the way. But most important, clients actually (1) experience the depth of despair that is associated with their patterns of avoidance, and (2) feel renewed hope as they cope with difficulties they usually avoid, first during the therapy hour, and later in their larger social environment. This is the point at which the renewed, vital sense of self is fashioned by clients and their particular concerns, not the force of the verbally persuasive therapist.

Our clinical illustrations are saturated with examples of the therapist functioning as an expert teacher. These include (a) teaching clients the value of being able to accurately describe their behavior and its underlying meaning, (b) teaching clients that self-evaluative thoughts and feelings accompany their patterns of behavior, (c) teaching clients that avoidance is associated with self-disapproval, whereas coping tends to breed self-approval, and (d) teaching clients that personal approval and disapproval are more a function of coping and avoidance than of favorable or unfavorable outcomes, the ease or difficulty of the task, or almost any other set of external considerations.

Notice, however, that these principles are not taught didactically. The therapist does not explain them to the client or, for that matter, even suggest them. The client actually experiences them, and then the therapist intervenes so that these events are accurately labeled to facilitate understanding and long-term retention. The continuous interchange between the therapist as an expert teacher and facilitator of experiential learning becomes more frequent in the second half of the session.

**Summary.** In this section, we have suggested that the therapist is both an expert teacher and a facilitator of experiential learning. The therapist is a teacher because the therapy process is structured in such a way that clients are taught generalizable principles regarding the management of their psychic lives. But what clients actually understand as these principles are taught is more experiential than cognitive, and what clients learn is more particlar than general. The therapist's role as an expert teacher is most obvious when he or she applies general principles in the treatment sessions in such a way that clients both experience and understand the value of the principle being taught. The therapist's role as a facilitator of experiential learning is most obvious when the therapist helps clients understand the particular meaning of, and the consequences that attend, their particular style of coping and avoidance.

## Client Content or Personality Style

We clearly emphasize personality style over client content. Even a casual reading of our earlier case illustration reveals the therapist's reluctance to attend to the literal meaning of the content used by the client to define her problems. Instead, the therapist postponed any significant interventions until some of her more enduring personality patterns started to appear. Eventually, these patterns were described and labeled and became the core considerations throughout the session. To illustrate the influence of this focus on the form and substance of this session, simply try to imagine what this session would have been like if the therapist had pursued the literal meaning of the content presented by the client with equivalent focus and intensity. Without getting into value-laden arguments about which is better, it is probably clear that the different emphases of these two approaches would yield quite different types of therapy hours. Because our emphasis consistently favors dealing with styles of coping and defense over the literal meaning of client content, we offer the following guidelines for your consideration.

1. Asking clients to clearly identify and accurately describe their styles of avoidance is an inherently difficult and anxiety-arousing task. The results of this process can have many beneficial results, but the threat that can accompany the level of insight and self-disclosure required to complete this task should never be underestimated by the therapist. The general quality and rapport of the therapeutic relationship is obviously important. Engaging in this process can also help create a therapeutic relationship that is high in candor, trust, and intimacy.

2. Paradoxically, we do not believe that therapist reassurance, encouragement, coaching, or sympathy is useful in helping clients through the difficult task of identifying their own patterns of avoidance. If clients resist or avoid this task, no matter what the

reason, they should be allowed to do so—maybe even encouraged at times. Even the most subtle forms of therapeutic pressure should be scrupulously avoided by the therapist. Instead, the focus should be placed on having clients describe how they are going about avoiding the task while the avoidance is taking place. Implicitly, the therapeutic message is that avoidance is really OK, maybe even necessary as long the client is willing to own up to it and understand it. Note that we did not suggest that clients be asked *why* they are avoiding, only *how* they are avoiding in the moment.

3. The therapist's own feelings about the necessity of this process are important considerations. Watching clients experience intense and negative self-evaluative thoughts and feelings can be very difficult. Many therapists instinctively want to rescue clients from intense suffering. In the model we have proposed, however, suffering is the raw material from which coping responses are experientially forged by the client, and because of this, we have every expectation that significant suffering precedes significant improvement. Our comfort with client suffering is seldom misperceived by clients, and we have come to believe that our comfort is a source of unspoken reassurance to them at their periods of greatest vulnerability. We would add that therapist comfort in the face of client suffering needs to be an expression of conviction and confidence to help clients through difficult phases of therapy, not a role-playing technique.

In the clinical case illustration we have been using, it is fairly clear that (a) the therapist was responsible for getting the client to eventually identify, describe, and label her enduring patterns of avoidance, (b) this process was both difficult and upsetting to the client, (c) the therapist was clearly task oriented, reasonably understanding, but seldom reassuring, (d) the absence of reassurance and encouragement by the therapist did not hinder client progress, and (e) the client's rapid improvement was a direct result of facing, experiencing, and then resolving her own feelings of personal disapproval.

**Summary.** Enduring patterns of client coping and defense are the staple ingredient in the treatment model we are presenting. This approach requires a therapeutic relationship that is high in

(a) task-centeredness, (b) trust, candor, and risk taking, and (c) therapist comfort in the face of client distress.

## Individual Autonomy: High to Low

Generally speaking, client autonomy is fostered in most therapeutic relationships by minimizing the structure of the treatment approach, minimizing the demands on client behavior, and working in a treatment format that is either (a) client centered or (b) intentionally ambiguous. It is generally assumed that in either of these two conditions the client is more likely to provide, or at least make a major contribution to finding, a personally relevant and psychologically meaningful direction for the therapy process. One of the frequently accepted indicators of clients' autonomy is their ability to be self-directing within the therapeutic relationship. We agree with this view.

The intervention strategies we have described in this book have high as well as explicit demand characteristics for client behavior. These are not the psychological conditions typically associated with high levels of client autonomy. Paradoxically, our ideal therapeutic relationship is one that is intended to foster and, certainly, require high levels of autonomy. Obviously, we have a bit of explaining to do. We will focus our discussion on the assumptions that are at the heart of this apparent contradiction.

Our conceptualization of the means by which client autonomy can be created, maintained, or both in a therapeutic relationship departs from the traditional views on this topic. A careful analysis of the assumptions of these traditional views reveals the basis for our disagreement with them. It also clarifies the origin of our own views. Essentially, therapeutic structure and high demand characteristics are usually assumed to be incompatible with the development of client autonomy. The logic of this assumption is simple and straightforward. It is believed that clients will be more self-directing in a less structured therapeutic environment simply because there are fewer external cues to respond to. Of course, this view is based on the assumption that systems of psychological treatment differ substantially with regard to levels of treatment structure. Many describe treatment approaches based on their inherent levels of structure and ambiguity. Treatment systems with high levels of structure typically refer to the behavioral and cognitive-behavioral approaches. Client-centered and analytical orientations are generally considered to be less structured and more ambiguous.

The assumption that treatment orientations differ substantially with regard to levels of treatment structure is flawed both semantically and conceptually. Structure literally refers to an "organized entity" or an "organization of interrelated events." The opposite of structure is not ambiguity; it is chaos and disorganization. It is a lack of conceptual orderliness and consensual meaning. In our view, theories of therapy do not simply vary on a continuum of structure–ambiguity; all approaches to psychological treatment are highly structured intellectual products. And the intellectual structure inherent in these theories is always conveyed to clients, sometimes implicitly and inefficiently, other times explicitly and efficiently. But any approach to psychological treatment that warrants the title of "theory" (in the most casual meaning of the term) has rather clear expectations of how clients should behave during the therapy process if they are to improve. We suggest that systems of psychological treatment do not vary on levels of structure nearly as much as they do on the clarity and explicitness with which they make their expectations known.

For example, it is clear with even a modest understanding of classical psychoanalytic theory that client insight is a staple element in the cure, and client introspection and self-exploration are essential ingredients in the process. The treatment process is also highly structured, so that clients are encouraged to respond to internal cues and stimuli as a means of enhancing insight, introspection, and self-exploration. During treatment sessions, the therapist maintains a neutral posture because neutrality is assumed to be the optimal condition for encouraging material to come bubbling up from the client's unconscious for review. Note that all of these conditions are structured for the client. Actually, this treatment orientation is highly structured, with the appropriate behavior of the client and therapist well defined. It is misleading and unfortunate that this treatment has mistakenly been referred to as "unstructured," and by implication, a treatment with low demand characteristics for client behavior. Its demand characteristics are high, as is its level of imposed structure.

The same analysis applies to client-centered approaches. Again, we find that theory sets the expectations for client and therapist behavior in a series of highly organized and interrelated psychological events. Therapists are expected to listen attentively, nod reassuringly, be responsive to client initiatives, and be open and candid with their enduring feelings about the client. Clients are expected to self-disclose, express feelings as they occur, and select the topics for discussion that are most important to them. This treatment, as are all others, is theory centered, not client centered. And because of this, it is a highly structured treatment system with unique demand characteristics for client behavior.

In essence, we are suggesting that any intellectually respectable system of psychological treatment cannot vary on a continuum of structure–ambiguity. Ambiguity, as we have stated, is not the opposite of structure. Besides, all treatment systems are highly structured patterns of thought and behavior, and vary mostly with respect to their completeness and the clarity with which they make their behavioral demands explicit. Ambiguity probably refers to treatment systems with vague rather than explicit demand characteristics, and gradually and unintentionally became a descriptor of the treatment itself.

These are consequential arguments. If they are accepted, they redefine the appropriate role of treatment structure and client demand characteristics in the development of client autonomy. Originally, client autonomy was assumed to be best served in a treatment format with minimal structure, minimal demand characteristics on client behavior, and high client-centeredness. We suggest that the development of client autonomy can best be served in a therapeutic relationship that is highly structured for the precise purpose of increasing client autonomy and that uses influential and explicit demand characteristics for client behavior designed specifically for that purpose. Client-centeredness is an irrelevant consideration and ambiguity is a major distraction. In this context, the therapeutic relationship we consider ideal rates extraordinarily high on client autonomy. The expectation of high levels of client autonomy is in evidence throughout the clinical illustrations we have been using. Clients are continually asked to decide such important matters as (a) the accuracy of descriptive labels, (b) the amounts and levels of emotional intensity they can tolerate during the session, (c) the types of behavior they most disapprove of in themselves, (d) the ways they would need to change so that they could approve of themselves, (e) their willingness to move on to new tasks clearly defined as difficult, and, most important, (e) their acceptance of appropriate levels of personal responsibility for problem solving within the therapeutic framework provided.

## Summary

We have challenged the traditional view, which suggests that client autonomy is enhanced in a therapeutic environment that is unstructured and has low demand characteristics for specific types of client behavior. It has generally been assumed that clients will be more autonomous and self-directing in this type of environment simply because there are fewer external cues to guide their behavior. This point of view seems seriously flawed for several reasons. First, all systems of psychotherapy are highly organized (highly structured) systems of thought, with rather clear expectations for both client and therapist behavior. Some of these expectations may be more vague than explicit, but that does not alter either their existence or influence. Second, because of this we suggest that calling any system of psychological treatment unstructured with low demand characteristics for client behavior is inaccurate and misleading. And, third, we propose that client autonomy is most effectively enhanced by using a treatment format explicitly structured with obvious demand characteristics designed expressly for the purpose of increasing client autonomy.

## Uniqueness of the Therapeutic Relationship

Seemingly, each of our bipolar dimensions for describing different types of therapeutic relationships is technically relevant, but collectively they omit some important considerations. Some of the most important events that take place within a therapeutic relationship occur only because of a special feeling of trust and confidence that exists between the client and therapist. This trust must be earned by both parties, and it is usually the result of intense levels of intimacy and conflict resolution. And, it is this feeling, which is so difficult to describe but which clearly exists, that allows clients to say out loud what they are terrified to even think, or for the therapist to push and have clients respond to what they have always avoided. Most remarkable, however, is for the client and therapist to spontaneously laugh when others would cry, and cry together when others couldn't understand why. This is a relationship quality that transcends our technical relationship dimensions and reflects the feelings and attitudes that bond a client and therapist together in trust as they walk together in the client's psychic mine field.

Orlinsky and Howard (1986) have suggested three principal components derived from an extensive analysis of research data that seem to be essential to the type of therapeutic bonding we are discussing. These three components are (1) role investment, (2) empathic resonance, and (3) mutual affirmation. These principles are described below:

**1. Role investment.** There is an intense and affective investment of energy in relationship roles, evident in both the patient's self-expressive emotional attachment to the therapist and the therapist's active collaboration through whichever technique he or she feels most capable of and confident in using.

**2. Empathic resonance.** A second element associated with cohesiveness of the social bond in beneficial psychotherapy is the good personal contact and the solid grounding in one another that is made by the participants. This personal contact is characterized by mutual comfortableness and trust, a lack of defensiveness on both sides (seen in the patient's spontaneity and the therapist's genuineness), and also by a strong and sensitive rapport, a sense of being on the same wavelength, that arises through empathic resonance and reciprocal understanding.

**3. Mutual affirmation.** There is, finally, an expansive mutual goodwill mobilized between participants in beneficial psychotherapy, a strong sense of affirmation that is not merely acceptance, but acceptance and encouragement of independence, that can be challenging as well as supportive out of concern and respect for the other person's basic interests and autonomy.

It is only within a relationship framework such as the one just described that our specific relationship attributes can be properly understood. Confrontations that take place in this context may not feel very confrontational to the participants, and the exchange of emotionally charged feedback can occur graciously, appreciatively, and comfortably.

Paradoxically, it must be noted that the so-called high-risk behaviors that are so central to our treatment methods are both a cause and a consequence of the developing therapeutic relationship. Gradually, increasing levels of authenticity, congruence, and general risk taking in the relationship usually breed higher levels of interpersonal trust, and higher levels of trust gradually reduce the perceived risk of authenticity and congruence (Bednar, Melnick, & Kaul, 1974). In our view, a healthy therapeutic relationship is one in which moderate levels of risk taking gradually improve the therapeutic bonding, and the improved therapeutic bonding gradually decreases the perceived risk for even the highest levels of psychological risk taking. The therapeutic relationship, then, is both served and serviced by the ever-increasing levels of psychological risk taking we consider essential to effective treatment.

Eventually, clients come to feel sufficiently safe in the therapeutic relationship to deliberately and, at times, even eagerly expose the patterns of thinking and behaving that are the source of their recurring psychological difficulties. This is precisely the context in which client learning becomes optimal. The therapeutic relationship allows clients to face themselves candidly, and in this process the therapist teaches clients the value of self-approving behavior and its consequences at the precise moment it occurs. This is a therapeutic relationship that preserves the role of the therapist as an expert teacher, but what is taught is far more experiential than cognitive and tailored precisely to enhance the client's disposition to cope rather than avoid.

# 9

# Family Relations and the Development of Self-Esteem

The impact of parents' behavior upon the child's self-esteem is undeniable; given the immaturity of children, however, parents' expression of their own resolution of the self-esteem question is far more influential than what they teach verbally. Evidence suggests that children are unable to conceptualize a self until age 8 or older (Harter, 1983). Moreover, it is not until a child reaches adolescence that he or she can truly use such cognitive material to produce behavior-influencing understanding (Selman, 1980). Thus, while parents may understand and attempt to teach valuable concepts of self-esteem, for the child these concepts must be translated into experiences and feelings rather than verbally described.

## The Therapeutic Task

Because this is a book about self-esteem and psychotherapy, the task for the therapist treating self-esteem difficulties in children or in the family becomes even more complex than treating individual adults. First, where in the family structure does the therapist intervene—with the child individually, with the family as a group, or with the parents as a consultant? Second, ingredient in the choice is another question: What is the nature of the therapist's influence in each grouping?

There are, of course, major philosophical schools of thought that address these questions, so we will not attempt to answer them here. Indeed, the choices may already have been predicated by the values of the graduate program the therapist attended. However, inasmuch as the positioning of the therapist in the relationship is a critical consideration in this book, let us examine very briefly one conceptualization of the factors involved in treating children.

We suggest there are three components: (1) the knowledge component, (2) the insight component, and (3) the intervention component. The *knowledge* component considers this question: What do the therapist or the parents need to know about the psychology of children and adolescents or the particular child? By definition children are immature organisms whose phenomenological world differs from that of adults. The component assumes that expert understanding fosters effective intervention as well as emotional acceptance and patience. Through family therapy or consultation, parents respect the child's immaturity, recognize the relevant psychological issues in the child's developmental stage, and discern how they are being seen by the child. They can then match their teaching or their actions to the child's needs.

The *insight* component is a question directed primarily at the parents: What do parents need to learn, recognize, or change about themselves that will affect their influence attempts? As will be discussed in greater detail later in the chapter, parents bring their own history to the interaction process. By virtue of their early experiences, they will be differentially sensitive to particular issues in the child's life. As they understand themselves better through the therapeutic process, parents experience greater freedom to modify their approach to again match the child's need.

The *intervention* component poses the most complex question for treatment of children, indeed, perhaps for the entire enterprise of psychotherapy: How do therapists structure their interventions to maximize the opportunity for beneficial change? By choosing to see children individually, therapists focus both the knowledge and insight component upon themselves, reparenting the children, as it were. Therapists emphasize their impact upon the affective qualities of the relationship, as models to be imitated or as counselors to children.

If therapists choose to see the family, they spread their influence, affecting the interactions of the family. Here they are likely to employ both the knowledge and insight components in the immediacy of communication. The therapist's personality and demonstration of interactive processes continue to serve as a model but more distantly than in individual therapy. Intervention in the family presumes to develop skills, entailing an active, often directly or indirectly instructional stance for the therapist.

As consultants, therapists assume that their focused influence upon the parents will affect the child or children indirectly but powerfully, because of the intensity of the parental relationship as well as the sheer number of hours of interaction. In effect, the therapist assumes that change in the parent will have a reverberating effect in the family.

Finally, a secondary prong of the intervention component entails this question: What form of communication most effectively produces behavior change? Many years of discussion and debate have been devoted to this issue, particularly as regards children. Again, while we will not attempt to describe the polemic, we suggest that a fundamental error is committed by many parents and some therapists: They assume that accurate dispensing of the knowledge component *should* provide the necessary and sufficient conditions for change. In other words, they believe that telling equals teaching and teaching equals behavioral change. It does not, because a part of anything learned entails an affective element as well as a cognitive one.

An example can be seen in the father "teaching" his child to swim. When the child is frightened of the water, he says to relax. But instructions to relax are generally insufficient modifiers of something as primitive as anxiety about water. When the child continues to be afraid in spite of the father's instruction, he becomes irritated, increasing the volume of his "solution" and the anxiety of the situation for the child. Soon the child is more afraid of the father than of the water, looking for any avenue of escape from the situation or dissolving into tears if that is impossible. The child probably will *not* learn to swim, at least in that session.

In other words, the problem for the therapist and parents is the affective "packaging" of the knowledge or insight. Because behavior change always entails both affective and cognitive parts, influence attempts must consider both in the communication. In the example above, the father correctly recognized that the child needed to relax in order to learn to swim, but doing nothing more than saying so was useless and even counterproductive. The father's real task was to create a learning situation calculated to help the child relax, perhaps by play or initially letting the child ride his back while he swam. The therapist's task is analogous: whether working directly with the child or consulting with the parents, the therapist must construct interventions that will be "heard" both cognitively and affectively.

In this chapter we will speak primarily to the therapist as a consultant to parents. The therapist's interaction with the child will be in the role of an assessment expert, gathering information about the child's development and personality that will help the parents in their influence attempts. Utilizing that knowledge component, the therapist can then help the parents employ more effective parenting strategies. In addition the therapist speaks to the insight component, working directly to treat the parents' self-esteem difficulties, knowing that their influence will be greatest as models of self-esteem. Finally, the therapist can assist the parents to fashion their communications in ways that will match the child's maturity and personality to increase their influence effectiveness.

The structure of the chapter roughly follows the knowledge, insight, and intervention components for the therapist. First we consider more general issues of developmental processes and common parental practices. The second section focuses on the relevance of parental self-esteem and its consequences for the child. Next we describe a conceptualization of the changing roles of acceptance, power, and autonomy. The concluding section deals with strategies for implementing particular elements of the self-esteem model with children.

The immediate question is, of course: What are the implications for parent–child relations that obtain from the self-esteem model presented? While some of our suggestions coincide with those of earlier writers, it will be seen that the propositions of the model yield concepts that are substantially different from those of Coopersmith and others. We began this book posing a paradox: How is it that so many people who ostensibly have reason to feel a strong sense of self-esteem confess privately to such grave self-doubts and personal beliefs in their own inadequacy? The thematic thrust of our argument has been that the pivotal element in positive self-esteem (in adults, thus far), even the expression of healthy emotional behavior, is the moment-to-moment decision to confront and cope with difficulties rather than avoid them. Our question must be, then, *What can parents do to provide the best possible opportunity for children to develop a stable sense of self-esteem, which ultimately includes the predilection to cope with difficult situations rather than avoid them?*

## Assumptions and Caveats

Several assumptions must be mentioned that are integral to our propositions. First, the entire process of developing self-esteem assumes a caring relationship. The qualities of affection and concern for the welfare of the child are so fundamental that we have little to say to parents who are not so emotionally invested. Similarly, therapists' care for their clients is axiomatic. No ethical therapist would presume to treat parents or families without at least a modicum of regard for their well-being.

Next, the development of self-esteem must be considered within the larger developmental process of the child. The nature of the parent–child relationship as well as the tasks of healthy development must change over time. An effective relationship at one time will not necessarily be as worthwhile an influence at a later stage of development. Also, general principles may be functional, yet their expression may need to take a different form. While we suggest, for example, that acceptance is always important, its communication changes dramatically. (The 2-year-old boy may thrive on a direct "I love you," while the strapping 16-year-old may prefer "Hey, big fella, how's it going today?") The acceptance is identical, but the language has changed. Other relationships, such as the control dimension, shift in both expression and substance to match the child's developmental needs.

A corollary to the developmental assumption is this: Parents all too frequently choose their parenting styles not from a consideration of the child's present need but from the unexamined reservoir of their own experiences in being parented. Having been learned at a more primitive level, their initial, "reflexive" response to exigencies of the moment will be either to repeat their analogous experience or, if they had a strong negative reaction to the event, to react in an opposite fashion, equally without planning. Because parents draw from their affective summary of what it was like for them as a child, then, what the child usually receives over time is a thematic and somewhat homogeneous experience. Thus, even caring parents are apt to be more effective at some stages of the child's development and less so at others.

Another assumption is illustrated in this truism: In order to treat your children the same, you have to treat them differently. Children vary considerably, even within families. A parenting strategy employed with good effect on one child at age three may be inappropriate for a sibling at that age. Excellent longitudinal studies (Thomas, Chess, & Birch, 1968; Thomas & Chess, 1977) clearly indicate temperamental differences that must be taken into account. In the adolescent years, what is coping for one child may be avoiding for another. Dependent, anxious children will fear challenging or disagreeing with others, whereas the oppositional child whose interpersonal strategy seems to be that the-best-defense-is-a-good-offence (misspelling intended) may be most fearful of a warm, cooperative relationship.

A final assumption: We freely admit that we have been describing an agentive theory in this book. Children, albeit influenced greatly by parents, are not caused. In spite of their best efforts, some children will not choose the outcomes parents have prepared for them, or interpret the parents' persuasions as they intended them to be perceived. Other significant people (i.e., teachers, peers, even strangers) affect the lives of children in both beneficial and harmful ways, and, in the case of hurtful experiences, children's interpretations may not be completely countermanded by the efforts of parents or therapists. Such is particularly the case in adolescence, when, for most, there is a dramatic resurgence of the need to be accepted. Issues relevant to self-esteem, resolved successfully in childhood, resurface in the search for identity, at a time when parental influence may be seen as a threat to self-definition.

Thus, the most expert counsel does not produce inevitable results. But it may increase understanding, foster planning by parents, and emphasize critical learning experiences at the appropriate developmental stage, thereby increasing the chances for fostering self-esteem.

## Common Assumptions About Parenting and Self-Esteem

Most of the commonsense approaches to developing self-esteem are based on the expectation that children gradually internalize beliefs about themselves that are communicated to them by their social environment. The reader already knows that the model presented emphasizes the internal nature of self-esteem in the adult. However, the tasks of parenting are particularly complex because children are initially developmentally incapable of responding to an internal set of expectations. Parents cannot simply determine to teach children to cope and confront issues as they themselves are doing, because the child's balance between the control of emotions and the control of thinking is so much different. Fostering a general sense of positive self-feeling requires an overarching strategy, a *Weltanschauung* or worldview, that takes into account developmental immaturity as discussed earlier and planning for parental activities, *which strategically change as the child matures.*

The importance of the parents' viewpoint and its predicating influence may be illustrated by the humorous experience of a colleague and friend. He had just finished his PhD in child psychology. As sometimes happens, he found that his training was looked at with some suspicion by his relatives, particularly his in-laws. (Perhaps it is an occupational hazard that, using Cooley's looking-glass self-concept, one's extended family members expect dentist in-laws to be looking at their children's teeth and psychologist in-laws to be "analyzing" their children's behavior.) At the conclusion of a visit from one such in-law, the mother observed her 3-year-old son riding his cousin's tricycle with great enthusiasm. With some delight at the opportunity for a challenge of my friend's skill (now that he was so smart that he had a PhD in the subject), she said, "Since you are the expert, let's see how you get Johnny to give up the tricycle and come with me." My friend responded, "I'll do what I know how to do." He walked over to Johnny, told him it was time for him to go home now, to please come again some time, and lifted him, screaming, into his mother's car. Johnny's mother drove away, nonplussed, with Johnny still crying mightily. In retelling the story, my friend remarked that it seemed that the goal of many parents was to have their child grow up without crying. His relative may have assumed that the "expert" parent can and should somehow manipulate the child into accepting unpleasant experiences without protest, a goal devoutly desired by most parents by late afternoon.

This story is symbolic of several child-rearing styles of parents, who, though certainly caring, raise children at risk for the chronic difficulties of low self-esteem discussed in this book. Let us consider several parenting theories.

**Unconditional love theory.** First is the belief that the kids with high self-esteem are those who have been raised with so much love and praise that they are somehow failure-safe, embarrassment-proof, and humiliation-protected. This unconditional love theory of building self-esteem sometimes uses a metaphor: the love bucket. If parents keep this love bucket full to overflowing, nothing can go wrong. Disappointments must be assuaged and smoothed over quickly, as though they were dangerously infectious. Parents must work overtime to construe reality so the child will never question the self or its abilities. They therefore must singlehandedly compete against the possible ego bumps and bruises outside of the family.

The error, of course, is that complex problems, especially human ones, are seldom solved by simply lavishing more praise, or more love, or more money on them. It is, in its nucleus, a defensive, avoidant decision that fears coping with what may be a child's very real shortcomings. This parenting style, therefore, contains the very ingredients that we have suggested foster low self-esteem.

No parent can successfully hover close enough to protect a child from those less caring and less admiring. Nor is it helpful. Self-esteem must be of a more robust construction than a child's dependence upon parental praise. Indeed, Adler (Ansbacher & Ansbacher, 1956) wrote eloquently of both the dangers of indulging a child and the beneficial psychological stance inherent in accepting imperfection in oneself. And Baumrind (Baumrind, 1963, 1966, 1971, 1975) found preschool children of indulgent parents to be the most unhappy and insecure of the groups she studied. Parents must not teach the child to avoid the honest need for self-appraisal and change.

We have suggested earlier that accurate, negative feedback is a reality for most people. It can be a healthy, if unpleasant, part of the self-evaluation process. Furthermore, parents who unfailingly pursue a course of attempting to contradict external negative feedback will find that the child considers them a less and less credible source of evaluation. Adolescents frequently do anyway, indicating their suspicion of parents' feedback with something like, "Oh, you always say I look good. That's just because you're my mom."

**Self-esteem-equals-success theory.** A second erroneous theory for developing self-esteem is that parents must see that children have so many training opportunities—dancing, music lessons, athletics, or preschool—that they will be guaranteed some arena in which they are more successful than age-mates. They must be winners in order to feel good about themselves. The self-esteem-equals-success theory assumes that positive self-feeling is in short supply and is available only to the victorious. (Philosophically, William James may be blamed to some extent for the theory. Recall his successes/pretensions ratio. Our self-esteem depends upon what we back ourselves to be. If we are successful, we have a right to feel self-love.) Parents subscribing to this theory have the oppressive responsibility to assess the child's gifts and provide the all-important head start in training that will save the child from the dangers of competing without an advantage. Children of average or less than average endowment are doomed to either the tension-ridden effort to become more than they are or to the resignation of inferiority.

The error in this theory is a fundamental and critical one, we believe, one that pervades much of the adult business world. It entails a mistaken focus on *outcome,* the belief that self-esteem is constructed by the result, the end point, or so-called bottom line of an endeavor. Self-esteem is thought to be a by-product of winning or achieving some goal, a competitive process in which trust and cooperation are irrelevant goals. While some portion of the assumption is true, in that success brings a sense of accomplishment, we have again suggested that it is neither necessary nor sufficient to produce lasting self-esteem. If children must always win in order to continue to feel good about themselves, they and their parents must constantly experience the stress of having to do as well or better each time they compete. (Again, we are reminded of one of James's solutions to problems of self-esteem: Abandon some of our pretensions.)

We have asserted, instead, that the *process* is the essential element: choosing to cope, to face the difficult challenges. Children can take pride in the effort and the desire they committed to the activity, without being dependent upon external judges declaring them the winners. (When the judge is another child or set of peers, a positive evaluation is risky, at best.) Indeed, we have suggested that positive, self-affirming thoughts and feelings occur when we confront issues, regardless of the outcome. The experiment described in Chapter 3 noted that people viewed themselves positively for coping in spite of the anticipation that their coping response might have no effect on the outcome. As T. S. Eliot has said, "For us, there is only the trying. The rest is not our business" (Eliot, 1940).

**The social invulnerability theory.** A third parenting theory, somewhat similar to the one preceding, assumes that self-esteem equals socialization. That is, if children can be trained so carefully and so well that their behavior is unassailable, they will be safe from the pangs of low self-esteem. This social invulnerability theory negates the possibility of a positive, confident sense of self in favor of protection from criticism. Like the earlier theory, it implies that the evaluation of the self resides in others' judgment, not in one's own. The emotional goal that these parents project onto their children is the absence of dread that one is vulnerable to attack. (The work of George Herbert Mead bears some distant but recognizable philosophical relationship to this theory and the one following. Recall that he suggested that we internalize the voices of significant others; therefore, in order to feel good about ourselves we must adapt ourselves sufficiently to persuade the voices to approve of us. By that mechanism we can come to say approving things of ourselves.)

Here it would seem that the error is more obvious. Striving for invulnerability generates the very anxiety that intensifies the likelihood of avoidance, which we have suggested is the seedbed of pathological behavior. The commitment to impression management as a style of life is evident, as are its deleterious consequences, so amply described by Rogers (1950). By contrast, attempts at definition of the concept of self-esteem in psychological literature usually have described self-esteem positively, as a confidence-building, "freeing" experience, attended by feelings of competence and self-control. The essential choice to face difficulties requires a willingness to view criticism as an acceptable, even integral (albeit not sought-after), part of the decision. Doing things less than perfectly is "part of the territory."

**Self-esteem-equals-belonging theory.** A final mistaken child-rearing theory, following the description of Mead's theory above, suggests that since the source of self-esteem is positive affirmation from others, children with high self-esteem are those who are successful at winning approbation. Abandoning the goal of invulnerability as impossible to reach, this self-esteem-equals-belonging theory emphasizes "fitting in," teaching children that they can feel good about themselves when they can get others to accept them. Emphasizing obedience and conformity, these parents teach great sensitivity to social nuance and custom. Children are trained to consider offending someone as the source of greatest social danger; they will experience anxiety or a sense of threatening obligation until the breach of acceptance is healed. The family ethic, spoken or unspoken, is, "What will people think?"

This style of seeking positive self-feeling is as futile as the effort to be invulnerable because it also depends totally upon the appraisals of others. Impression management is ingredient in the life-style because children must mold and adapt themselves to meet the perceived demands of those from whom they have chosen to seek approval.

Referring to our earlier discussion, genuine positive feedback is apt to be received with disbelief because children may conclude that the praise is due only to their skill at presenting themselves. Individuals cannot experience more than a fleeting sense of self-confidence when they are aware that their position depends upon pleasing an audience. By definition they have created a position in which they are inferior. They cannot rely upon their own internal feedback because others are always the final judges of their performance. Constantly seeking feedback from others, therefore, they can never be sure of its veracity when they are so certain of their own dissembling.

Parenthetically, as clinicians we have frequently observed that clients who in therapy describe themselves as pleasers have a deeply felt wish to be accepted just as they are. They express their fatigue and resentment at "having to put on a show" for everyone. Yet, when asked to describe who they really are, they seldom can express a definition, having devoted themselves so exclusively to impression management. While initially they seem unacquainted with their own self-evaluative thoughts, some practice produces a realization of intense self-disapproval.

We do not wish to denigrate the importance of belonging. Choosing to listen only to one's own feelings or fearing intimate, and therefore binding, relationships is not an answer, representing instead a different form of insecurity. We assume that positive self-esteem includes belonging, but that it is accompanied by the feeling of being equal to others, not dependent. If one's essential definition is that of being equal to others, he or she can listen to both inside and outside voices.

While there certainly are other, similar theories regarding the development of self-esteem, we consider the four listed as being the most common. Note that our focus was upon strategies of caring parents who want happiness for their children. We have not considered the effects of destructive styles, when parents are indifferent or even hostile to the child's welfare. We do so now briefly.

**Indifferent and hostile parenting styles.** It goes without saying that parental attitudes of neglect and cruelty do *not* enhance self-esteem (either in the child or the parents). We earlier noted evidence that children before the age of 8 are incapable of articulating a separate sense of self (Harter, 1983), and they are hence unable to define themselves otherwise than that which is communicated by parents. Thus, indifferent or rejecting parents variously teach children that they are intrusive burdens to be borne, or incompetent competitors for the scarce resources of the family, or somehow even that they are enemies within the family, deserving of the parents' vituperation. Inside the cognitive immaturity of the young child, the interpretation of events requires causes, usually one-dimensional, sequential explanations. Therefore, being hurt, chastised, or pointedly ignored is equivalent to being pun-ished, and being punished means to children they must have done something wrong. Unable to recognize the possibility that their parents' responses to them may be coming from the parents' own unresolved difficulties, the children blame themselves, coming to believe that they are somehow defective, unable to be good enough to be loved.

It is interesting to note that, in spite of such difficult beginnings, some children from neglecting or abusive backgrounds emerge from childhood surprisingly intact. We suggest that there are two crucial, related elements that may explain such survivors of dele-terious child-rearing environments: consistency and a distorted form of non-impression-management parenting. Parents who are consistently harsh provide at least a predictable environment from which children can learn skills and *must* learn self-reliance if they are to survive. They may indeed develop a certain resil-ience from being forced to cope with their nonsupportive sur-roundings. (The damage to their emotional-affectional lives as adults is often serious, however.)

Secondly, parents who make no pretense of their hostility to-ward their children are similarly predictable. In that sense these parents do not attempt to manage impressions of themselves to the children, and, for their part, the children may learn to cope with their parents' response to them. On the other hand, parents who insist verbally on their love and concern while betraying their hostility in other subtle ways present the child with a much more complex and threatening task. Indeed, early research in psy-chopathology suggests that a totally unpredictable environment may be the circumstance of most harm to psychological develop-ment (Bateson, Jackson, Haley, & Weakland, 1956). Consider the observations of Johnson, Giffin, Watson, and Beckett (1956) re-garding 27 schizophrenic child patients and their families:

> When these children perceived the anger and hostility of a parent, as they did on many occasions, immediately the parent would deny that he was angry and would insist that the child deny it too, so that the child was faced with the dilemma of whether to believe the parent or his own senses. If he believed his senses, he maintained a firm grip

on reality; if he believed the parent, he maintained the relationship but distorted his perception of reality. Repeated
parental denial resulted in the child's failure to develop
adequate reality testing. (p. 143)

Thus in an extreme and backward fashion, these observations
illustrate the fundamental error in choosing impression management as a means of pursuing self-esteem, either personally or as
a parent.

## Discussion

Except for the indifferent and hostile parenting styles just described, there is an underlying theme for each strategy we have
considered that harks back to the summary of early writers on
self-esteem in Chapter 2: Rejection and the fear of rejection are
twin sides of *the* malevolent force that destroys positive self-
feeling. Simply put, people fear being pushed away and alone.
(Recall William James's comment quoted earlier: "No more fiend-
ish punishment could be devised, were such a thing physically
possible, than that one should be turned into society and remain
absolutely unnoticed by all the members thereof.") The experience of self-esteem is assumed to be ultimately social, therefore,
referenced and calibrated by the response from other people or in
comparison to them.

We do not argue with the fundamental importance of acceptance and nurturance. But the assumptions have not gone far
enough. Greenwald and Breckler (1985) described the development of the self proceeding through four stages: the *diffuse* self,
or a self that has not been differentiated; the *public* self, which
derives its definition from the feedback of others; the *private* self,
wherein true self-definition commences and an identity is established; and the *collective* self, in which the self becomes egoless,
identifying with concerns of larger groups. We have suggested
earlier that the child grows up needing acceptance, but that the
balance between acceptance and individuality shifts gradually toward individuality and a greater need for acceptance from oneself. It is the internal decision of what one must do to approve of
oneself that is the touchstone for self-esteem in the adult. *Thus,*

*the critical mistake in the common parenting styles is that parents oriented toward avoiding rejection train only for the development of the public self. The question of fostering the child's development of a private self may remain unasked, let alone unanswered.*

Of course, some of the blame for parents' focusing exclusively on the development of the public self rests with the fact that they have not been focusing at all. They want the children to be happy and successful, but they also don't want them to be a source of trouble or concern. Like the mother of the child on his cousin's bicycle, a parent's de facto goal may be to raise the children with as little difficulty as possible, preferring pleasing, obedient children to ones who, in their adolescence, become responsive to their own approval. It is disconcerting even to democratic parents to have their children reach conclusions different from the ones they themselves have. Solipsism, the problem of assuming one's conclusions are the only correct ones, is not limited to the young.

Parenthetically, an important, usually overlooked consequence of this generic "pleasing-us-is-best-for-you" expectation is an interesting incongruity: parents expect their sons or daughters never to disagree with them, *yet to be noncompliant* when pressured by peers to use drugs or violate other family values. Although these children may in fact refuse to participate in such situations, they are simply unprepared by experience to know how to disagree amicably. Later in the chapter we will discuss the proposition that parents must foster the opportunity for the child to learn to say no, based on merit and rationality, to significant others.

Here, then, is one of the fundamental elements to the answer to our question of developing self-esteem: *Parents must planfully attend to the process of fostering the development of the internal component, the private self, which enjoys acceptance but is prepared to prefer self-approval to that of others when necessary.*

## Concept Summary

Having considered a number of general issues relevant to the process of parents' fostering self-esteem in their children, let us summarize concepts thus far that the therapist can utilize in treatment of families with self-esteem difficulties:

1. Child-rearing strategies of parents must accommodate both the developmental stage and the individual personality of the child. The therapist can assist parents in assessing the unique position of each child in the family to develop a conceptualization of his or her present needs. As in our earlier discussion of intervention, the therapist can coach parents in the language of its presentation, especially when the language must be long-term, nonverbal, or even nonconceptual.

2. Through the interview process, the therapist can help parents evaluate their own "childhood-constructed" expectations about parenting, assisting them to become more aware of their communication style and planful in modifying it to meet their child's needs. Not infrequently, the therapist can do much to help the child by helping the parents work through unresolved issues in their own lives. Through consultation with the therapist, parents can learn to be more consistent and predictable, providing a collateral benefit for the child.

3. For the sake of both the child and the parents, the therapist must stress the value of focusing on process, not outcome. Parents must accept the agency of the child, recognizing that their best efforts may not be immediately or even ultimately successful in enhancing the child's self-esteem. However, they will foster their own self-esteem by remembering that they also must focus on process, not outcome, coping with what the child may need as well as the possible frustration attendant upon the child's not utilizing the experiences for growth. In addition, the therapist can teach parents both to encourage the child to focus on trying and to learn themselves to take pride in the process of the child's activities rather than the end-point achievements.

4. The therapist must model as well as teach the positive, robust nature of self-esteem, in which negative as well as positive feedback is an accepted ingredient, shortcomings are essential parts of being human, and displeasure, even rejection, of some people is to be expected and accepted.

5. The therapist can help parents become aware of the importance of the child's developing the private self as adolescence approaches. They must expect and teach that the child does not always have to please them. When parents respect the child's need to develop individuality, the child becomes more aware of

and responsive to inner direction. A particular strategy, illustrated in greater detail later in the chapter, may be to deliberately encourage the child to disagree on merit.

6. The therapist's most important task with parents is to attend to the parents' authenticity, emphasizing the fundamental bankruptcy of impression management, a recurrent theme of this book.

## Parental Self-Esteem

We propose that the degree to which parents have resolved their own questions of personal self-esteem will have more influence on their children than anything they might attempt to teach them verbally. Let us consider the proposition and its implications for treatment of self-esteem difficulties in the family. In a broad sense we speak now to the insight component described in the early pages of the chapter.

Several lines of evidence in psychology converge to underscore the importance of the parents' example in teaching self-esteem. We noted earlier Harter's (1983) conclusion that children before the age of 8 are generally maturationally unable to recognize a separate sense of self. In other words, the formation of an "I" who observes and influences the "me" does not occur until at least middle childhood. Even then, developmental theories of both cognition (Flavell, 1985) and personality (Erikson, 1968) suggest that it isn't until adolescence that children become truly self-conscious, employing the capacity of self-reflection to study themselves and thereby choose to alter behavior. This is not, of course, to suggest that children are not learning about the self. Hardly! The major proportion of the self-definition upon which the adolescent and adult reflect is formed in the early years. It is simply that the learning comes primarily from observing parents and significant others and receiving messages about oneself through their actions. It is as though, when adolescents are prepared to use the skills of self-reflection, they find much of the basic structure of the self already in place, as though their self-beliefs were unquestioned givens.

A related conceptual track emphasizes the power of modeling in influencing behavior (see Bandura, 1986, for a review). The role of observation and imitation is amply demonstrated as one of the fundamental sources of learning for the child. Moreover, the elements that increase the model's influence—warmth, identification, and prestige—are all present in the healthy parent–child relationship.

Therefore, parents must recognize that their children will learn more from their example than from anything they will tell them. The parents' actions, their problem-solving approaches, and their responses to stress represent a one- or two-person seminar on life. For the young child, whose self-esteem so fundamentally pivots on being accepted, parents' attitudes toward themselves—whether prizing or indifference or rejection—are unavoidably communicated.

The most central aspect of the modeling process, therefore, focuses upon the parents' congruence, their personal demonstration of authenticity, or, on the other hand, their dissimulation and pretense in avoiding issues. So many parents assume that they must pretend to be what they are not *for the sake of the child.* We suggest that what children will learn, then, is *to pretend to be what they are not,* with all the consequences that the choice of impression management entails. Contrary to expectation, we propose that, for the sake of the child, parents permit the child to observe their struggles, their difficulties, and their conflicts *because struggling is a primary coping response.*

Thus, the parent's authenticity—the willingness to face difficulties, to recognize methods of avoidance and seek congruence—is critical. In that sense, all the apparently adult concepts of the book are indirectly but clearly influential in developing self-esteem in children. Children may not be able to describe how they feel about themselves for choosing to avoid problems, but they will most surely observe its effect.

It is ironic that some parents see healthy self-esteem for themselves as a wishful dream but are most anxious to do anything they can to protect their children from similar pain. They may view a search for their own positive self-feeling as being egoistic, detracting from the needs of their children. Their message is masked as self-sacrifice, but ultimately is perceived by the child as evidence that the world's demands are threatening. Worse still, the client is asked to learn to cope with those demands while observing a most intimate model who does not.

## Autonomy

Coopersmith, Baumrind, and other theorists of parental antecedents of self-esteem agree that competent, high-self-esteem children experienced parental respect for their individuality. Thus, juxtaposed with the bonding and controlling elements that, left unmitigated, would foster the pathologically enmeshed family, parents' active willingness to encourage differentiation adds the vital dimension of autonomy. Recall that Carl Rogers (1950) premised much of his theory of psychotherapy on the need of individuals to respect their personal uniqueness.

Earlier in the chapter we described the unfortunate sequelae to persons, who, having tried hard to meet others' definitions of worth, had never developed their own. Parents must encourage, not just passively allow, differences to foster children's skill in hearing their own voice, recognizing what they themselves feel and desire. What initially may appear to be willful egocentricity in young children gives way to an interactive process between parents and children by which they learn to know themselves. The interaction of learning to differentiate self from others continues with peers and finally becomes the internal dialogue that builds the self-definition known as identity.

Given the overall thrust of the book, it is not surprising that we see this element of parenting as fundamental to the development of self-esteem. Indeed, we have even suggested and will elaborate in the next section the importance of the child's learning to disagree in the family. Moreover, we have proposed that the amelioration of self-esteem difficulties requires that the therapist assist the client in recognizing the self-evaluative processes. Any person must be reasonably sensitive to his or her own feelings and values to ask, What must I do in this situation to approve of myself?

*3. The control relationship between parent and child shifts gradually to match developmental needs.*

It is within the control dimension that parents are required to be most alert to the child's maturing; more strategic alterations in their parenting are dictated here than in the other dimensions. Parents whose goal it is to prepare the child to be an adult with good self-esteem must planfully modify their control of the child's life to match his or her readiness for responsibility and decision making. It is a complex task for several reasons. First, the learning residue of the parents' history is particularly germane to the issue of control. The amalgam of childhood memories is apt to foster a homogeneous, even rigid, response to the task of disciplining one's children. Much of a family therapist's work, where adolescents are involved, focuses on the issue of control—parental domination or abdication of control, and the child's rebellion or anxieties created by parental control.

Second, parents apply their experience with older siblings to the younger ones even though it may not be appropriate. Unfortunately, the trauma of an older brother's or sister's mistakes sometimes impels parents to knee-jerk, unwarranted attempts at control, which may provoke in the younger siblings the very situation the parents sought to avoid.

Finally, almost by definition the maturation process dictates that children will test limits. Parents must be sensitive to the child's development, discerning between the child's desire for power and his or her readiness for the attendant responsibility.

With those complexities in mind, we suggest in broad outlines a declining power curve in which parental control shifts gradually from total control (vertical) to influence by permission (lateral).

**Infants.** Schematically, the relationship during infancy is vertical, or nearly so, as shown in the diagram below:

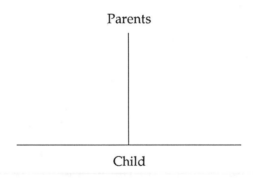

Parents

Child

At this stage the child is completely dependent upon the parents for nurturance and protection. We have suggested that the major component at this age for later self-esteem is the child's sense of being loved and belonging in the family. Erikson's (1963) theory of developmental stages emphasizes the essential need for the child to reach out for acceptance and have the parents reach back. The child's latitude for expressing individuality at this stage may be limited to that which is already present by virtue of biological temperament.

Yet, even in such immaturity the thrill of growing and doing for oneself is clear. Anyone who has observed the total delight of a child taking his or her first steps can see the power of functionally autonomous reinforcement. In those moments the child may appreciate praise but does not need it. Indeed, research on intrinsic versus extrinsic reinforcement (Lepper, 1983) suggests that children feel more motivation to continue to achieve if they experience their own reward rather than being rewarded by parents. It is certainly true that many a parent, thinking to encourage a child who is singing in solitary play, offers praise, only to find that the child stops upon recognizing that he or she is being observed.

**Preschoolers.** As children grow, emerging abilities provide opportunities for developing age-appropriate competencies and learning socialization such as sharing and cooperative play. Their cognitive immaturity still dictates that most of the control for their lives must be external, residing in parents, older siblings, or teachers. As mentioned, Baumrind (1975) found that preschool children were already the beneficiaries of parental styles that combined warmth with high expectations for maturity and respect for individuality. In the preschool period, the power relationship might be visualized as shown in the diagram below:

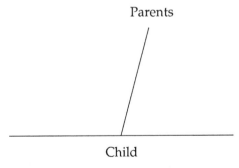

Parents

Child

The parents' focus for the child at this age begins to combine acceptance with expectations for performance, even though performance may be somewhat limited, such as to self-help, obedience, and basic socialization skills. Autonomy issues also have their beginnings. Parents must decide how to deal with the child's dislike of certain foods. Particularly important is the confusion between feelings and actions. Although it may be several years before the discrimination is well learned, the child can hear that it may be acceptable that he or she is experiencing anger, but it is unacceptable to act out those feelings in certain ways.

The continuing parenting principle is to balance control, which provides clear expectations and boundaries, with appropriate latitude to match the child's readiness for expression of responsibility and individuality. Thus, parents discuss and agree upon what the child can be expected to do, and they provide the training necessary for the child to meet those expectations. They designate activities in which the child may choose without interference. They continue to respect age-appropriate immaturity, recognizing that growth is saltatory, not continuous. In other words, parents accept that the child will occasionally disappoint them; however, those lapses in maturity do not cause them to rescind opportunities immediately.

**Midchildhood.** Midchildhood, or the latency period, is a time in which the development of skills is essential in establishment of self-esteem. Children are now in school, comparing themselves daily to peers. Total acceptance by parents without regard to accomplishment becomes suspect as the demand increases for the child to accept his or her place in a larger group. Harter's (1982, 1983) research evidences the emergence of the importance of competence for feelings of self-worth. Now, praise or expressions of affection can be more effectively tied to actual activities by which the child can acquire a sense of efficacy. Parental time with the child also shifts somewhat from entertainment time together to learning and skill-building time. Participation in household and personal maintenance increases the child's sense of belonging as a contributing member. Presumably, the child's sense of self emerges during this time; in Greenwald and Breckler's (1985) terms, the public self is the focus of development.

Individual differences continue to gradually set the trajectory for the child's later definition of self as a unique personality. While the potential for rebellion is still relatively small, parental respect for the child's expression of preferences, within limits, can "put money in the bank" for the relationship when the feelings of need for latitude intensify. That is, parents' willingness to understand and respond respectfully to their children's choices gives the parents leverage when they must ask the children to do things they don't want to do.

The power relationship may look something like this:

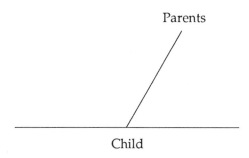

Parents

Child

**Preadolescence.** As the latency period of a child wanes, there are important value issues that are nonnegotiable, but the parents realize that the child's growing cognitive abilities permit generalization. Parents can now expect children to recognize general principles of the family's values; they can give up reciting rules in favor of asking children to judge their own behavior. Belongingness in the family is assumed, and the parents' nurturance has shifted somewhat to create an image for the child of a "safe place" to discuss the challenges and disappointments of the outside world. That does not mean that the child is protected from negative feedback; it is, instead, an integral part of the atmosphere of the home. The high levels of trust ensure that feedback is seen as task-oriented requests for change, not hurtful personal criticism.

At this age a critical element for the establishment of the private self emerges. Up to this point, the parents' agenda for the child has been the process of teaching skills, teaching rules and then principles, and teaching the self-discipline that accompanies obedience. The child will have learned the confidence that attends knowing what is appropriate in given social circumstances.

Now the child enters the time in which the parents allow enough latitude to learn the essential skill of *disagreeing* amicably. As one of the distinguishing features of our model, we suggest that a fundamental way of fostering self-esteem overlooked by most parents is the skill of expressing differences with others rationally. Beginning at a time when the child's desire to please is still strong and authority is accepted, parents can agree that, in some arenas of behavior, the child can choose *and win* an argument in spite of their objections. This process assumes that parents are communicating their willingness to respect the child's individuality.

It is not only important that children learn to reasonably disagree, but that they experience making a choice that is at variance with their parents' counsel yet still maintain as strong a caring relationship with them. Children learn that differences can exist without endangering their sense of belonging to the family, that sometimes they have to (and have the right to) make decisions at variance with those they would like to please. Thus, children begin to learn the complex, important skill of recognizing internally how they feel and arguing rationally for respect for their choices. And by the time peers attempt to persuade them to take drugs, children can be comfortable refusing. They will already have had the experience of being noncompliant with people whose acceptance is much more important than that of peers. As the diagram shows below, the power relationship continues to become more lateral:

Parents

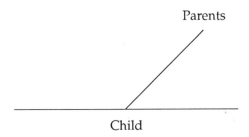

Child

Parents' choices of appropriate arenas for disagreement are important, of course. They must not give children latitude to make choices where they are not willing to let them experience the results of an ill-advised choice. Nor is it helpful for children to experience more power than responsibility. If parents accede to children's irrational, emotional demands, later hurt is guaranteed when they encounter authorities such as schoolteachers, coaches, or police. The opportunities that the parents choose as appropriate for disagreement may seem trivial to the onlooker, but it is in exactly those small issues that the child can enjoy developing confidence in being different without threatening fundamental family values. For example, the child may want to buy shoes that the parents think are too expensive or that might not be appropriate for their intended use. In that arena, they can ask the child to justify buying the shoes and to deal with their objections. Then they may respond with, "Although we don't agree with you, if that is what you want, we will buy the shoes and you can earn the money for the extra amount." Children thus experience their parents' trust in making their own decisions (in certain arenas), and they experience the accomplishment of listening to and representing the self when it would be safer to acquiesce.

**Adolescence.** During adolescence, when the child may be in the throes of self-questioning, it is important that the power relationship have shifted laterally enough that differentiation from parents is an accepted process and that it is not being confused with the turmoil of other value choices. When adolescents believe the parental control/respect-for-individuality ratio is unfair, they may come to define parents' love in terms of, "Don't you trust me?" Adolescents are by now well aware of their parents' values. If adolescents decide to force a more lateral relationship in a power conflict, they are well prepared to hurt the parents, violating the parents' most important values as a weapon in the conflict, even though the adolescents hold the same values themselves. The schematic of the relationship may look like this:

Parents

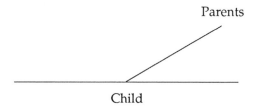

Child

Also, if parents have accepted the differentiation process, they are in a position to be confidantes to their children, because the children will know that discussing concerns with their parents will not limit their latitude to choose. Thus, as mentioned, parents may be of considerably more influence than they would be if they had continued to intrude in the children's lives. They do not abdicate being parents, retaining the responsibility to demand respect for critical family ethics. There are still some nonnegotiable values. Nor do they attempt to be laissez-faire buddies who do not disagree or who hope to wield influence by passive unconditional acceptance.

Recent research regarding the development of the self (Harter, 1983) suggests a resurgence of the child's concern for acceptance during adolescence, with the significant difference being that the judges of acceptability now are the child's peers. The parents' control of the child's sense of self via their nurturance wanes and may even become suspect during the most turbulent times of striving for identity. It is hoped, however, that the necessary tools for the continued construction of self-esteem are in place.

A second theme relevant for self-esteem that is proposed to emerge during adolescence is that of the development of self-control. Several theoretical concepts converge here: the individual's striving for identity, the quest for self-consistency, and, presumably, the development of the private self. While we will suggest that it begin earlier, it is at this stage that parents can most effectively employ the verbal procedures of the self-esteem model, assisting the adolescent to recognize self-evaluative processes and their consequences for self-esteem.

Toward the end of adolescence, the parental power relationship will be complete, and it will look something like the diagram below:

Parents

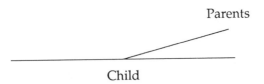

Child

The parents will still be viewed as parents, but their role will be approximately that of beloved advisors or mentors. The relationship will never be completely lateral because of the child's respect for the history of the parents' commitment. Children know they are free to ask for their parents' counsel and equally free to choose their own direction. And they know the parents' commitment is abiding. Again, they recognize that commitment comes with expectations. The violation of particularly deeply held family values cannot be tolerated, and children know that, while they are free to choose, those violations would, out of mutual understanding, require that children live out of the home. For the parents, relinquishing the need to control is their best assurance that the children's choices will be rational, not reactive.

## Intervention Component Issues

In therapy as in life, there is always too much information being communicated from moment to moment to use it all. The therapist must deliberately choose the point of entry, the strategic portions of the event flow on which to apply change techniques. We have already suggested that the most important task for the therapist in treating self-esteem difficulties in the family is to assist the parents in resolving their personal self-esteem problems. Now we turn to two final considerations, one in which the task is little more than helping parents recognize the implications of the choices in the parenting dimensions, and another that transposes some of the verbal concepts of the model for parents.

*1. If parents must choose among parenting dimensions, the acceptance/bonding dimension is the most important.*

Given that therapists will be working with families because something has gone wrong, they must frequently assist the family to restore or, perhaps, create for the first time the balance of the parenting dimensions discussed. We suggest that many parents come to therapy agitated because their control techniques are not working. Their predictable response to problems with children is to intensify their efforts, in effect to try harder to do *what is already not working.* Therapists must frequently assist parents to choose a more adaptive ordering of priorities among the dimensions, "picking their fights," as it were. While it is certainly true that occasionally parents may need to intensify their control of the child, we propose that most often the primary dimension to restore is the sense of acceptance and belonging, which provides leverage for parental control.

Parents certainly have had more experience than the child with the exigencies of life, and their relatively broader purview provides perspective that the child does not possess. Their influence on the child as guides in developing self-esteem obtains as they continue to be accepted as credible authorities. Yet the time comes in all children's lives when the only reason they will continue to value their parents' counsel or direction is that they cannot deny their parents' commitment to them. Other parental means of exercising control, such as intimidation or guilt, diminish with the child's developing maturity and frequently even become the sources of unreasoning opposition. Adolescents especially are sensitive to disingenuousness, reacting immediately to the perception of being manipulated, even when they know it may be in their best interests. (Ironically, a son may express the effectiveness of Dad's modeling by being as stubborn and willful as he is; Dad's determination to control is vitiated by his very demand.) Manipulation is anathema to a person engaged in defining the self as an individual. Thus even parents who perceive themselves as desiring their child's success may find themselves shut out by dint of their overweening attempts to control. Again the importance of the personal authenticity of parents looms large.

Children who enjoy a strong sense of identification with and respect toward their parents will feel the pull of reciprocity to be considerate of their parents' wishes, because the children recognize the parents' desire to be responsive to legitimate concerns. Children can trust their parents' motives for them, knowing that they are prized but acknowledged as separate entities. Children will feel free to express concerns, doubts, or hopes when they know their parents will not attempt to force their solutions to problems on the children. Parents will find that their counsel, while it must compete with other sources as the child grows, maintains its favored position of trust. Just as importantly, they will find the child apt to forgive parental mistakes, recognizing their abiding concern in spite of occasional lapses.

*2. As the child matures, parents can utilize the verbal concepts of the model.*

Herein, the therapist can act somewhat like a behavioral coach. Earlier we discussed how important it is that the parents are authentic themselves. The degree of their congruence and self-esteem will do much to encourage the child's own efforts. The child, observing and identifying with the parents' determination to face conflict situations, will be more apt to accept the anxiety inherent in such circumstances as unwanted but also unavoidable and therefore acceptable.

Parents must use their experiences and those of the child as they observe them to talk about the events, their feelings, and their perception of the outcome. Without preaching, they can use activities as they occur as in vivo experiments in self-esteem enhancement. Knowing that they serve as models for imitative learning, parents can augment the learning effect by verbalizing the process as it takes place.

An example might be: The parent verbalizes the conflict situation. "I think there is a misunderstanding between me and Mrs. Jones, our neighbor. I need to talk to her about [situation]." Next the parent verbalizes the anxieties attendant on coping with the conflict. "But I don't want to say anything about it. I might get mad and say something I would regret, or she might misunderstand me and the situation would get even worse. I wish she would just realize [solution]. I get nervous when I think about having to say something difficult to someone I don't know well." Now the parent verbalizes the consequences of avoiding the conflict and models the decision to confront instead. "But I know if I don't say anything, probably nothing will improve. And I won't feel good about myself, because I never feel good about me when I feel as though I've been too afraid to do what needs to be done. So I'm going to do my best to work this out with Mrs. Jones. It still may not work, but I'll feel better for having tried." Of course, it is essential that the parent then proceed to confront the situation and report its consequences, emphasizing self-evaluative thoughts. "Well, I'm really glad I did that. [Describe the resolution.] You know, whenever I face these situations instead of avoiding them, I feel good about myself. I feel as though I can handle the problems that occur."

Thus, children will become familiar with the concepts as well as their own self-evaluations, moving toward the quintessential question for the model: "What must I do in this circumstance in order to approve of myself?"

Recognizing the importance of facing and coping with difficult situations, parents will also watch for situations in which children feel anxiety and unwillingness to face something; the parents then support them as they face it anyway. It is most important that parents gently and judiciously insist that children face their conflict circumstances. The parents can then discuss the process of coping, helping the child to learn the difference between having to do something that isn't easy or is unpleasant and having to do something that is "awful." Then, as they see the child facing issues, parents can ask, "How do you feel about yourself for [doing what needed to be done]?" They can help children to recognize and notice self-approving feelings, and emphasize their consequences. Parents can help children realize that they will feel stronger, more courageous, more in control, and that they won't need parents or anyone else at those times to tell them.

Similarly, when the child is struggling with decisions, parents can ask, "What do you have to do to approve of yourself in this situation?" When the child is clearly avoiding an issue, they can increase the child's accountability to the self by asking, "How do you feel about what you are doing right now?" While this process requires a relatively high level of cognitive and emotional maturity, the children will "teach" their parents their readiness for such reflection by their response to the process. There are times, of course, when the child knows the process well enough that repeating the probing questions may be not only unnecessary but provocative. The parents' knowing smile and continued insistence on coping will convey the message without occasioning resentment.

## Summary and Conclusion

The therapist's tasks in treating self-esteem difficulties in the family are diverse—as an assessment expert, teacher, model of attitudes, behavioral coach, and therapist to parents. The most important therapeutic goal, we have suggested, is that parents recognize *and cope with* the fundamental importance of their own authenticity, in the presence of their children. In addition but subsidiary to the parents' self-esteem, we have described parenting dimensions and a developmentally paced process for inculcating relevant attitudes about self-esteem in the child or adolescent. Assuming the parents' genuine desire for the child's welfare, the therapist can utilize the concepts presented as a template by which to prepare a treatment plan for the family.

Finally, a note to the therapist. To the degree that a therapist acts as a substitute parent (*in loco parentis*) to a client, we believe it to be important that he or she follow the principles of parenting set forth in this chapter. The therapist's behavior, like that of the parents, serves as a model for the child. If the therapist is to be a good model, that behavior ought to be similar to that of parents of high-self-esteem children—that is, it should combine warmth with high expectations and high respect for individuality. We further suggest that it is incumbent on the therapist to be authentic and to shun impression management. It is vital that the therapist achieve congruence in the therapeutic relationship: actions must match words and the therapist must embody the behavior he or she wishes to teach. Only then will the therapist be truly able to assist in the client's struggle toward identity, self-consistency, and self-esteem.

# Afterword

In this volume we have described our ideas about the role of self-esteem in the treatment of emotional problems. Although a number of theorists emphasize the importance of self-esteem in their work, to the best of our knowledge the mode of therapy we have described here is unique.

Obviously, any mode of treatment, like science itself—indeed, like therapy itself—is an evolving, growth-oriented process. We fully expect to further refine our model as we continue to work with clients and as other clinicians who apply our methods report their experience. It is our sincere hope that, by pursuing the issue of self-esteem and making it the core of our model, we have been able to build a credible, viable mode of treatment that will eventually take its place alongside other major therapeutic strategies.

# References

Adler, A. (1964). *Superiority and social interest* (H. L. Ansbacher & R. R. Ansbacher, Eds. and Trans.). Evanston, IL: Northwestern University Press.

Adler, A. (1979). *Superiority and social interest* (H. L. Ansbacher & R. R. Ansbacher, Eds. and Trans.). New York: Norton.

Allport, G. W. (1937). *Personality: A psychological interpretation.* New York: Holt.

Allport, G. W. (1961). *Pattern and growth in personality.* New York: Holt, Rinehart & Winston.

Allport, G. W. (1962). Psychological models for guidance. In R. F. Carle, C. D. Kehas, & R. L. Mosher (Eds.), *Harvard Educational Review,* 32(4), 373–381.

Ansbacher, H. L., & Ansbacher, R. R. (1956). *The individual psychology of Alfred Adler.* New York: Basic Books.

Bandura, A. (1977). Self-efficacy: Toward a unifying theory of behavioral change. *Psychological Review, 84,* 191–215.

Bandura, A. (1986). *Social foundations of thought and action: A social cognitive theory.* Englewood Cliffs, NJ: Prentice-Hall.

Bateson, G., Jackson, D., Haley, J., & Weakland, J. (1956). Toward a theory of schizophrenia. *Behavioral Science, 1,* 251–264.

Baumrind, D. (1963). Authoritarian vs. authoritative parental control. *Adolescence, 3,* 255–272.

Baumrind, D. (1966). Effects of authoritative parental control on child behavior. *Child Development, 37,* 857–907.

Baumrind, D. (1971). Current patterns of parental authority. *Developmental Psychology Monographs, 41*(1), Part 2.

Baumrind, D. (1975). Some thoughts about childrearing. In U. Bronfenbrenner & M. Mahoney (Eds.), *Influences on human development.* Hinsdale, IL: Dryden Press.

Beck, A. T., Rush, A. J., Shaw, B. F., & Emery, G. (1979). *Cognitive therapy of depression.* New York: Guilford Press.

Bednar, R. L., Burlingame, G. M., & Masters, K. S. (1988). Systems of family treatment: Substance or semantics? *Annual Review of Psychology, 39,* 401–434.

Bednar, R. L., & Kaul, T. J. (1978). Experiential group research: Current perspectives. In S. L. Garfield & A. E. Bergin (Eds.), *Handbook of psychotherapy and behavior change: An empirical analysis* (2nd ed.). New York: Wiley.

Bednar, R. L., & Lawlis, F. (1971). Empirical research in group psychotherapy. In A. E. Bergin & S. L. Garfield (Eds.), *Handbook of psychotherapy and behavior change.* New York: Wiley.

Bednar, R. L., Melnick, J., & Kaul, T. (1974). Risk, responsibility, and structure: Ingredients of a conceptual framework for initiating group counseling and psychotherapy. *Journal of Counseling Psychology, 21,* 31–37.

Bem, S. L., & Lenney, E. (1976). Sex-typing and the avoidance of cross-sexed behaviors. *Journal of Personality and Social Psychology, 38,* 48–54.

Benedict, R. (1934). *Patterns of culture.* Boston: Houghton Mifflin.

Cannon, W. B. (1939). *Wisdom of the body.* New York: Norton.

Carp, F. M., & Carp, A. (1981). Mental health characteristics and acceptance-rejection of old age. *American Journal of Orthopsychiatry, 51*(2), 230–241.

Cooley, C. H. (1902). *Human nature and the social order.* New York: Scribner's.

Coopersmith, S. (1967). *The antecedents of self-esteem.* San Francisco, CA: Freeman.

Coopersmith, S. (1969, February). *Implications of studies on self-esteem for education research practice.* Paper presented at the American Educational Research Association Convention, Los Angeles, CA.

Covington, M. V., & Beery, R. G. (1976). *Self-worth and school learning.* New York: Holt, Rinehart, & Winston.

Daly, M. J., & Burton, R. L. (1983). Self-esteem and irrational beliefs: An exploratory investigation with implications for counseling. *Journal of Counseling Psychology, 30*(3), 361–366.

Eliot, T. S. (1940). *T. S. Eliot: The complete poems and plays.* New York: Harcourt, Brace.

Ellis, A. (1962). *Reason and emotion in psychotherapy.* New York: Lyle Stuart.

Ellis, A. (1973). *Humanistic psychotherapy: The rational and curative approach.* New York: McGraw-Hill.

Epstein, S. (1973). The self-concept revisited: Or a theory of a theory. *American Psychologist, 28,* 404–416.

Epstein, S. (1979a). Natural healing processes of the mind: I. Acute schizophrenic disorganization. *Schizophrenia Bulletin, 5*(2), 313–321.

Epstein, S. (1979b). The stability of behavior: I. On predicting most of the people much of the time. *Journal of Personality and Social Psychology, 37,* 1097–1126.

Erikson, E. (1963). *Childhood and society* (2nd ed.). New York: Norton.

Erikson, E. (1968). *Identity: Youth and crisis.* New York: Norton.

Fish, B., & Karabenick, S. A. (1971). Relationship between self-esteem and locus of control. *Psychological Reports, 29*(3), 784.

Flaherty, J. F., & Dusek, J. B. (1980). An investigation of the relationship between psychological androgyny and components of self-concept. *Journal of Personality and Social Psychology, 38,* 984–992.

Flavell, J. (1985). *Cognitive development* (2nd ed.). Englewood Cliffs, NJ: Prentice-Hall.

Ford, D., & Urban, H. (1963). *Systems of psychotherapy*. New York: Wiley.

Frank, J. D. (1973). *Persuasion and healing* (Rev. ed.). Baltimore: Johns Hopkins University Press.

Frank, J. D. (1982). Therapeutic components shared by all psychotherapies. In J. H. Harvey & M. M. Parks (Eds.), *The master lecture series: Vol. I. Psychotherapy research and behavior change* (pp. 5–38). Washington, DC: American Psychological Association.

Freud, S. (1937). Repression. In J. Rickman (Ed.), *A general selection from the works of Sigmund Freud*. Garden City, NY: Doubleday Anchor Books. (Original work published 1915).

Freud, S. (1957). Recommendation to physicians practicing psychoanalysis. In J. Strachey (Ed. and Trans.), *The standard edition of the complete psychological works of Sigmund Freud* (Vol. 12, pp. 109–120). London: Hogarth Press. (Original work published 1912).

Freud, S. (1961). On the grounds for detaching a particular syndrome from neurasthenia under the description "anxiety neurosis." In J. Strachey (Ed. and Trans.), *The standard edition of the complete psychological works of Sigmund Freud* (Vol. 3, pp. 87–117). London: Hogarth Press. (Original work published 1924).

Friedenberg, W., & Gillis, J. (1977). An experimental study of the effectiveness of attitude change techniques for enhancing self-esteem. *Journal of Clinical Psychology, 33*(4), 1120–1124.

Friedenberg, W., & Gillis, J. (1980). Modification of self-esteem with techniques of attitude change: A replication. *Psychological Reports, 46*(3), 1087–1095.

Garfield, S. L. (1986). Research on client variables in psychotherapy. In S. L. Garfield & A. E. Bergin (Eds.), *Handbook of psychotherapy and behavior change* (3rd ed.) (pp. 213–256). New York: Wiley.

Gauthier, J., Pellerin, D., & Renaud, P. (1983). The enhancement of self-esteem: A comparison of two cognitive strategies. *Cognitive Therapy and Research, 7*(5), 389–398.

Greenson, R. R. (1967). *The technique and practice of psychoanalysis*. New York: International Universities Press.

Greenwald, A. G., & Breckler, S. J. (1985). To whom is the self presented? In B. R. Schlenker (Ed.), *The self and social life*. New York: McGraw-Hill.

Hamachek, D. F. (1978). *Encounters with the self* (2nd ed.). New York: Holt, Rinehart & Winston.

Harmm, M. H. (1980). The Barron Ego Strength Scale: A study of personality correlates among normals. *Journal of Clinical Psychology, 36*(2), 433–436.

Harter, S. (1982). The perceived competence scale for children. *Child Development, 53*, 87–97.

Harter, S. (1983). Developmental perspectives on the self-system. In E. M. Hetherington (Ed.), *Handbook of child psychology, Vol. 4. Socialization, personality, and social development* (4th ed.). New York: Wiley.

Hetherington, E. M., & Parke, R. D. (1986). *Child psychology: A contemporary viewpoint*. New York: McGraw-Hill.

Higgins, E. T. (1983). *A theory of discrepant self-concepts*. Unpublished manuscript, New York University, New York.

Higgins, E. T., Klein, R., & Strauman, T. (1985). Self-concept discrepancy theory: A psychological model for distinguishing among different aspects of depression and anxiety. *Social Cognitions, 3*, 51–76.

James, W. (1890). *Principles of psychology*. New York: Holt.

James, W. (1981). *Principles of psychology*. Cambridge, MA: Harvard University Press. (Original work published 1890).

Johnson, A., Giffin, M., Watson, E. J., & Beckett, P. (1956). Studies in schizophrenia at the Mayo Clinic: II. Observations on ego functions in schizophrenia. *Psychiatry, 19*, 143–148.

Kaul, T. J., & Bednar, R. L. (1986). Experiential group research: Results, questions, and suggestions. In S. L. Garfield & A. E. Bergin (Eds.), *Handbook of psychotherapy and behavior change* (3rd ed.). New York: Wiley.

Kazdin, A. E. (1980). *Research design in clinical psychology*. New York: Harper & Row.

Kelley, G. (1955). *The psychology of personal constructs*. New York: Norton.

Kennedy, J. F. (1956). *Profiles in courage*. New York: Harper.

Kolb, B., & Wishaw, I. Q. (1985). *Fundamentals of human neuropsychology* (2nd ed.). New York: Freeman.

Korchin, S. J. (1976). *Modern clinical psychology*. New York: Basic Books.

Lepper, M. R. (1983). Extrinsic reward and intrinsic motivation: Implications for the classroom. In J. M. Levine & M. C. Wang (Eds.), *Teacher and student perceptions: Implications for learning*. Hillsdale, NJ: Erlbaum.

Lieberman, M., Yalom, I., & Miles, M. (1973). *Encounter groups: First facts*. New York: Basic Books.

Linton, R. (1956). *Culture and mental disorders*. Springfield, IL: Charles C Thomas.

Loevinger, J. (1976). *Ego development: Conceptions and theories*. San Francisco: Jossey-Bass.

Lynn, D. B. (1959). A model man for applied psychology. *American Psychologist, 14*, 630–632.

Mahoney, M. J., & Thoresen, C. E. (1985). *Self-control: Power to the person*. Monterey, CA: Brooks/Cole.

Markus, H., & Wurf, E. (1987). The dynamic self-concept: A social psychological perspective. In M. R. Rosenszeig & L. W. Porter (Eds.), *Annual Review of Psychology, 38*, 299–337.

May, R. (1953). *Man's search for himself*. New York: New American Library.

May, R. (1983). *The discovery of being*. New York: Norton.

May, R., Angel, E., & Ellenberger, H. (Eds.). (1958). *Existence*. New York: Basic Books.

McCall, R. J. (1975). *The varieties of abnormality.* Springfield, IL: Charles C Thomas.

McKee, J. P., & Sherriffs, A. C. (1957). The differential evaluation of males and females. *Personality, 25,* 356–371.

Mead, G. H. (1934). *Mind, self, and society.* Chicago: University of Chicago Press.

Meichenbaum, D. B. (1977). *Cognitive-behavior modification.* New York: Plenum.

Millon, T. (1969). *Modern psychopathology: A biosocial approach to maladaptive learning and functions.* Philadelphia: Saunders.

Millon, T. (1981). *Disorders of personality: DSM III Axis II.* New York: Wiley.

Orlinsky, D. E., & Howard, K. T. (1986). Process and outcome in psychotherapy. In S. L. Garfield & A. E. Bergin (Eds.), *Handbook of psychotherapy and behavior change* (3rd ed.). New York: Wiley.

Patrick, J. (1984). Predicting outcome of psychiatric hospitalization: A comparison of attitudinal and psychopathological measures. *Journal of Clinical Psychology, 40*(2), 546–549.

Prochaska, J. O. (1984). *Systems of psychotherapy: A transtheoretical analysis.* Homewood, IL: Dorsey Press.

Rimm, D. C., & Masters, J. C. (1979). *Behavior therapy techniques and empirical findings* (2nd ed.). New York: Academic Press.

Rogers, C. R. (1950). The significance of the self-regarding attitudes and perceptions. In M. L. Reymert (Ed.), *Feelings and emotions: The Mooseheart Symposium.* New York: McGraw-Hill.

Rogers, C. R. (1951). *Client-centered therapy.* Boston: Houghton Mifflin.

Rogers, C. R. (1957). The necessary and sufficient conditions of therapeutic personality change. *Journal of Consulting Psychology, 21,* 95–103.

Rogers, C. R. (1959). A theory of therapy, personality, and interpersonal relationships as developed in the client-centered framework. In S. Koch (Ed.), *Psychology: A study of a science: Volume III. Formulations of the person and the social context* (pp. 184–256). New York: McGraw-Hill.

Rogers, C. R. (1961). *On becoming a person.* Boston: Houghton Mifflin.

Rogers, C. R. (1980). *A way of being.* Boston: Houghton Mifflin.

Rosenberg, M. (1979). *Conceiving the self.* New York: Basic Books.

Sandler, J. (1985). *The analysis of defense.* New York: International Universities Press.

Sathyavathi, K., & Anthony, T. (1984). An attributional approach to locus of control, self-esteem, and alienation: A clinical study. *Psychological Studies, 29*(1), 76–82.

Satir, V., Stachowiak, J., & Taschman, H. A. (1975). *Helping families to change.* New York: Aronson.

Schlenker, B. R. (1985). Identity and self-identification. In B. R. Schlenker (Ed.), *The self and social life.* New York: McGraw-Hill.

Seeman, J. (1959). Toward a concept of personality integration. *American Psychologist, 14,* 633–637.

Selman, R. L. (1980). *The growth of interpersonal understanding.* New York: Academic Press.

Shoben, E. J. (1957). Toward a concept of the normal personality. *American Psychologist, 12,* 183–189.

Singh, U. P., Prasad, T., & Bhagalpur, U. (1973). Self-esteem, social-esteem, and conformity behavior. *Psychologia: An International Journal of Psychology in the Orient, 16*(2), 61–68.

Steger, J. H., Simmons, W. L., & Lavelle, S. (1973). Accuracy of prediction of own performance as a function of locus of control. *Psychological Reports, 33*(1), 59–62.

Stockton, R., & Moran, D. C. (1982). Review and perspective of critical dimensions in therapeutic small group research. In G. M. Gazda (Ed.), *Basic approaches to group psychotherapy and group counseling.* Springfield, IL: Charles C Thomas.

Strauss, A. (Ed.). (1964). *George Herbert Mead on social psychology.* Chicago: University of Chicago Press.

Sullivan, H. S. (1962). *Schizophrenia as a human process.* New York: Norton.

Thomas, A., & Chess, S. (1977). *Temperament and development.* New York: Brunner/Mazel.

Thomas, A., Chess, S., & Birch, H. G. (1968). *Temperament and behavior disorders in children.* New York: New York University Press.

Truax, C. B., & Carkhuff, R. R. (1967). *Toward effective counseling and psychotherapy: Training and practice.* Chicago: Aldine.

Tyler, L. (1978). *Individuality: Human possibilities and personal choice in the psychological development of men and women.* San Francisco: Jossey-Bass.

Wegrocki, H. J. (1939). A critique of cultural and statistical concepts of abnormality. *Journal of Abnormal and Social Psychology, 34,* 166–178.

Wiener, N. (1948). *Cybernetics, or, Control and communication in the animal and the machine.* New York: Wiley.

Wylie, R. (1961). *The self-concept: A critical survey of pertinent research literature.* Lincoln, NE: University of Nebraska Press.

Wylie, R. (1974). *The self-concept: A review of methodological considerations and measuring instruments* (Vol. 1, Rev. ed.). Lincoln, NE: University of Nebraska Press.

Wylie, R. (1979). *The self-concept: Theory and research on selected topics* (Vol. 2). Lincoln, NE: University of Nebraska Press.

Yalom, I. D. (1985). *The theory and practice of group psychotherapy* (3rd ed.). New York: Basic Books.

York, P., York, D., & Wachtel, T. (1982). *Tough love.* New York: Doubleday.

# Author and Subject Index

# About the Authors

RICHARD L. BEDNAR is Professor of Psychology and Director of the Comprehensive Clinic at Brigham Young University. Prior to that, he was Director of the Clinical Psychology Training Program at the University of Kentucky. He has published consistently for over 20 years, with recent chapters in the *Annual Review of Psychology* and the *Handbook of Psychology and Behavior Change*. His research has appeared in numerous journals, such as the *Journal of Consulting and Clinical Psychology* (for which he has also been a consulting editor), the *Journal of Counseling Psychology*, and the *Journal of Applied Behavioral Science*. A noted guest speaker, he has been invited to Hebrew University (Israel), Beijing University, and many other international conferences.

M. GAWAIN WELLS is an Associate Professor of Psychology at Brigham Young University and a Core Faculty member of the University's Comprehensive Clinic. His research interests range from psychotherapy to emotional development in children. His interest in self-esteem has been stimulated by 10 years of practice with children and adolescents. He has been a psychological consultant to drug abuse agencies, residential schools for adolescents, and private schools. He is currently on the medical staff of the Utah Valley Regional Medical Center.

SCOTT R. PETERSON has been with Research and Staff Development of LDS Social Services for 10 years. He has developed and presented experiential and video-based training programs for clinical social workers on the diagnosis and treatment of psychological disorders. He has had primary training responsibility for field application of *DSM-III-R*, marriage and family communications, treatment of personality disorders, and emotional implications of infertility. A freelance writer, he is coauthor with Dr. Bednar and Dr. Wells of the forthcoming book, *Face Up or Foul Up: The Intimate Secrets of Self-Esteem*.